Bill Hamilton on the Western Frontier

THE AUTHOR

Bill Hamilton on the Western Frontier

An Adventurous life of a Trapper, Scout and Indian
Fighter, 1822-1908

ILLUSTRATED

My Sixty Years on the Plains Trapping, Trading,
and Indian Fighting

and

A Trapping Expedition, 1848-9

and

A Trading Expedition among the Indians in 1858
from Fort Walla Walla to the Blackfoot Country
and Return

W. T. Hamilton ("Bill Hamilton")
&
Edited by John H. Lewis

LEONAUR

Bill Hamilton on the Western Frontier
An Adventurous life of a Trapper, Scout and Indian Fighter 1822-1908
My Sixty Years on the Plains Trapping, Trading, and Indian Fighting
and
A Trapping Expedition, 1848-9
and
A Trading Expedition among the Indians in 1858 from Fort Walla Walla to the
Blackfoot Country and Return
by W. T. Hamilton ("Bill Hamilton")
&
Edited by John H. Lewis

ILLUSTRATED

FIRST EDITION

Leonaur is an imprint of Oakpast Ltd

Copyright in this form © 2025 Oakpast Ltd

ISBN: 978-1-916535-86-2 (hardcover)
ISBN: 978-1-916535-87-9 (softcover)

http://www.leonaur.com

Publisher's Notes

Contents

Introduction to the Leonaur Edition (2025)

As most readers of Leonaur books are aware, we usually attempt to augment our titles with another complimenting text. This may be, for example, an historical record to add context to an eye-witness account. It may be a contrasting perspective on the same events described in the first work. In those instances, the second text will usually be the work of another author. It is, however, our usual practice to investigate whether the principal author has written other works which will expand, enhance or contribute further valuable detail to the initial text. Once we have discovered that such a text does exist, then the task is to actually find it, for these are regularly written pieces of some longevity. As a result, the outcome of our investigations regularly ends in disappointment, because obscure texts are, by their very nature, elusive.

In the case of W.T. Hamilton's narrative we were able to discover that he had, indeed, written accounts which filled in the gaps or expanded in valuable detail, aspects of his comparatively well-known book, 'My Sixty Years on the Plains'. Reference to Hamilton's intelligence gathering mission concerning the actions of potentially hostile tribes undertaken on behalf of the United States Army was discovered comparatively readily and sourced. This is a sizeable narrative in its own right and, as one may expect is written in the author's engaging style including many interesting incidents and further adventures. This long narrative is undoubtedly a worthy contribution, the final one chronologically and holds that place in this edition.

Readers may be aware that much of the principal narrative concerns Hamilton's younger days. So, it was both a surprise and revelation when we discovered that there existed yet another additional narrative of the author's exciting recollections that chronologically fitted prior to the recorded expedition into the Blackfoot country.

This narrative may well be recorded elsewhere, but we can only confess that we had not read about it before own discovery. So, it was in a spirit of some pleasure that it was sourced and added into its rightful place within these pages.

These additional Hamilton pages have increased (in this edition) Bill Hamilton's familiar published adventures by approximately 40%. Since his accounts of experiences as a trapper, trader and Indian fighter in on the western frontier can be described as nothing less than riveting, we hope the present reader will enjoy them now in full measure.

John H. Lewis, 2025

Introduction to the Original Edition(1905)

The Western Mountaineer

In writing this book the author had only one end in view, that of relating in a simple way his experiences as a mountaineer. In these days, when such experiences are fast becoming a thing of the past, the story is of special interest.

The mountaineers as a class were unique. Life itself had little value in their estimation. They were pushing, adventurous, and fearless men, who thought nothing of laying down their lives in the service of a friend, or often, it might be, only as a matter of humanity. Theirs was a brotherhood in which one man's life was entirely at the service of any of its members, regardless of friendship or even of acquaintanceship.

Equipped with nothing but their skill and endurance, a few ponies, a gun or two, and provisions enough to last them for the day, they set out to make their way through a vast wilderness that held all the terrors of the unknown. They became self-reliant, and encountered obstacles only to overcome them with a dash and courage which amaze and delight us.

Mr. William T. Hamilton is a living example of this type of men. He is now in his eighty-third year, (as at 1905), and is still in full possession of his acute intellect. He is a general favourite wherever he is known, and is familiarly styled "Uncle Bill." He spent his whole life, from the time he was twenty, on the plains, and is an authority on Indian life and customs. He was also acknowledged by all to be the greatest sign-talker on the plains, either Indian or white; and was able to converse with all tribes. All Indian tribes use the same signs, though speaking a different language.

Sign-talking among Indians will soon be a lost art, for the present generation is not handing its knowledge down to its children. In 1882, while Mr. Hamilton was a witness in the Star Route trial in Washington, the Smithsonian Institution endeavoured to photograph these signs, but with indifferent success.

The author has been extremely modest in describing the Indian fights, stating only the simple facts. These simple facts accentuate the valour and intrepidity of the trappers, when brought to bay by hostile tribes.

His story also gives, for the first time, an account of three years of the life of the great scout and mountaineer, Bill Williams, one of the prominent figures in the early history of the plains.

To the efforts of these heroes, we owe the great advances civilization has made in the West. They reclaimed this vast and valuable territory from the outlaws and the Indians. They "blazed the trail" that was to lead the frontiersman to valuable deposits and rich agricultural regions. They set an example for courage and perseverance which will keep their memory always bright in the hearts of true Americans.

Hilma S. Sieber.

Park City, Montana, August, 1905.

CHAPTER 1

The Vote that Made me an Indian Fighter

On the River Till, in Cheviot Hills, Scotland, in the year 1825, twenty-five men formed a company for the purpose of emigrating.

These men built themselves a bark, and when ready to sail held a council to determine whether their destination would be India or America. A vote was taken, which resulted in a tie, thus forcing the captain to cast his ballot. He voted for America, and by so doing destined me to fight Indians instead of hunting Bengal tigers in India. My father was one of the company, and his brother was the captain.

I was just two years and ten months of age when we landed at New Orleans.

My father had means and we travelled all over the States, finally settling in St. Louis eighteen months later. Here I remained until I was twenty years of age, receiving five years of schooling.

In the meantime, chills and fevers were undermining my constitution, and the doctor ordered a change of climate. My father made arrangements with a party of hunters and trappers, who were in St. Louis at the time, to allow me to accompany them on their next trip, which would last a year.

The party consisted of eight men, all free trappers, with Bill Williams and Perkins as leaders. These two men had had fifteen years' experience on the plains amongst Indians, and had a wide reputation for fearless courage and daring exploits.

A good trading outfit was purchased, one third of which my father paid for, giving me a corresponding interest in the trip.

We started in the spring of 1842 with wagons and pack animals, making for Independence, Mo., which was the headquarters for all mountaineers in those days. At Independence we sold our wagons and rigged up a complete pack outfit, as our route would take us where it would be difficult for wagons to travel.

I was still wearing my city clothes, and mountain men present asked Williams what he was going to do with that city lad in the mountains. This remark cut me deeply, and I hurried to the frontier store and traded all my fine clothes, shirts, and dickeys, which were worn in those days, for two suits of the finest buckskin, such as these merchants always kept on hand to fleece greenhorns like myself, making five hundred *per cent*, profit in the trade. Next morning I appeared dressed *à la prairie*, and the old trappers noticed the change and said, "Williams, that boy of yours will make a mountaineer if he catches on at this rate."

We all went to work getting our pack outfit ready, which was accomplished before night. Next morning, the 15th of March, 1842, we started, bidding *adieu* to the remaining mountain men, who were all making preparations to start on their different routes for trapping and trading. The trappers and traders of that day were brave and reckless men, who never gave a second thought to the danger in their calling.

We made good time and reached Salt Creek on March 20th. Camp had just been made when we saw in the distance a small herd of buffalo coming directly towards us. Williams gave orders to corral all stock. No second order was needed with these mountain men, who acted in unison like a flash when occasion called for action. The stock was barely secured when the buffalo passed in close vicinity of camp, followed by thirty painted Kiowa warriors. A wild and savage-looking outfit they were. I had seen many Indians in St. Louis at different times, but none so wild and savage as these were. It was at this time that I received my first lesson in how to deal with wild Indians, or, more properly speaking, how to control their overt acts.

Our packs were placed in a triangle, answering in case of need to a good breastwork. Each man was armed with a rifle, two pistols, a tomahawk, and a large knife, commonly called "tooth-picker." Besides this, two of our men had bows and arrows, and were experts with them.

The Indians came up and examined our outfit and demanded pay for passing through their country. Williams gave them to understand that they could not go through the outfit, nor would they receive pay for passing through the country, informing them that this was Pawnee country. The Kiowas at that time were semi-hostile, robbing and killing when it could be done with impunity.

12

I stood by Williams during the parley, much interested in the conversation, which was entirely by signs. The rest of the men were in what we called our fort, with stern and savage looks on their faces.

Williams was well up in Indian ways and treatment in any and every emergency, and finally gave the leader, or chief, as he called himself, some tobacco. They departed, looking daggers at us.

Williams informed me that there was no chief in the outfit, and that it was only a small thieving party led by a young brave, who had two feathers stuck in his scalp-lock.

We kept close watch during the night, expecting that the Indians would attempt to steal some of our stock or attack camp. Old experienced mountain men leave nothing to chance. Many outfits, within my knowledge, have come to grief through placing confidence in the red man, who always covets the belongings of the paleface.

Nothing disturbed us during the night, and in the morning, we started down Salt Creek to the Platte River, where Williams expected to find Cheyennes, hoping to trade them out of some furs. We travelled up the Platte River to Cherry Creek, seeing plenty of fresh Indian signs, but no Indians.

The camp was kept well supplied with buffalo and antelope steak and ribs. The ribs are specially fine, and are highly appreciated by everyone, whether mountaineer or dweller in civilization.

We camped on the North Platte River about two miles below where Cherry Creek empties; and about sundown three young Indians, who had been scouting for hostiles, rode into camp. They were Cheyennes, and the very ones that Williams was looking for, as they were generally well supplied with all kinds of furs. The Indians told us that their village was a short distance up the creek. Williams gave them tobacco for their chief, old White Antelope, and told them that we would visit the village on the following day. He then invited them to supper for the purpose of finding out what the tribe was most in need of, which is quite a trick in trading with Indians, though I believe the same rule works with white men. At all events, I never knew it to fail to bring a good trade.

We packed up early the following morning, but not before a few Indians had paid us a visit. They were elated at our coming, for they were acquainted with Williams and Perkins, with whom they had often traded, and were on what is called friendly terms. Perkins was the equal of Williams in knowledge of Indian science and, like him, was brave, cool, and ready in extreme danger.

We arrived at the village about eleven o'clock, preceded by our leaders, who wished to select the most advantageous camp, as it was our intention to remain several days.

We unpacked and put up a wall tent, which we used for a store. Our stock was put in the chief's care; and we supplied the women with all the necessaries for a feast. This is always customary if you wish to stand well, and must be given offhand and with generous impulse. Indians are close observers, and if they see that you give with a niggardly hand, they will say, "These white men love their goods, and will give us poor trade. Let's trade nothing but our poorest furs." Such an unfavourable condition must be avoided at any cost, as any trader will agree who has had experience among Indians.

Williams and Perkins had but a limited knowledge of sign-language, but sufficient to do the trading. All these signs I learned easily, much to their astonishment. They both claimed that they would never become experts, but that if I kept on in the way I had started I would soon be the most perfect of any white man on the plains. It came to me without any effort and certainly surprised me. The other men had been observing my aptness and were astonished. They were indifferent sign-talkers, but good in everything else that goes to make a thorough mountaineer. It has always appeared strange to me that so many intelligent men, who had been for so many years among Indians, trading and otherwise, were so deficient in knowledge of sign-language. Some assert that facility in the language is due to linguistic talent; but be that as it may, as I said before, the art was acquired by me without any effort.

All the principal chiefs assembled in White Antelope's lodge, where the customary smoke was indulged in, during which we were questioned as to what our outfit consisted of. Then came the feast, which included buffalo tongue, the choicest of meats, coffee, hardtack, and molasses. This last article is a favourite with all Indians.

In the meantime, Noble, Docket, and myself spread on blankets the various goods which Williams had selected for this trade—powder, half-ounce balls, flints, beads, paint, blue and scarlet cloths, blankets, calico, and knives.

A certain rule must be complied with in trading with Indians, which is that you must not pay one Indian—man or woman—one *iota* more for a robe or fur of the same quality than you pay another. If you do, you ruin your trade and create antagonistic feelings throughout the village.

The Indians stood in need of all the articles named, and by sundown our tent was full of furs of the finest quality. We then adjourned for supper, which was prepared by the women.

After supper I accompanied the chief's son, Swift Runner, through the village. He was about my own age and took a great liking to me, taking considerable pains in teaching me signs. He introduced me to all the leading men in the village, telling them that I was his friend. I took special notice of a tall young boy with a particularly large nose, a magnificent specimen of a coming warrior. He was known as Big Nose; but I firmly believe he was the famous Roman Nose, who was killed by General Forsyth on the Republican River in 1868.

Swift Runner told me that a large hunting party was going to start the next morning after buffalo; and that if I would like to go, he would furnish me with a good buffalo horse. I asked permission of Williams, and he consented, saying, "All right, boy; you can take my horse; he is one of the best buffalo horses on the plains." I thanked him, saying that Swift Runner had promised me one of his. The evening passed very pleasantly for me, as the young folks entertained me to the best of their ability.

I was considered fairly good-looking, with smooth face, agile and quick in movements. I was the youngest child and my parents had allowed me every indulgence. They owned a farm just outside of St. Louis, and I always claimed that I was a country raised boy. Foxes, deer, and coons were in abundance, and it followed that every boy would own a pony, providing, of course, that the parents could afford it. At all events, I possessed one of the best mustangs in Missouri—a little devil, which would kick at everything and everybody who approached him except myself. My brothers would say that we were a well-matched pair, both little devils.

At home we indulged in all kinds of athletic exercises, such as dumb-bells, boxing, trapeze, and single-stick; and then we had constant practice with rifle and pistol, in all of which I became very proficient. I believe that all boys should be taught in the same way. It is productive of longevity, all things being physically equal. I am at this writing past eighty-one, straight as an arrow, supple and quick. I have never had use for glasses. Almost every day someone asks me to what I attribute my suppleness and eyesight, and I answer that "commonsense philosophy conforms to the teachings of hygiene."

CHAPTER 2

Buffalo Hunt with Cheyennes

The next morning, before daylight, fifty hunters and about twenty squaws with pack animals were assembled, ready to start on the buffalo hunt.

We travelled about ten miles, when the scouts discovered a herd and reported their location to the hunting chief. He was thoroughly acquainted with the topography of the country and led us on a long detour, so as to get on the leeward side of the herd. As soon as we reached there, the Indians stripped to breech-clout and advanced, leading their running horses.

The chief now divided the hunters in two divisions, in order to get what buffalo were wanted in the smallest possible area. It is necessary to approach as close as possible before raising the herd, for when raised they travel fast and no laggard of a horse can overtake them.

Generally, each division has a leader, who gives the order to go. We rode to within a quarter of a mile of the herd before the word was given.

Here would have been a grand scene for an artist to put on canvas—this wild array of naked Indians, sending forth yell after yell and riding like demons in their eagerness to bring down the first buffalo. For this is quite a feat and is commented upon by the whole village.

Swift Runner and his cousin had the fastest horses in our division and brought down the first buffalo, much to the chagrin of many a young brave, who coveted that honour that they might receive smiles from their lady loves.

My pony was close, on the heels of the leaders, and Swift Runner pointed out a fat cow for me. In a few jumps I was alongside and fired, greenhorn like, at the cow's kidneys. As luck would have it, however, I broke her back and she dropped. Swift Runner gave a yell of delight at my success. I should have put the shot just behind the shoulder.

There was yelling and shooting in every direction; and many riderless ponies were mixed in with the buffalo, with Indians after them, reckless if they in turn were dismounted as their friends had been, by the ponies stepping into prairie-dog or badger holes. Many an Indian has come to grief by having an arm or leg broken in this way. Ponies are sure-footed, but in a run such as this one, where over a thousand buffalo are tearing at full speed over the prairie, a dust is created which makes it impossible for the ponies to see the holes, hence the mishaps, which are very common.

All the meat required lay in an area of three quarters of a mile. I had brought down four and received great praise from the Indians. I could have done much better, but, boy-like, I wanted to see the Indians shoot their arrows, which many of them used. One arrow was sufficient to bring the buffalo to its knees. They shot behind the shoulder, sending the arrow deep enough to strike the lungs. One shot there is enough for any animal in the United States.

Now came the butchering, which was completed in two hours, and each pony was packed with three hundred pounds of the choicest of meat.

Several Indians who had been thrown, limped somewhat, but none were seriously hurt.

We arrived at the village about sundown and found the whole tribe lined up to greet us and to ascertain how successful we had been.

A feast had been prepared and was awaiting our coming; and as for myself, I was "wolfish"—which is a mountain man's expression for hungry—for I had tasted no food since five o'clock in the morning.

After supper incidents of the hunt were gone over, and listened to with interest by all. Our party congratulated me warmly on my success, and it was commented on also by the Indians, which pleased the boys immensely. If a white man fails to acquit himself creditably it invariably casts a reflection on all whites.

The Cheyennes were and are today, (1905), a proud and brave people. Their domestic habits were commendable and could be followed to advantage by many white families. To violate the marriage vow meant death or mutilation. This is a rule which does not apply to all tribes. Meat is their principal food, although berries of different kinds are collected in season, as well as various roots. The kettle is on the tripod night and day. They use salt when they can get it, and are very fond of molasses, sugar, coffee, and flour. They are hospitable to those whom they respect, and the reverse to those for whom they

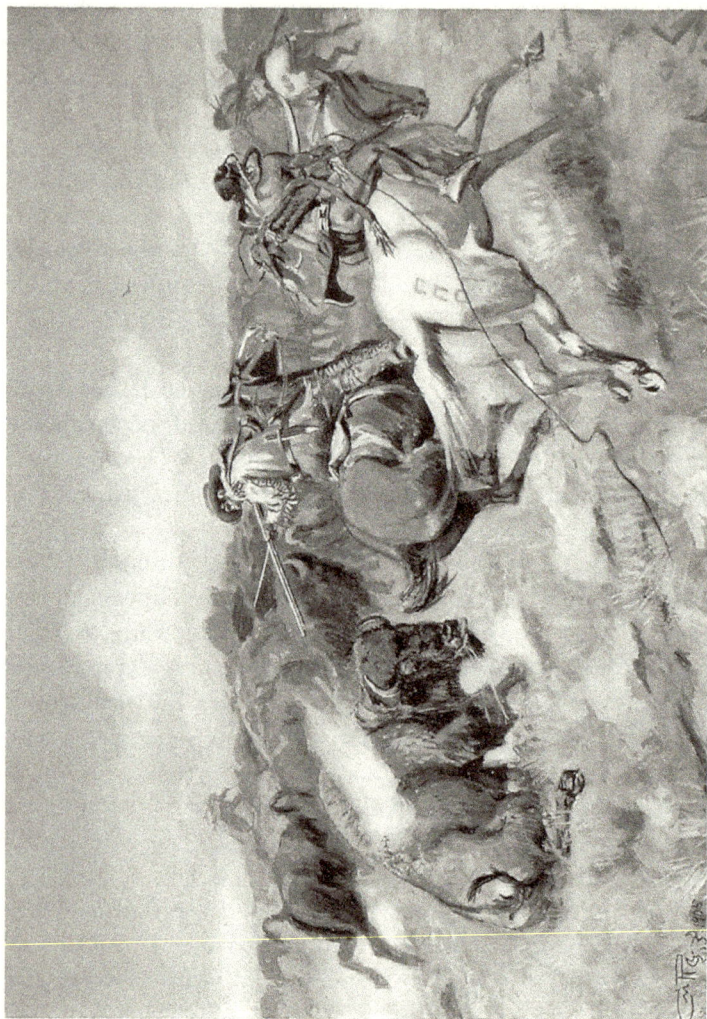

I BROKE THE COW'S BACK

have contempt.

Most tribes of plains Indians dry their meat by cutting it in thin flakes and spreading it on racks and poles in the sun; although in damp or wet weather it is put inside of lodges, where it will dry, but not so well as in the sun. Mountain men follow the same practice and use the meat when game is scarce, and this often occurs.

Pemmican is manufactured in the following manner. The choicest cuts of meat are selected and cut into flakes and dried. Then all the marrow is collected and the best of the tallow, which are dissolved together over a slow fire to prevent burning. Many tribes use berries in their *pemmican*. Mountaineers always do unless they have sugar. The meat is now pulverised to the consistency of mincemeat; the squaws generally doing this on a flat rock, using a pestle, many specimens of which may be seen on exhibition in museums.

A layer of meat is spread, about two inches thick, the squaws using a wooden dipper, a buffalo horn, or a claw for this work. On this meat is spread a certain amount of the ingredients made from the marrow and tallow, the proportion depending on the taste. This same process is repeated until the required amount is secured. One pound of *pemmican* is equal to five pounds of meat.

Buffalo tongues are split the long way and dried for future use, and thus prepared are a delicacy fit for a prince.

Another important article of food, the equal of which is not to be had except from the buffalo, is "*depuyer*" (*dépouille*). It is a fat substance that lies along the backbone, next to the hide, running from the shoulder-blade to the last rib, and is about as thick as one's hand or finger. It is from seven to eleven inches broad, tapering to a feather edge on the lower side. It will weigh from five to eleven pounds, according to the size and condition of the animal. This substance is taken off and dipped in hot grease for half a minute, then is hung up inside of a lodge to dry and smoke for twelve hours. It will keep indefinitely, and is used as a substitute for bread, but is superior to any bread that was ever made. It is eaten with the lean and dried meat, and is tender and sweet and very nourishing, for it seems to satisfy the appetite. When going on the war-path the Indians would take some dried meat and some *depuyer* to live on, and nothing else, not even if they were to be gone for months.

I have been asked many times regarding *depuyer* by different ones who have been astonished when told of its merits as a substitute for other food, and surprised that it was so little known except by mountain men and Indians. Trappers would pay a dollar a pound for it, and I do not believe that bread would bring that price unless one were starving. As I have said, it is a substitute for bread; and when you are invited to an Indian lodge your host will present you with *depuyer* just as you would present bread to a guest. You may be sure should they fail to present you with *depuyer* that you are an unwelcome guest.

Williams concluded to move the next day, so he traded for a few ponies, sufficient to pack the furs for which we had traded.

When we were ready to start, the leading chiefs assembled to say goodbye (*"how"*), and the women presented me with a half-dozen pairs of beautifully embroidered *moccasins*. This tribe excels all others in beadwork as well as in garnishing and painting robes. One must bear in mind, however, that the Cheyennes of 1842 must not be classed with the Cheyennes of today.

When I parted from my young Indian friend Swift Runner, he presented to me the pony which I had ridden on the buffalo hunt. I named him Runner.

CHAPTER 3

My First Shot at an Indian

It was the intention of Williams to strike for the South Platte River, in the vicinity of Laramie River, where he expected to meet with fur buyers, who would be returning to Green River; and either to dispose of our furs or have them forwarded to St. Louis, which at that time was the principal fur-buying city in the United States.

A few days' travel brought us to the South Platte River, and at a point fifteen miles east of Laramie River we found a Sioux village. Big Thunder was the chief, and he requested us to camp as his people wanted to trade. The Sioux were friendly in those days, especially to traders and trappers, and we had a royal time.

Just before daylight the following morning, an alarm was given in the village and all the men hurried out, to find that the Pawnees— mortal enemies of the Sioux—had run off about one hundred head of ponies which had been turned out to graze a short distance from camp. The number included two mules and three ponies belonging to our outfit.

As soon as the news was received, fifty young warriors hastened to saddle their best ponies. Williams signified his intention of going, but I told him that he was too old, and that Noble and myself would go and bring back the stock.

We started with the Indians, under the leadership of Young Thunder, a fine specimen of a coming chief. I rode my pony, Runner.

We soon struck the trail of the Pawnees and followed it down the south side about ten miles, and then crossed to the north side of the river. We could tell by the appearance of the trail that they were only a short distance ahead of us.

The Sioux now discarded all their clothing, excepting leggings and breech-clouts, and mounted their war-horses, which had up to this point been led.

I put a pad on my Runner. These pads are made by filling two sacks with antelope hair. The sacks are generally made of buckskin, are seven or eight inches in diameter, and rest on each side of the horse's backbone, being sewed together on top with buckskin. Material is fastened to each side for stirrups and cinch. They would be a curiosity in the East, but are light and elastic, and a horse feels no inconvenience from them and can travel twenty miles farther in a day than under a saddle.

We started at a canter. Young Thunder in the lead. After going about eight miles, we noticed that sand was still sliding in the hoof-tracks ahead. This was a sure indication that the Pawnees were but a short distance in advance. We now went at about half speed, the Indians becoming alert.

Passing over a divide we could plainly see a cloud of dust about two miles in advance. At about the same time the Pawnees must have discovered us, for there appeared a scattering just as if stock was being urged to greater speed.

We gained rapidly on the Pawnees, and were soon close enough to determine that the party consisted of twelve. They were trying their best to get the herd to a cottonwood grove on a bend of the Platte River.

It was at this time that I discovered the wonderful endurance of the Indian pony. Young Thunder gave a war-whoop, which was the signal for a charge. The ponies bounded forward as an engine when the throttle is thrown wide open.

The Pawnees heard the yell and left the herd of stolen stock and made for the grove, frantically urging their ponies to greater speed. Two of them went to sleep before they reached cover, ten getting safely to the grove, thankful of saving their lives, knowing that the Sioux would be satisfied with the two scalps and the recaptured herd.

Several of the ponies were close to the grove, and Noble and I dashed at full speed and turned them away. The Pawnees fired several shots at us, but the bullets went wide of their mark. As we were within one hundred yards of the timber, I wheeled and shot, but it was a waste of ammunition, as no Indians were in sight.

When we returned to our party, they had the two Pawnees stripped and scalped. I asked the Sioux if they did not intend to charge the Pawnees in the grove. Young Thunder, who had been a close observer of our actions in recovering the ponies, smiled, and shook us by the hand.

It is a question in my mind if the Sioux would have recovered these ponies but for us. They will not approach a solid body of timber with a heavy growth of underbrush. I thought then that Indians were not such terrible fighters as some writers made them appear; and my first impressions have never changed, although I have contended against some who apparently knew no fear, but they are exceptions.

We reached the village in due season, Young Thunder leading the party, the warriors following singing scalp songs and carrying the Pawnee scalps tied on the end of ' *'coup'*" sticks. The whole village turned out to greet us, and all were yelling like furies. They could tell by the song of the warriors that no loss nor damage had been sustained, which is not always the case.

Pandemonium reigned all night, with singing and dancing and the recounting of the warriors' bravery in taking two scalps and recapturing the ponies stolen by those "dogs of Pawnees."

When Williams heard of my going close to the timber, he said: "I shall have to keep you at home next time, if I expect to return you to your parents. You are a young fool to approach close to timber where hostile Indians are concealed."

I told Williams that three of our ponies were in the bunch and that I did not want to return without them. I thought the Sioux were cowards, but I have learned by experience since that a white man, on the plains at least, will risk where an Indian dreads.

The Pawnees had not acted with good judgment in trying to drive off one hundred head of horses so near daylight. They should have realised that the Sioux would be on their trail in a short while, mounted on their best horses.

Indians are credited with being extraordinarily cunning in stealing horses, the Pawnees especially so, which is the reason other tribes call them "Wolf Indians." The sign for wolf is the index finger and thumb spread apart, other three fingers ends to palm, the hand held up to the side of the head. This is the uniform sign both for wolf and for Pawnee.

I have made mention of *coup*-sticks. While all tribes do not call it by the name ' *'coup*," the custom and usages of all are identical. These sticks are generally made of willow, and are from seven to ten feet in length and one inch in diameter. The bark is peeled and they are painted with vermilion, after the fashion of barbers' poles. Warriors invariably carry these sticks in action, and when a foe falls the one who strikes him with a stick claims the *"coup,"* or one brave action done. A brave's valour is determined by the number of ' *'coups"* he has to his credit. Sometimes a half dozen Indians strike the same foe, and each one claims a *coup* and is entitled to and gets part of the scalp.

CHAPTER 4

War-Parties and Singing

We started the next day for the Laramie River, where we expected to visit another Sioux village, whose chief was Black Moon; also, to meet some traders from Green River, men representing the Northwest Territory Company, and some opposition traders. There existed great rivalry among them to secure their furs and robes from "free trappers," as our outfit was classed. Corporate companies were not friendly to free traders and trappers, and made it very unpleasant for them when opportunity offered. In those days the cream of men in the mountains belonged to the free traders and trappers, and it followed that corporations had no "walk away," as mountain phrase had it.

The Sioux were very wealthy from an Indian standpoint, owning vast numbers of horses and mules and furs and robes and they were generally considered "*nabobs*." They roamed the plains with their villages, so as to be in close proximity to buffalo, of which they required large numbers, as meat was their principal food, and sent out war-parties against their enemies, who were numerous and included Pawnees, Crows, Utes, and Iowas.

So, it followed that they kept constantly on the go, and for recreation, when a war-party had returned from a successful raid, bringing back scalps and ponies, all women related to the party would decorate themselves in all their barbaric finery and promenade through the village singing and chanting the bravery of their lovers and husbands, and making all the other women in the village feel abashed. This is the secret spring of war-parties constantly going out. The singing, dancing, and feasting are continued several nights and days.

Very different are the conditions when war-parties return defeated. A gloom is cast over the village. Relatives of those who are slain or are missing cut off fingers and in other ways mutilate themselves; and a council is held by the medicine men to devise some plan by which they may get revenge on the enemy. Bear in mind—and this is true of all tribes, notwithstanding contrary statements by some writers who have had no general knowledge of the character of the Indian, either on the plains or in the mountains—an Indian never for a moment considers himself the aggressor. Sufficient for him is the fact that some member of the village has been lost.

We reached Black Moon's village on the Laramie River the next day, camping near the chief's lodge.

The story of our recovering the stock and the taking of two Pawnee scalps had preceded us, and the young warriors wanted to see the young paleface who had ridden close to the grove. They looked upon that as a great feat, though I failed to see it in any such light. As it was, it made me many friends among the young men. The older ones, however, said that I was a young fool and would lose my scalp someday.

We traded for considerable fur at this camp, which somewhat astonished Williams, as there were three traders on the Platte River. The reason was, as I have already stated, that the traders were not up to their business in such ways as paying uniform prices for furs of the same quality.

A war-party of young men came into camp that night from the Sweetwater River and informed us that a trader with wagons would be along the next day.

The next morning, we unpacked all our furs, classifying and rebaling them. Williams took great pains to instruct me in all this, saying that he intended to make me the equal of anyone in the business, as it might be useful in later years. I often think that he had a presentiment that I would never return to civilization.

In the afternoon an old trader named Vasques arrived with wagons and oxen, and was astonished to see all the furs we had collected. He looked surly, but this did not worry Williams, who understood his disposition. Williams should have been engaged by the government as a diplomat, for he could outwit any and all of these arrogant corporate traders. At any rate, Vasques saw that his only chance to get furs and robes was to curb his temper and come to terms, which he did, paying us $750 in cash for the beaver and other small furs, and a quantity of Indian goods, of which he had a fine assortment, for the robes.

Williams got the best of him on every turn. He either had to trade with us or haul his Indian goods back to the States, which he was not inclined to do.

When departing the next day, Vasques said that he would make this business of free trading most interesting for all concerned. I admired Williams's reply, which was, "Good, Mr. Vasques; remember I will be on hand to take an active part in the matter when it occurs."

We now had fourteen pack-horses, loaded with a fine assortment of Indian goods, and moved up the Platte River to the mouth of the Sweetwater. While making camp six young Arapahoes put in an appearance and told us that their village was a short distance up the Platte River. It consisted of one hundred lodges, with Yellow Bear as chief. This was old Yellow Bear, father of the one killed on Sand Creek by Colonel Chivington.

Williams rode back with the Indians to their village. His object was to have the Indians bring their robes and furs to our camp, as we intended making a long detour before reaching Green River. Yellow Bear and his son returned with him to inspect our goods, and, being satisfied, returned to the village. We stood guard that night, as we were in a country dangerous from outside war-parties.

The next morning the village arrived early. They were wild-looking Indians, and not to be trusted. They were a thieving outfit, as the whites found out in after years.

Trade opened at once, and by noon we had one hundred robes and a quantity of other furs. Then came a feast and a smoke with the chiefs, after which they all returned to their village. We hurried in packing up, for Williams wanted to reach the Independence Rock crossing of Sweetwater River as soon as possible. He was in hope of meeting another wagon outfit that might be coming from Green River, and to which we might dispose of our furs. We reached the crossing the next day at noon, but found only Vasques's wagon trail.

It was while at this camp that I had my first introduction to Crow Indians, when Williams halted a war-party, or, more properly speaking, a thieving party of twenty-three, within fifty yards of camp. We had all our packs placed in a square, the robes making a fine breastwork.

The Crows were very insolent and came very near bringing on a fight. In the first place, they wanted a feast. Then our best horses, giving in exchange poor ones. They also demanded blankets and furs, all of which Williams gave them to understand they could not have. They next wanted to examine our outfit and trade, but Williams knew that they had nothing to trade and he told them so, and also advised them to leave. At this they became more insulting.

We had two large, shotguns which we used on guard at night, as they were most effective weapons at close range, being loaded with a half-ounce ball and five buckshot. One tall Indian, diabolically painted, stepped towards where I was standing and I brought my gun to bear upon him. At this he said, "*Mas-to-shera mo-mo-nar-ka*," and retreated. Perkins told me that meant, "White man fool."

Finally, the Crows asked for some tobacco, which Williams gave them with the understanding that they were to leave at once, and they did, casting in sign to us, "Mean white men," all of which I understood.

I felt very much like resenting, but was restrained by Williams, who said that I must not heed such things from Indians. After many years of experience, I fully agree with him.

We remained in this camp two days and then started for the upper Wind River country, hoping to meet the Shoshones, who frequently remained in that section until May, furs still being in their prime. It is amusing to hear men from the East claim that beaver and otter are only trapped in the winter. Such is not the case, as beaver and otter trapped in April and May are classed A1. I have sold to expert fur buyers furs trapped in June, and these same buyers credited themselves with being able to tell, by the appearance of the fur, in just what month in the year the furs were trapped.

On our third day's travel we met a trader named Pomeroy, who had Indian goods on hand, expecting to trade with the Indians on the trip to the States. Williams told him that all the Indians he would be liable to meet were without furs, which was stretching it somewhat. We then unpacked our furs and robes and offered to trade for cash or goods. It required half a day to consummate the trade, we receiving $300 in cash and a quantity of Indian goods. Williams told me afterwards that Pomeroy would not make much on that trade.

I think that Williams must have hypnotised Pomeroy, as he overlooked the important fact that at this season of the year Indians were still dressing robes and would continue to do so for six weeks to come, and Pomeroy would have had plenty of opportunities to trade with villages on his way down Platte River. But Williams made him believe that the villages were leaving for buffalo, which was not so, as they had an abundance of meat and buffalo were close by.

Williams was the soul of honour, and when I questioned him about his statements to Pomeroy, he smiled and said, "Diplomacy." I have never forgotten that, and after years of observation I find that honourable merchants follow the same tactics. Self-interest predominates among all, from the highest to the lowest. They evade the literal truth, calling their conduct "business diplomacy."

CHAPTER 5

In a Dangerous Country

We continued on towards Little Wind River and crossed a most rugged and romantic country, whose lofty sky-piercing peaks ascended to and above the clouds. On the northwest were the Wind River Mountains, which are the main Rockies; to the eastward the Big Horn Mountains, world renowned in their isolated grandeur;—the home of all noble game, such as buffalo, elk, antelope, deer, and bear. It is a hunter's paradise. Here the different tribes of Indians met on their annual hunt, and the meet was often the scene of conflict.

We saw no Indian sign until we reached Little Wind River, where Evans and Russell picked up a *moccasin*. This was dangerous country. Hostile war-parties were numerous, and were liable to make their appearance at almost any hour of day or night.

Williams selected a strong position for camp, as he considered this the most dangerous country on the plains, being constantly invaded by war-parties of Blackfeet, Bloods, Piegans, and Crows. The trappers and Shoshones were kept constantly on the alert, to avoid losing their stock and even their scalps. Williams was of the opinion that the tracks discovered were made by a party of Blackfeet, as they almost always went to war on foot.

Beaver and otter seemed plentiful, and the men set traps. That night we slept with arms by our side ready for instant action; and kept close guard, as it was almost a certainty that the Indians had discovered us and would try for our stock. Noble and I stood first guard, and Evans and Russell second.

About four o'clock in the morning two shots brought us all to our feet. Immediately after the shots we heard yell after yell from the Indians, and they began firing at the camp with guns and bows and arrows. Evans and Russell had killed two Indians with their first shots. We fired at the flashes of the Indian guns; these were Hudson

28

Bay flint-locks and made a very decided flash when discharged. The weapon is not over-effective, but will do damage at short range. Some of our shots must have taken effect, as the Indians fell back, though they continued sending shots to camp until close to daylight.

Several of our men, myself included, wanted to charge, but Williams would not allow it, as he considered it dangerous charging an unknown number of Indians at night, although he had concluded that there were not more than a dozen in number, if so many.

Just before daylight the Indians attempted to recover their slain comrades. They are expert in crawling through grass, but our men were up to all their tactics and prevented them and added one more to keep company with the two already sent to their happy hunting-grounds. The Indians gave a yell of despair and departed, sending after us a few parting shots.

Daylight was now appearing in the east and objects could be seen at a distance. Noble and Russell "lifted the hair" of the three dead Indians, and as they had had some experience in scalping it was easily accomplished. The method of scalping was to run the knife around the head under the hair, cutting through to the skull bone; then taking hold of the scalp-lock and giving it a quick jerk, the scalp would come off and was afterwards dried on a hoop.

The reason that mountaineers scalped Indians was in retaliation, and also because Indians dread going to their happy hunting-grounds without their scalps. For this reason, they will risk a great deal to get their slain after a battle.

We discovered a trail of blood leading down the river, from the place where they had fired the shots into camp, showing that some of our return shots had been effective.

Five of our ponies had been wounded, one so severely that we killed him to put him out of misery.

Williams, enraged at the injury that had been done, was determined to punish the Indians still further. Leaving two men in camp he ordered the rest to follow him.

The experienced mountain man is as keen as an Indian on a trail, and no difficulty was found in following this one.

About five miles down the river a small stream put in from the north side. This stream was about two miles in length, and at its head was a spring surrounded by a small grove of quaking aspens. The Indians had gone up this stream, and we were soon close upon them.

Going at a rapid rate for nearly a mile, we came to a rise, and when on top we were within plain view of the Indians, who were hurrying along, trying to get two of their wounded comrades to the grove. They were about half a mile in advance of us. To keep them from reaching the grove, Williams dashed to the right, where there was a level bench or prairie, so as to give our horses a chance to go at top speed.

The Indians saw in a moment that they would be cut off from the grove, and they made for a patch of willows and stunted box-elders just below.

There were eleven of them, and we had them cornered, as trappers say.

From the brow of the hill on our side to the Indians in the willows it was about one hundred yards, and Docket tried a shot. The Indians returned fire, wounding him in the thigh. It was a flesh wound, but bled freely. As there were a quantity of boulders close by, Williams gave orders to roll them up to the brow of the hill for breastworks.

Leaving Evans, Russell, and Docket behind this breastwork, with orders to keep shooting at the Indians, Williams told Noble and me to follow him to the grove without letting the Indians notice our departure.

In the grove we *cached* ourselves, although I did not understand Williams's plan. Its wisdom was soon apparent.

The men on the brow of the hill kept up a steady fire, and the Indians realised that they would be annihilated if they remained in their present position.

Six of them made a dash for the grove, and when they came within one hundred yards Williams gave orders to shoot. We made a lucky shot, and three of them fell face down. The other three gave a yell of despair and ran up the hill. We mounted and dashed after them. The Indians were panic-stricken when they saw us so suddenly mounted.

I now saw what Williams was in a fight. Reckless to an extreme, he dashed at the Indians, who wheeled and shot but missed. A tall Indian was in advance and Williams made for him, and in a shorter time than it takes to write it, there were three more dead Indians. Williams had identified them as Blackfeet, and this was afterwards confirmed by the Shoshones when shown the scalps.

Williams now said: "Boy, this is your first opportunity. Lift the scalp from that buck. It belongs to you."

Of course, I knew how to scalp, and soon accomplished the feat, much to his satisfaction, for he said, "You are broke in now. You will do."

Flattering, I thought, coming from such an old Indian fighter as he was. We went after the first three and then returned to the men at the breastwork and found them waiting for us.

Many men would have left those five Indians in the willows, satisfied with the revenge. Not so with Williams.

Some of our men told me that he was considered the hardest man on the plains to down in a fight with the Indians. He was never known to quit when once started. It was a fight to a finish.

It struck me forcibly in this instance, when he replied to my question of what he was going to do. He looked at me peculiar like and said: "There are five Indians down there who shot at and insulted us. They shall have what they would have given us had they been successful in their attack. Boy, never, if possible, let an Indian escape who has once attacked you." I was receiving a practical lesson.

He now said: "I want one of you to go with me. The rest of you throw some shots at the Indians while we get to the gulch and approach them from below."

But these fearless trappers held Bill in too great estimation, and they all said, "Once, old chieftain, your orders will be disobeyed. We cannot afford to lose you."

Russell said, "Evans and I will undertake that job. You cover us."

Down they bounded to the gulch below. Both were quick on foot, with eyes like eagles. They had been in many desperate fights, and understood the danger of approaching Indians in ambush. A wounded Indian is a dangerous animal when approached by an enemy.

We kept up a steady fire until our men were seen to be close to the willows. Evans and Russell now shot and bounded forward, yelling like Indians.

We also rushed down. One wounded Indian had arrow in bow, ready to shoot, but he was not quick enough. In a very short time, all was over.

We found in the plunder two fine rifles, ammunition, knives, and other articles belonging to trappers. Williams said that some small party of trappers had been surprised by these Blackfeet, and in a few days, we found that such was the case.

After collecting all the plunder, we returned to camp. When Perkins saw what we brought back he said, "Well done, chieftain! Blackfeet had better give you the go-by."

Williams smiled and answered, "No better than you would have done." Either one of these men would have died for the other.

As we were "wolfish"—a mountain phrase for hunger—we did ample justice to the feast which had been prepared.

The men then went to look after the traps, and as I wanted to know all about trapping, I accompanied them. They made an excellent catch of beaver and reset the traps. I observed closely the manner of setting and baiting. This is done in different ways, according to the condition of the banks of the creek, the dams, the depth of water, and whether there is a muddy or gravelly bottom.

Trapping is a science only to be acquired through long practice. I am considered one of the best, yet I am constantly experimenting. "Medicine," which is of various kinds, may be good on one river or creek, but not effective on others.

To skin, flesh, and stretch beaver and otter is quite an art, in which many trappers never become proficient.

CHAPTER 6

We Trade our Blackfoot Plunder

We remained in this camp three days, and Williams was constantly on the lookout for Shoshones or trappers, climbing up on high knolls and using a spyglass.

On the morning of the fourth day, we moved down Little Wind River to where it forms a junction with Big Wind River, and saw no Indian signs.

There is here one of the grandest and most romantic warm springs to be found on this continent. It is situated on the south side of the Little Wind River, about nine miles from the mountains. Its mineral properties are unexcelled, and according to scientific men it is the equal of any spring in what is now known as the National Park. The spring is on the Shoshone reservation. I have been told that New York capitalists are willing to pay the government one million dollars for it. The country from Owl Creek range to the base of the Great Wind River Mountains is called warm land by the Indians.

We stayed in this camp two days, keeping a sharp lookout, especially for war-parties. Here I set my first traps for beaver and caught two and one foot out of three traps set, which made me feel very proud. In those days beaver brought from $8 to $16 a hide. Dark otter skins brought a good horse from the Indians, or $10 to $12 from traders.

We next moved up the river about twenty miles, scouting the country towards Owl Creek Mountains, but saw no fresh Indian sign.

Here was a beautiful and strong camp, which could repel an attack from any number of Indians. Williams said we would have to remain here until we met the Shoshones, or ascertained if they had left for Green River by some other route. They avoided the plains as much as possible on account of the numerous war-parties to be found there.

On the fourth day, at evening, a scouting party of Shoshones was discovered by Williams. I was with him and we were some distance from camp. Williams said, "Shoshones." I asked him how he could tell, and he answered that it was by the way they acted, which he said denoted that they were the advance-guard or scouts of a village. They always have scouts out when moving villages, so as to be prepared for enemies.

We galloped towards them, firing a shot. The Indians saw us and heard the shot and understood that we were friends. There were nine in the party; they were acquainted with Williams, and seemed really glad to meet him. They asked him who I was, and were told that I was a friend from the States. They accompanied us back to camp, where we had a feast and a smoke.

Their curiosity was greatly excited on seeing our captured trinkets, and Williams recounted the whole circumstances of our trouble with the Blackfeet. They were the most excited Indians I have ever seen from that day to this. When shown the scalps, many of them yet stretched on hoops to dry, they jumped up and gave a ringing war-whoop.

These same Blackfeet had killed two trappers on Gray Bull Creek, and had gotten away with five horses.

Williams told the Shoshones that the Blackfeet who had attacked us had no horses. They answered that we had not seen all of them; and that they had stolen seven horses from their village. According to the Shoshones' statement the war-party had split, and there must have been about thirty of them in all. The other Blackfeet were around, they said, and it made them uneasy. They wanted us to pack up at once and join their village. Washakie, one of the most remarkable Indians, was their chief, and he was a great friend of the whites.

Williams told the Shoshones to return to their village, taking two of the Blackfeet scalps, and to notify Washakie that we were camped here and wanted to trade. They departed saying that their village would be with us the next day.

We scouted the country for quite a distance up the river, but saw nothing. It does not follow because one sees no Indians that none are about. It stood mountain men in stead to be constantly on the alert, Indians or no Indians. Many a poor outfit has come to grief by not taking the mountaineers' advice.

We were not disturbed during the night, and in the morning put everything in order to receive Washakie and his village.

Williams told the men that they could have all the plunder captured from the Blackfeet, and that the Shoshones would pay good prices for it. He told me that I could get a good horse for my two scalps. Docket gave me a fancy scalp, saying, "Now, young chief, you can buy a squaw."

About three o'clock Washakie, with a bodyguard of twenty men, rode into camp. It was a pleasure to see that noted chief and Williams meet. Long-parted brothers could not have been more affectionate.

We soon had a feast prepared, and after the feast a smoke.

In the meantime, the village made its appearance, and lodges were put up above and below our camp. We were, in fact, corralled.

The plunder was all spread on blankets, and as Indians are more acquisitive than whites, a lively trade sprung up, particularly with the women. They would give a pair of fancy *moccasins* for almost anything that had belonged to the Blackfeet.

The chief's son brought a good horse and presented it to me. Anyone acquainted with Indians knows that a present from them means that you own something that they want. I soon found out that it was the scalp he wanted and I gave it to him. He was a noble young man, with the characteristics of his father.

The Shoshones were delighted at my proficiency in sign-language, for by this time I was able to converse on any and all subjects.

It must have been very amusing to hear the many questions the women asked me. "What tribe had I been raised with?" "Where was my woman?" "Had I left her?" They would not believe that this was my first experience.

Trade continued until dark. The Indians exchanged *moccasins*, beaver hides, mink, martin, and buffalo robes.

Williams bought all the furs and robes from our men, paying them cash. They had no interest in our stock of goods, but were paid to accompany us. Any furs which they caught in traps belonged to them. They were all old acquaintances of Williams and Perkins.

The Indians stood guard that night, and in fact every night while we were in this section. It stood them well in hand to do so. Kalispell Indians generally paid this country a visit every spring to take a few scalps and ponies. The Kalispells were enemies to all Indians on the plains. When they and Blackfeet war-parties met there was sure to be a clash, and this happened frequently.

Williams and Perkins held council most all night, while scalp dances and war songs were being indulged in by all the young folks. It makes no difference with Indians whether they take the scalps or not, if only these had belonged to their enemies. I have heard people

WASHAKIE—CHIEF OF THE SNAKES

make statements to the contrary, but they knew not what they were speaking of. Hence many false ideas originate in the minds of many well-informed Americans.

The next day Washakie gave orders to his people to bring their furs and robes and give a good trade to their friends. This they did to our satisfaction.

Two mounted parties were sent out scouting for enemies, and a few to bring in meat. One of the parties met three trappers who belonged to the outfit surprised by the Blackfeet. An account of the troubles of these men will well illustrate the risk taken by trappers in collecting furs in those early days and even thirty years later.

The two trappers killed were off some distance from camp looking after their traps, when Indians surprised and killed them. The other three heard the shots and hurried to camp to secure what horses they could; but the Indians were able to run off five head and also to capture the two rifles which we had retaken. Williams returned the rifles and knives to the three men.

They were nervy, these three. One was a Scotchman, one a Frenchman from St. Louis, and the third came from Kentucky.

They said that when they heard the shots, they were aware that their companions had been attacked, so they rushed for their horses, securing six, the Indians getting three besides the two belonging to their dead comrades. "Kentuck" said they had no opportunity to render assistance to their fellows as the Indians charged upon them. They were camped in a thick grove of cottonwoods, and had prepared a breastwork for just such an attack. The Indians kept at long range, knowing that if they approached trappers' guns some of them would come to grief. All Indians dreaded trappers when once brought to bay. Any tribe today, (1905), will confirm this statement. A few shots were exchanged and then the Indians withdrew.

"Kentuck" was anxious to find out what had been done with the two trappers, so he climbed a high knoll and saw about thirty Indians making for the mountains, half of them mounted.

He then went down the gulch and found his two friends dead, scalped, and otherwise mutilated in a horrible manner. His eyes flashed when recounting the circumstances. The reader can well understand the just cause for trappers retaliating. Good for evil is hardly a trapper's creed when dealing with Indians.

After burying the men, they packed up and started to join the Shoshones, knowing where they were camped, and intending to remain with them until they reached Green River. They now joined our party.

In their possession were six packs of beaver of eighty pounds each, worth $9 a pound, making a total of $4320. There was good money in trapping, but the rewards hardly justified the risk.

I found the Scotchman and the Kentuckian well educated men. The latter presented me with a copy of Shakespeare and an ancient and modern history which he had in his pack.

We had an abundance of reading matter with us; old mountain men were all great readers. It was always amusing to me to hear people from the East speak of old mountaineers as semi-barbarians, when as a general rule they were the peers of the Easterners in general knowledge.

These three trappers had caught a beautiful white beaver, a fur which is very rare and valuable. This they presented to Williams and would take nothing in return, saying: "You keep this as a memento from us of the high esteem in which we hold you."

In the afternoon the other scouting party returned and reported that near Owl Creek Mountains they had had a fight with a war-party of Pend Oreilles, and that two of their number were slightly wounded.

These two appeared very proud of their wounds. All Indians have that weakness, showing their wounds to all and looking for smiles from their lady loves for their bravery.

CHAPTER 7

We Have a Close Encounter

The Shoshones expected to remain in this camp for several days, to give their women an opportunity to finish dressing robes and drying meat.

The grass was good, timber was plentiful, and a few buffalo were on the prairie. To supply the camp with fresh meat and to scout for war-parties would keep the young men busy, so Washakie said.

In the meantime, the Indians were having a joyous time dancing over Blackfeet scalps. I passed the time in visiting all the lodges, and studying the habits and customs. I was becoming interested and had a desire to learn everything pertaining to Shoshones, so that I could ascertain the difference between them and other tribes that I might come in contact with.

The scouts kept reporting fresh Indian tracks, but no Indians. This brought about a council between the Shoshones and our party for the purpose of devising some plan to rid this section of war-parties. We had more than a passing interest in accomplishing this. Not that we feared the war-parties, but we wanted to collect furs without being constantly annoyed.

Williams was the leading spirit in the council. After much deliberation it was decided to form three parties of twenty-five each, who should operate in conjunction, some of our party to be in each of the three.

By daylight the following morning all were ready, and we silently left the village, taking the routes selected.

Our company of Shoshones, including Williams, went to Bull Lake, as it was a favourite place for war-parties. Indian tradition had it that the father of all buffaloes roamed around this lake. From the high knolls surrounding the water one could sweep the country for miles with the aid of a spy-glass, and could readily discover any Indian village or trapping outfit.

When we reached Bull Lake Creek, where it forms a junction with Big Wind River, we saw fresh pony tracks coming from the east side of Big Wind River and going up the creek. It was impossible to tell the number, as they travelled in single file.

Every foot of this section was known to the Shoshones, which was of great advantage. We went up the creek for about three quarters of a mile, when the country became rough. Three of the young men now dismounted, stripped, and went on ahead to scout, we holding their horses. When we received a signal from the scouts, we would advance to the point explored.

It was just about this time that we heard shots from the east side of Wind River, and we felt certain that one of our parties had come in contact with hostiles.

Our scouts approached a high-timbered knoll and discovered a band of Indians running towards a high ridge, looking in the direction from which we had heard the shots. Our scouts returned on a run and mounted. Moonhavey, a noted chief and warrior, took the lead, keeping under cover so as not to be observed by the Indians on the ridge.

We continued on for half a mile and came to a crooked draw which headed up on the ridge. The chief wheeled and went up this draw for a quarter of a mile and halted.

Just ahead was a sharp bend, which when passed would bring us in full view of the Indians on the ridge.

The Shoshones stripped to breech-clouts in short order and mounted their runners. Moonhavey gave the signal for a charge and dashed around the curve.

Within two hundred yards were fourteen head of ponies under the care of two young men. They gave a warning cry to their comrades on the ridge, who fired several shots without effect as the range was too great.

With a furious yell the Shoshones charged on the two men, who tried their best to mount, but they were soon on their way to their happy hunting-grounds. The Indians on the ridge, seeing the two men fall, disappeared.

Our party divided, one going to the right and the other to the left, until about three hundred yards apart, when both parties started up the ridge.

Upon reaching the top, we saw the Indians about one quarter of a mile distant, making for Wind River, where cottonwood groves were visible. Once there they would be able to stand us off for some time and more than likely kill some of us.

The country was comparatively level to the river, with the exception of two steep draws, which we crossed at a run. If the war-party had used good judgment they would have taken possession of one of these draws, but their minds must have been set on the timber and river. The war-party next scattered, which was another blunder, as they must have realised that they could not reach the timber and that we outnumbered them two to one. They should have remained together and taken possession of some buffalo wallow, for there were plenty of these around. I fail to see the wonderful strategy with which Indians are credited. I had a quick eye and I observed every move of both parties.

When the Indians scattered, they were about two hundred and fifty yards ahead, and if the scene that followed could have been reproduced on canvas it would have been worth a fortune. It was a scene that occurs only in actual warfare.

The Shoshones gave yell after yell, charging madly and most recklessly. The chief warned them to be careful, but they paid no attention to him, for in a case like this it is a great feat to take the first scalp, and the successful warrior is greatly praised in their village. His lady love guys the other girls, claiming her lover as the bravest of the brave, first among their enemies. I believe the same rule exists among paleface girls, when a lover has performed an heroic act.

The war-party dropped blankets and war-sacks, which contained tobacco, pipes, *moccasins*, and other things, thinking that the Shoshones would stop and pick them up. But the Shoshones charged on, redoubling their yells.

It was a wild scene for a few moments, shots and arrows flying in every direction. Williams, Moonhavey and myself had the fleetest horses and reached the Indians first. Williams killed the first Indian, while Moonhavey and I both fired at the same time and both missed, which chagrined me greatly.

I dashed after a tall Indian, who had his arrow strung, passing him at a run. We both fired at the same time, his arrow lodging in the fleshy part of my horse's shoulder, which would have ruined him if the arrow had had force behind it, but the Indian was scared. My shot knocked him down, and I heard Williams yell out, "Well done, boy!" There were only three left and they were having a combat with a few young Shoshones who were doing poor execution. Some older men

41

His arrow lodged in the fleshy part of my horse's shoulder,

stepped in and put a quietus to any further fighting by sending the three to join their companions in the happy hunting-grounds.

After "lifting hair" and collecting plunder, we returned to where we had left the captured ponies. Seven of them belonged to the Shoshones, having been stolen by the Blackfeet. Five of them belonged to Kentucky's party, and there were two strange ones, which Moonhavey forced Williams and myself to accept.

The shots had ceased from the east, so the chief sent the wounded men to the village, and the rest of us started over towards where we supposed our second party was. We discovered them clustered together near a spring. One Shoshone was dying, having been shot through the lungs, and three others were wounded. They had come in contact with nine Blackfeet, who had taken possession of a rocky knoll and made a breastwork on it. The two opposing forces exchanged shots for some time without any apparent result, as fearless Evans remarked. Council was held, and it was agreed to charge the knoll from two sides.

Six Indians were left behind to cover the charge by continuous firing at the breastwork. With a yell and a rush, the knoll was charged, and a quietus was put on those nine Blackfeet in short order.

Evans had his cheek split open with an arrow, and "Kentuck" received a slight wound in the left arm. Williams always carried a supply of court-plaster, lint, and bandages for such emergencies, and soon fixed up the men.

After dressing the Indians' wounds, we took two long poles and fastened one on each side of a gentle pony, lacing a pair of blankets to the poles. On this we put the dying Indian and set out for the village. The other wounded Indians rode ponies and, fool-like, were proud of their wounds.

We reached the village at three o'clock and were met by half the tribe, who wanted to ascertain the cause of our slow approach. And now there was a mixture of joy and sorrow blended together; the relatives of the dead man mourning and making the night hideous with dismal howls, others singing, yelling, and sending forth war-whoops, parading the village, and recounting in detail all the incidents pertaining to the fight and the extermination of those "dogs of Blackfeet."

CHAPTER 8

My First Bear

The third party had not as yet returned. In going through the captured war-sacks we found two white men's scalps, which "Kentuck" recognised as belonging to his partners. He buried them, saying, "I am not acquainted with their relations, or I would send or take the scalps to them."

Williams assisted me in cutting the arrowpoint out of my horse's shoulder, and he soon recovered, which highly pleased me. He and I were greatly attached to each other, and I used to feed him sugar every day. Docket said that I gave him more sugar than the whole party used.

Williams would answer, "Let the boy alone, he will get over that in time." But I never did while I owned Runner. Sugar was then worth one dollar a pound.

"Scotty" and Russell were with the third party, and Washakie, with all the head men of the village, held a council with Williams and Perkins to talk over the situation.

They came to the conclusion that there were no more Blackfeet in the country, and that the third party had come in contact with Arapahoes, Crows, or Kalispells.

Washakie finally decided to dispatch half a dozen young men to scout the country as far as Owl Creek Mountains, a distance of twenty miles, and to return at once unless they discovered something which justified a further advance.

The party was led by the chief's oldest son, a brave and energetic young warrior, bearing a remarkable resemblance to his noted father. They left, leading their running horses, so that in case of emergency they could either fight or run as circumstances warranted.

In the afternoon of the next day, the third party was seen slowly approaching, and it was evident that it included some wounded. The Indian women who had husbands or lovers in the party became most anxious. Some of the Indians with spy-glasses ran to high ground to count their number, and soon made out thirty-three, which was the full complement, including the six young scouts.

On the arrival of the party in the village it was found to contain six wounded, including "Scotty" and Russell. The former was shot through under the left collar-bone, and Russell had received a glancing shot in the scalp. "A close call," as Perkins remarked.

They had met a war-party of twenty Piegans on the summit of Owl Creek Mountains. Shots were exchanged with little damage, and the Shoshones finally charged the hill. It was during this charge that "Scotty" and Russell received their wounds. The Piegans retreated, leaving two of their number. The Shoshones followed them about twenty miles, keeping up a running fight until the Piegans got into a strong position; then they withdrew. On the way back they lifted the hair of three killed in the running fight and two killed on the hill. They also collected considerable plunder, including five good ponies, giving "Scotty" and Russell their share.

The leading chiefs now held a council, and decided that there were no more war-parties in that section. All the Indians were jubilant and they went about saying that now all their enemies would fear them. They calculated without their host, as the saying is. When what had taken place became known among the Blackfeet and Piegans, they would be sure to hold a great council and concoct some plan whereby they could revenge themselves upon those "dogs of Shoshones" for the loss of their brave warriors. As I previously stated, Indians never consider themselves the aggressors. It is enough that they have lost warriors.

That same day we wound up our trade with the village and began to pack up. Williams induced Washakie to take all our furs to Fort Bridger, as well as the six packs belonging to "Kentuck's" party. The Shoshones intended to go by the South Pass route, while we purposed to cross the mountains and follow down Green River, collecting furs and bear hides *en route*. Bear hides were still prime in the mountains and were valuable. On the second day we parted company with our friends, who urged us to stay.

By this time, I was almost equal to the best sign-talker in the village. Bear in mind that not all Indians are good sign-talkers. Dunces among them are as common as among whites.

Washakie would look at me quizzically and ask me with what tribe I had been raised? He could not or would not believe that this was my first experience among Indians. He would say to Williams that I could ride a horse as well as any of his young men and was their equal in shooting; while in fact I was their superior with both rifle and pistol, thanks to my early training. I mystified and bewildered them by turning hand-springs. My health was splendid and I was surcharged with energy.

As we now had eleven in our party, we apprehended no more danger from war-parties, but traders and trappers never relaxed their vigilance in those days. He who did so often came to grief.

If asked to compare the horsemanship of the Cheyennes and the Shoshones, I should say that they were equally skilful. Both can accomplish the difficult feat of retaining their seat on a horse while life remains; and they are like a cat, tenacious of life.

When wounded they retain their seat by winding a hair rope around the horse's body; sometimes they put their legs under this rope, tight to the thighs; and sometimes bring the knees up so as to form an acute angle, the rope passing tight over the thighs and under the calf of the legs.

They can lie on the side of a horse in action, and if wounded will retain the seat until out of danger of enemies.

I have heard some men claim that an Indian could lie on the side of a horse and shoot under its neck with bow and arrow, without the use of pad, saddle, or rope! To my knowledge such is not the case. I have many times been in action with mounted Indians and I have never seen it accomplished.

An Indian dreads to use a rope when approaching trappers in a fortified position, or when brought to bay. Trappers will kill the horse first, and they are then sure to get the Indian.

As hunters and shots, the Shoshones are superior to the Cheyennes, for the reason that they are more of a mountain Indian and hunt more small game.

The domestic habits of the Shoshones are commendable for Indians. They are clean, inclined to be proud, and think a great deal of their women and children. They like to see them well dressed as Indian dress goes. Many of them have more than one wife, but one of the wives is superior to the others, who do all the hard work, such as dressing robes, collecting fuel, and packing the horses. Take them as a whole, the Shoshones are a contented and hospitable tribe and, no doubt owing to Washakie's great influence, friends of the whites.

We remained two days at Bull Lake and caught many beaver. I

was now becoming very successful in trapping, and caught as many as any of the outfit. Williams taught me to skin, flesh, and stretch, in all of which I soon became proficient. Furs indifferently handled always bring a low price on the market.

We next crossed the mountains to the west fork of Green River, and found furs in abundance. We also found black, brown, and silvertip bear, getting several fine hides.

I went with Perkins on my first bear hunt. We succeeded in coming upon two black bears and got within one hundred yards without the bears scenting us. Perkins told me which one to aim at, and we both fired at the same time. His bear made one forward jump and then rolled over. Mine fell forward, growling and trying to get up, but unable to do so. I put another shot in the bear's head to finish her. Of course, I felt very proud of my first bear, though in later years I learned that it was easier to kill a bear than an antelope, provided you know where to shoot it. You are sure to get any animal shot in the shoulder-blade, because they cannot travel.

It has often been said that bears are the most ferocious animals in protecting their young. Such a statement is false, as I have many times seen a she-bear run away from her young, which were picked up and carried away into captivity. The mountain lion, so much dreaded by many, is cowardly and is only dangerous when cornered. The great danger in bear-hunting is when a wounded one gets into a thicket. In such instances a good bear dog is needed. We shot two more bears that day, making a load for a pack-horse.

Perkins said to me after supper that night: "Now, young man, I am going to give you a practical illustration of how to shoot not only bear, but all other four-legged animals." He pulled out one of the bears and took the hide off. Next, he spread out the legs and put the bear on its belly. He then cut the ribs from the backbone, cut down the flank, and pulled down the sides, so as to give a view of the bear's internal organs. He then showed me where to shoot from any position that it was possible for the bear to be in, and told me particularly to note how low the vital parts lay.

I profited by that lesson and never forgot or deviated from it. I would advise all persons to do likewise with their first bear. I would also advise them never to go into a thicket after a wounded bear, and not to hunt bears at all unless they have confidence both in their rifles and their own nerves. Many men are used up by wounded bears through their own ignorance.

Our wounded men had by this time recovered sufficiently to take an active part in collecting furs. We caught a quantity of martin and a few fisher. The latter is classed as American sable, with a demand twenty times greater than the supply.

We remained in this camp on the west fork for six days, and then moved down-stream about twenty-five miles and camped in a most beautiful place: an ideal spot for the poet to become inspired with the beauty and grandeur of nature and to be awed by the lofty peaks which ascended above the clouds.

At this camp we made a great catch of bear, having piled up a lot of beaver carcasses to attract them. I became expert in bringing down bear with the first shot. The men were all fine shots. They could not be otherwise after such long experience. They often received great praise from people for their expertness with firearms, but no more than they merited, for an American mountaineer had no equal on the globe. It was necessary that they should be expert, for they carried their lives in their hands. At any moment they were liable to come in contact with roving war-parties, who were never known to fail to attack a trapping outfit if they dared. To be taken prisoner was to experience a death none desired. A slow fire is merciful beside other cruelties practised by Indians. All mountain men were acquainted with these facts, and therefore it was impossible for an Indian to capture a scout or a trapper—and scouts were invariably trappers. They knew what would follow.

I have often been asked why we exposed ourselves to such danger? My answer has always been that there was a charm in the life of a free mountaineer from which one cannot free himself, after he once has fallen under its spell.

CHAPTER 9

Exploration of the Yellowstone in 1839

We left this camp with regret and moved down the river about twenty miles. Here we saw pony tracks, but could not determine whether they were made by Indians or trappers. Selecting a favourable location for camp, we built corrals and turned loose most of the stock under guard, picketing half a dozen of our best horses in case of emergency.

Docket and I then mounted our horses and followed the pony tracks, receiving a caution from Williams to keep a sharp lookout. Docket was an experienced scout, well up in Indian strategy, and we apprehended little danger of being surprised by lurking savages. We followed the trail about six miles, and struck a creek which we followed northward about seven miles. Here we came in sight of a camp, which Docket pronounced to belong to trappers. Arrived there, we found seven free trappers, three of whom were acquainted with Docket. They were somewhat astonished at seeing us.

Two of their number were badly wounded, having been attacked about ten days previous, when they lost half their horses and some of their traps. The Indians had discovered their traps and raised (stolen) them. This often occurs. The outfit were very glad to meet us, as they were out of tobacco and ammunition. They said that they would move over to our camp the following day.

When asked if they knew what Indians had attacked them, they said no, but they supposed that they were Blackfeet. This tribe was the last to be out in the spring, its war-parties going in every direction, even as far as Salt Lake Valley and beyond, as all old mountain men can attest. There is a Blackfoot fort on a bench overlooking the great hot springs, north of where Salt Lake City now stands. The fort is still preserved, I have been told, as a memento of the old days. At all events, I myself, as well as many others, bathed in the spring and saw the fort long before any Mormons had reached Salt Lake Valley.

Leaving the valley Docket and I went across country, keeping a good lookout for bears, of which many signs were visible. About three miles from the trappers' camp, we discovered a she-bear with three cubs passing over a ridge. Hurrying to the ridge, we saw the bears about two hundred and fifty yards away, turning over rocks in a hollow. We dismounted and crept to within one hundred yards, when Docket said, "You kill the old one." Taking careful aim, I placed the bullet within an inch of the spot aimed for. She bounded forward and rolled over, with blood rushing from mouth and nostrils. Docket shot a cub, the other two running around thoroughly bewildered. We both shot again, each one getting his cub.

We took the hide off the old one and packed the young ones to camp. At this season of the year a cub is the daintiest of food, and one which few mortals have an opportunity of partaking of at the present day.

The other men had shot four bears, besides making a good catch in the traps. We were kept busy dressing and stretching until dark.

We stood guard constantly—one man at a time, and left nothing to chance. Just because no Indian sign had been discovered, it did not follow that no Indians were about or in the vicinity. If they were, they would have heard the shooting and would be sure to hunt up the camp before morning.

The next day the trappers whom Docket and I had met arrived and camped close to us. They traded several beaver hides for articles they stood in need of. They were a sunburnt, hardy and brave-looking lot of men, with erect forms and fearless demeanour. All but the two wounded ones were acquainted with our outfit. These two belonged in Santa Fé.

We remained in this camp eight days, and as the trapping season was over started for Fort Bridger, travelling by easy stages.

Here we found many trappers and traders who were having a high time, gambling and drinking. Many trappers became hilarious, but not offensive. A strict law prevailed among mountain men embodied in a few words: "Take nothing which does not belong to you without the owner's consent." A man who committed an offence would be fined about all he possessed, besides being ostracised. Far better to be dead than in that condition. He would never be allowed in a trappers' camp. His act would in a short time be known throughout all the camps.

It was at this time that I became acquainted with many of the old mountain men, such as Bridger, Anderson, and the Baker brothers. A great many trappers, such as Carson and Bent, resorted to Las Vegas and Santa Fé. There was a great rivalry among fur buyers at those places. Prairie schooners were constantly hauling goods from Independence, Mo., to the two towns.

Fort Bridger is on Black's Fork, a tributary of Green River, a beautiful location. Henry's Fork and other streams tributary to the same river contain the purest of water and an abundance of trout. Timber was plenty and the grass excellent for stock. It was an ideal place for a camp for either trapper or Indian. Washakie was camped about three miles from Bridger. He had not stored our furs at the Fort, but had them in his village.

Pomeroy and Campbell, agents for the Northwest Fur Company, were at Bridger, anxious to buy furs. They were acquainted with Williams, but were not on very friendly terms. In fact, they were not friendly with any free trader or trapper, but were too shrewd to show the dislike too plainly. They were arrogant, having a desire to control the actions of free trappers to their own personal advantage, something which they never accomplished. They struck Williams at once for a trade, and we packed all our furs from the Indian village to our camp. I observed closely the dickerings and tricks of those fur buyers on one side and of Williams on the other.

It took three days before the trade was consummated to Williams's satisfaction. Our men got Williams to handle their furs, as none of them were able to deal with these leeches of fur buyers. We had a few Indian goods left, so Williams traded for more to complete the assortment, as he expected later to meet the Utes and Navajos. Besides the Indian goods we received one thousand dollars in cash and three cheques on St. Louis bankers.

I mailed my cheque to father and got scolded for so doing when I returned for a thirty days' visit a few years afterward. I also wrote him that I should not return in the spring. I had become infatuated with mountain life and was enjoying splendid health. I would not have foregone the same for all the wealth in the universe.

Like Vasques, these traders threatened to make it very unpleasant for Williams someday. But this did not in the least disturb him. Perkins told them that they had better look out for Williams, as he had more influence with Indians than any of the traders.

"Kentuck" sold his furs and went back to the States, promising to rejoin our party in the spring. "Scotty" remained with us. Altogether there were about sixty trappers at Bridger besides a few Hudson Bay men. The order of the day was drinking, gambling, horse-racing, and shooting-matches. I believe gambling is contagious, for I could not resist trying my luck at target-shooting at five dollars a shot. I won two hundred and thirty dollars, much to the disgust of many old-timers, who thought they had an easy thing of it with a "boy." Our men all backed me heavily.

During the evenings I used to listen to old trappers relating stories, and they interested me greatly. From an historical point of view one in particular is worth recording.

In the year 1839 a party of forty men started on an expedition up the Snake River. In the party were Ducharme, Louis Anderson, Jim and John Baker, Joe Power, L'Humphrie, and others. They passed Jackson's Lake, catching many beaver, and crossed the Continental Divide, following down the Upper Yellowstone—Elk—River to the Yellowstone Lake. They described accurately the lake, the hot springs at the upper end of the lake; Steamboat Springs on the south side; the lower end of the lake, Vinegar Creek, and Pelican Creek, where they caught large quantities of beaver and otter. They also told all about the sulphur mountain, the Yellowstone Falls, and the mud geysers, and explained the relations of all these more lucidly than any map can show them.

They also described a fight that they had with a large party of Piegan Indians at the lower end of the lake on the north side, and on a prairie of about half a mile in length. The trappers built a corral at the upper end of the prairie and fought desperately for two days, losing five men besides having many wounded. The trappers finally compelled the Piegans to leave, with the loss of many of their bravest warriors. After the wounded were able to travel, they took an Indian trail and struck a warm-spring creek. This they followed to the Madison River, which at that time was not known to the trappers.

I listened with rapt attention when they described the wonderful springs at the Lower Basin, especially the one situated on the bank of the river called Fire Hole. It was this spring which gave the name Fire Hole Basin.

The description of the geysers on the upper Madison River astonished all the trappers present, and Williams advised me to take notes, as he wanted to visit that section.

Many years after I guided a party through that country and it lay as a picture before me. I used to describe in advance what we should see from day to day, and members of the party said: "How comes it, Hamilton? You said that you had never been in this section before, yet you go from place to place describing everything just as it is?"

In a very few words I enlightened them, and they thought it strange that the outside world had not earlier known about that wonderful Country.

I gave them to understand that the outside world would not believe stories told by trappers of the grand and romantic scenery to be found in the Rocky Mountains. Had this wonderland been described in St. Louis in the early forties, the reply would invariably have been, "Old mountaineer's story." There is plenty of proof of this assertion. Trappers as a rule were an independent set when relating truths which were not believed. It was the fault of our advanced civilization that this wonderland was not brought to the notice of the general public years before it was.

Give me the man who has been raised among the grand things of nature! He cultivates truth, independence, and self-alliance. He has lofty thoughts and generous impulses. He is true to his friends and true to the flag of his country.

Many Shoshones were present at Fort Bridger, and they asked me all kinds of questions by signs, all of which I answered correctly, to the astonishment of old trappers. Even Bridger asked me where I had learned sign-language. I pointed to Williams and said, "From him."

"Not so," said Bridger, "for you can teach him signs."

He asked Williams where I had come from and he was answered truthfully, but did not believe what he was told. Many old-timers thought I had been raised by some tribe. Even today, (1905), people believe the same. Enough of this—it is sufficient to say that in one year from the time I started I was considered the most proficient in sign-language of all white men on the plains.

We stayed at Fort Bridger about two weeks and then, with Washakie and his Shoshones, moved to Brown's Hole on Green River, which is about sixty miles from Bridger and was a trappers' rendezvous. A few Utes and Navajos came up on their annual visit with the Shoshones, to trade and to race horses. These Indians collect considerable fur and are keen traders. We opened up our goods in a tent, and I was placed in charge as trader, having by this time a fair idea of the quality and price of furs.

CHAPTER 10

Williams Leaves Us

We remained at Brown's Hole until the first of September, making several excursions to the Uintah Mountains, a beautiful and romantic country and then a hunters' paradise for small game.

Nothing occurred to mar the good feeling between the whites and the Indians. I spoke of this to Williams one day when the three tribes were parading on horseback. Indians and horses were decorated with paint and trappings of finery, according to the taste of the owner. Each man was trying to outdo the others in horsemanship, stopping ponies when in full career, halting at a mark, at a jump—the one who succeeded in stopping the nearest to the mark winning the trophy. I had seen Cheyennes and Sioux parade, but they were not equal to these.

The whites and Indians held shooting contests on horseback, and the former showed their superiority. Three posts were set in the ground, about twenty-five yards apart. They stood six feet out of the ground and were ten inches in diameter. The top of the post was squared for a distance of about twelve inches. The arms to be used were Colt's six-shooters. Horses were to be put at full speed, passing the posts not closer than ten feet, and the contestant was to fire two shots at each post.

Some of our party put two bullets in each post and all at least one. I tried it twice, and was somewhat surprised to find that the best I could do was to place one bullet in each post. The Indians had several pistols equal to ours, but only three of them hit each post, putting one shot in each. Many Indians hit but one post out of six shots.

With rifles the whites defeated the Indians still worse, shooting at all distances from twenty to three hundred yards. In those days the best rifles used were the Hawkins, and they carried three hundred and fifty yards. Wagers were always made, and the Indians always insisted that the whites should take first shot. Nine times out of ten the whites won, and then the Indians as an excuse would claim that "their medicine was not strong that day."

In riding bucking horses, the whites also came out ahead, and it is well known today, (1905), that the Indians never did equal them in this accomplishment.

I have already mentioned that two of our men were expert with bows and arrows. Russell was one, and Bowers, whom we called "Silver Tip," the other. They could hold their own against any of the Indians. In fact, we were all constantly practising with them. Today I can shoot an arrow-point through an inch and a half plank.

Our party now started to get ready for the fall trapping season, which opened in the mountains on the 15th of September. Williams had to go to Santa Fé on business, but he promised to be back in the spring and organise a party for a two-years expedition.

He traded his mule, which was a good one, for a Navajo's blanket. The blankets are world-renowned. It is a question if any manufactured by civilized men are their equal. They are absolutely water-proof, and are made by the women entirely by hand. The colours are fast, and the secret of the art is known only to the Indians.

Williams presented me with his, and I kept it many years, making a serape of it. This is done by cutting a slit in the centre large enough for the head to go through, and it will keep one perfectly dry in wet weather.

We traded all our furs to some buyers, taking in exchange sugar, coffee, salt, crackers, flour, ammunition, tobacco, knives, traps, etc., and cash, Perkins and myself taking the goods and Williams the cash.

The day before Williams started, he took me for a walk and gave me advice in many things. He looked upon me as his son, and few fathers ever gave their sons better advice.

He also told me that he was writing a history of his life among the Pueblo, Navajo, and Apache Indians, and when completed he would give it to me, which he did many years afterward. I firmly believe that it was the only true history ever written of the characteristics, habits, and customs of these three tribes. In 1873 I was appointed United States Marshal, to look after some bad men and Indians at the Crow Indian Reservation on the Yellowstone River. Major F. D. Pease was agent at the time. For security I placed Williams's manuscript in the safe and three days later the Agency burned down. At the time of the fire, I was on the trail of some cattle thieves, otherwise I would have saved a manuscript that can never be replaced.

CHAPTER 11

Trapper Life in a Hostile Indian Country

For the next ten days we were very busy getting into shape and organising. Perkins was selected as leader. The party was made up of twenty trappers, and included our old men with "Scotty." A council was held on the 16th of September and it was decided to explore Salt Lake, Weber, Bear, and Malade Rivers, and other streams, as circumstances and amount of furs should warrant.

The next day we started, a wild and motley-looking outfit I thought. The Indians all crowded up to shake us by the hand and to warn us to look out for the Blackfeet.

Nothing of interest took place until we reached Weber River, which rises in the Wahsatch Mountains and empties into Salt Lake. We followed the river down, passing through the canon, and came in sight of the Great Salt Lake Valley, spread out in all its primitive grandeur. I said to Perkins, "Here is a scene fit to be viewed by the gods."

Perkins and the other men laughed, saying, "Bill is becoming poetical." It was no longer "Boy." "Bill" had taken its place.

Perkins wanted to visit a stream south of where Salt Lake City now stands, and on our way there we camped at the hot springs, noted before, taking a plunge or bath before the Mormons ever heard of that country. We also examined the Blackfoot fort on the bench overlooking the springs.

The next morning some Utah Indians called on us and wanted us to pay for being in their country. Such a thing could not be thought of for a moment. These Indians spoke the Shoshone tongue, which many of our men understood. They were also very fair sign-talkers. When informed that they would receive no pay, their chief, who was called Old Bear—and bear he was by his looks, for a more surly look-

Next morning some Utah Indians called on us

ing savage was never seen—ordered us to leave immediately. He had with him some thirty warriors, who had a few flint-lock guns, bows and arrows, lances, knives, and tomahawks. They were thus fairly well armed, but by no means equal to our party.

Perkins, who was an expert in dealing with turbulent and insulting Indians, having great patience, tried by every means to pacify them and make friends, but without success. He made the Indians keep back from our outfit, and then they would spit at us and make signs meaning "dogs," which we all understood. I expected every minute to see the fight commence. We were prepared at every point, and our arms were in prime condition.

Perkins cautioned the men to have patience, for many of them were becoming nervous at the insults from the Indians. Trappers would not brook insults from anyone, and as I saw these men grow more and more angry and bite their lips, I thought it commendable in them to curb their feelings. All this time Perkins was trying his best to make peace. He filled his pipe, lit it, and offered it to the chief, who refused with contempt, saying, "Big Chief never smokes with white dogs."

Perkins's patience was now exhausted, and he told the chief in pretty plain language to get out. When the Indians saw our men prepare for action by standing in open order and bringing their guns down to bear on them, they mounted their ponies; and casting all kinds of insults at us, both in signs and in spoken language, they departed, going south, the very route that we wanted to take.

After they had disappeared, we held a council, and Perkins thought that we would have to give up going any farther south, as their village was located somewhere in that direction. We were not afraid of the Indians, but we wanted to collect furs and would have no opportunity to do this without being greatly annoyed.

As things stood it was a certainty that the Indians would follow us, and that a fight could not be avoided. We concluded to take the back track, a thing that trappers seldom do, except under extreme conditions such as those just related.

The reader may be interested in knowing just how a company of twenty trappers divided the work in the business of collecting furs among hostile Indians.

In the first place, everything was held in common, which means that the value of all furs trapped was equally divided. All the men could not trap, for a picket had to be constantly on duty. A guard remained with the horses during the day. Dining the right the horses were corralled. One man had to take care of camp, and generally two men acted as skinners and caretakers of all the furs brought in. The remainder set traps, and all kept a sharp lookout for Indians. No shooting was allowed while setting traps, as a shot signified Indians, at which signal all were on the alert.

A general rule that was followed by all mountain men was to strap stay-chains or trace-chains to the horses' fetlocks. It was impossible for them to stampede with such a fixing. When trappers lost their horses, they were obliged to go to some rendezvous and restock, as furs could not be collected without horses.

We camped in a strong position on a sharp bend in the Weber River, where the banks were steep and the waters deep, so that in case of an attack the Indians could not approach from the river side. Perkins thought that the Indians would undoubtedly hold a council in their village and concoct some plan whereby they could capture those "white dogs" and get all their horses. All this we understood, but, as I have said before, they calculated without their host, as the sequel will show.

Beaver signs were plentiful here, and after camp was made the men went out and set traps. At supper all hands were in camp.

We passed many jokes that evening, "Silver Tip" taking the lead, for he was by long odds the most humorous and comical member of the party.

Personally, I was engaged in making a close study of all our men, particularly the new ones, and I came to the conclusion that they were a noble-looking body of men. With high foreheads and with calm and fearless eyes, their demeanour was that of gentlemen. I had read of Daniel Boone and Simon Kenton, and in my mind, I began to make comparisons, wondering whether Boone or Kenton were any nobler-looking than these men.

Then I thought of Leonidas and his handful of men repelling Xerxes and his immense Persian Army. Could they be any braver or of finer metal than these trappers? As such thoughts passed through my mind, I came to the conclusion that the American nation might well feel proud of her mountaineers, who fearlessly explored the un-known wilderness, encountering and overcoming untold difficulties and dangers by the mere force of their own indomitable will-power and courage.

The true mountain men have never received the credit which they justly merited for their part in bringing this unknown country to light.

We only put up one ten-skin lodge for our effects, sleeping outside with arms in hand. Two guards were put on duty, to be relieved at midnight.

Perkins said that it was customary for the Utahs to attack just before daylight. It is at this time that Indians expect to find whites fast asleep.

A little before day two or three wolf howls were heard by the guards, who immediately notified Perkins, and he soon had all the men up. Our packs were placed in a semicircle as a breastwork, and twenty of our best horses were saddled and tied in a thicket, to protect them as much as possible from Indian bullets and arrows. About the only protection the Indians would have in approaching camp was the sage-brush which stood on the flat.

We had a fairly well-fortified position, and it stood us well in hand to have it so. The Indians, knowing our number, would attack us seven or eight to one, and perhaps more.

Trappers in those days were obliged always to contend against overwhelming numbers; but they never hesitated, and it was always a fight to win, for defeat meant death.

The first wolf howls were soon followed by others, coming from points nearer and in a semicircle. Indians are expert in imitating the cries of wolves or coyotes, and it is very hard to distinguish them from the cries of the real animals. On the other hand, even after years of practice, few whites can successfully imitate these animals. The hooting of the owl is frequently used as an Indian signal in attacking camps. All these signals are carefully studied by trappers and scouts, who are rarely deceived.

The Indians must have located our camp from the mountains, which were at no great distance, as our one lodge was set up in a Cottonwood grove, which concealed it.

We had not long to wait before the attack commenced. Just at break of day the signals ceased, and the trappers knew that the crisis was at hand.

The Indians crept to within one hundred yards of camp before they gave the war-whoop. Then they came madly charging, fully one hundred in number.

The trappers had their rifles in hand and their pistols out of their scabbards ready for instant use after the rifles were discharged.

We let them get within fifty yards before delivering a shot, and at the discharge of the rifles many fell. Three of our men were armed with double-barrelled shotguns, loaded with a half-ounce ball and five buckshot, deadly weapons at close quarters. These were now discharged and the Indians halted. Immediately the trappers began with their six-shooters, one in each hand, for as a result of long and constant practice they could shoot equally well with either. Every condition of his life obliged the trapper to be expert in the use of firearms.

At receiving so many shots from twenty men the Indians became panic-stricken. They had not calculated on the trappers having two pistols each—twelve shots apiece after the rifles were discharged. They had expected to exterminate us before we could reload our rifles.

The Indians retreated, assisting many of their wounded. Perkins had hard work to keep the men from charging, for our fighting blood was up. Had we charged, we would have lost several men, for the sagebrush was alive with Indians.

Several in our party received slight wounds, but none that were serious. An arrow went through my fur cap.

It was now getting daylight, and several wounded Indians lying close to our breastwork began shooting arrows at us, but our men soon quieted them.

When the sun was about two hours high, the Indians sent a messenger with a rag tied to a stick. Perkins met him outside. He said the Indians wished to make peace and that they had lost their chief, Old Bear, as well as many of their bravest warriors.

This was merely a sham. All they wanted was to save their slain from being scalped.

Perkins told the Indian to remain outside until he held council with his men. He was quite a diplomat, and made a strong speech to the effect that it would be best to make peace. It would certainly be to our advantage in collecting furs. The Indians had received a repulse which they had not expected. They would now return to their village, taking their dead and wounded, and mourn for many days. This would give us time to trap the Malade River and other streams before they got through mourning.

A vote was taken and resulted in seven wanting to continue the fight and thirteen declaring for peace. We did not fear the Indians, but we wanted to collect furs, not to fight. Perkins told the Indian to go back and bring five of his comrades to our camp.

In the meantime, we cooked breakfast, keeping a sharp lookout all the while, for under no conditions do trappers trust Indians after a fight.

We did not have long to wait for the six Indians, who came up looking crestfallen at their failure. Perkins smoked with them and gave them some tobacco. He then told them that if they molested us any more or stole any of our horses, he and his men would wipe out their village.

"Big talk," Docket said; "twenty men wiping out six hundred."

However, they appeared mighty glad to get possession of their dead and they made signals to other Indians to bring up ponies, and they soon had the dead lashed to the ponies and departed. I counted thirty-two, which rather surprised us, as we had thought the execution very much greater. Had they attacked camp a half-hour later, in the same manner, their loss would have been doubled.

The next year we learned that many of the wounded had died, and that the Utahs declared that they had lost many of their best warriors. This tribe had frequently robbed small parties of trappers, many times killing them, and this was the first severe lesson that they had ever received. After this occurrence they invariably gave the well-organised bodies of trappers the "go by."

If any reader of this should doubt the fighting quality of the trapper, let him go among any tribe of Indians today, (1905), and ask them what they think of it. They will invariably answer that it "costs too much blood to fight trappers."

This band was of the same Indians that gave the Mormons so much trouble a few years later.

CHAPTER 12

A Terrible Storm

We finished our trapping in this section without being molested further, and then moved to Bear River. At this camp we came in contact with the Bannocks, whose chief was named Pocatello. It was he who fought Connor and his California volunteers in 1862. The result of the fight was that the Bannocks were simply annihilated. Pocatello escaped by swimming down the Bear River with the thermometer at 38° below zero, unusually cold for that country.

These Bannocks made annual visits to the plains after buffalo, and were expert in the making of *pemmican*. They were also adept in collecting fine furs, more expert than any other tribe I have ever known.

It was now October and furs were beginning to get prime. We trapped Bear River and Malade River with good success; and then crossed Goose Creek Mountains and trapped Goose Creek and Raft River.

Here we met some Pah Utes, a branch of the Shoshones, but the Shoshones do not affiliate with them. They were a primitive race, making fire by friction between two sticks. We visited their village, as I wanted to see how they conducted their domestic affairs. They could not be compared to Sioux, Cheyennes, or Shoshones, for they were careless in habits. Their cooking utensils were primitive in construction. For spoons they used the hoofs of elk and the horns of mountain sheep. They are credited with manufacturing pottery, but I visited many lodges and saw none. They had a few kettles, which appeared to me all they desired. Their arms consisted of bows and arrows and a few indifferent flint-lock guns. Many arrows were pointed with flint, which they poisoned by dipping the point in liver which had previously been poisoned with rattlesnake venom. I have heard that they extracted a poison from roots, but this I very much doubt.

They collect quantities of berries, and for meats they have deer, antelope, mountain sheep, jack-rabbits, and ground squirrels. The last two are evidently their favourite food, for I noticed large numbers of them hung up in the village. They hunt squirrels with blunt-pointed arrows. They are great beggars and thieves, and we caught them trying to steal our horses.

The streams were now beginning to freeze up, and we started for the Brown's Hole rendezvous, arriving there the latter part of November.

Several traders had come from the States with supplies, and there was quite a rivalry among them for our furs. Bovey & Company were the most liberal buyers, and we sold them the entire lot.

Besides the trappers there were at the rendezvous many Indians—Shoshones, Utes, and a few lodges of Navajos—who came to exchange their pelts for whatever they stood in need of. Take it all in all, it was just such a crowd as would delight the student were he studying the characteristics of the mountaineer and the Indian. The days were given to horseracing, foot-racing, shooting-matches; and in the evening were heard the music of voice and drum and the sound of dancing. There was also an abundance of reading matter for those inclined in that direction.

Perkins had a fly-tent put up and made a counter out of dry-goods boxes, and then said:

"Now, young man, you take charge of the store. You are the best sign-talker in the camp and can out-trade me. Besides, the Indians and trappers are all fond of you."

I was the youngest man in the camp and full of the Old Nick, the men would say, for I was continually playing some prank.

On January 20th a fearful storm began, which raged for six days, scattering most of the horses in the hills, and made both trappers and Indians uneasy, as Blackfeet, Bloods, or Piegans were often in this section at this time of the year. These tribes are winter Indians, and storms and severe weather do not affect them in the least.

On the seventh day the storm abated, and about seventy-five trappers and Indians started out to gather stock. All our horses except six were missing. Among the six was my Runner, and mounting him I joined one of the parties composed of twenty whites and five Indians.

At Cedar Creek we struck fresh tracks of a large number of horses making due east to a comparatively level country. The Indians said to me in signs, "Blackfeet." We travelled at half speed for the next twelve miles and came to a ridge, from the summit of which we could see some Indians driving horses about one and a half miles away.

A draw to our right led towards the spot, so we turned up and at a rapid pace followed it to its head without being discovered by the Blackfeet.

When we reached the head of the draw, a Shoshone dismounted and crept to the brow of the hill and discovered the Blackfeet going over a hill beyond. Watching until they disappeared behind the hill, he signalled and we hurried forward to the next ridge.

From this ridge we could plainly see them and counted eleven. They had just halted to change horses, and when they caught sight of us, they hurried to remount.

Our horses were the swiftest and we soon overtook them. They had no possible chance of escaping, and getting rattled they separated, which was just what we wanted them to do. Had they staid together and fought they might have done some damage. As it was, they became panic-stricken at our sudden appearance. Here was a practical illustration of the efficiency of pistol practice at stumps. The trappers did not for a moment hesitate to charge the scattered Blackfeet; but each one selected his man and passed at full speed, delivering pistol shots at from twenty to forty feet distant.

Almost every shot brought down an Indian, who in the meanwhile attempted to fight with his arrows. In less than three minutes there were eleven dead Indians.

There was one Blackfoot mounted on a pinto pony who was leading the others, and as my Runner was the swiftest horse in our outfit the men yelled, "Bill, catch that pinto with that devil of yours."

The Indian at this time was two hundred yards distant, and I headed for him, and it was a grand race for a quarter of a mile.

I then spoke to my pony—"Catch him." He needed no whip nor spur, and I never saw him do better. When within fifty feet the Indian wheeled and let fly an arrow, but Runner would spring to the right" or left by pressure of my knee and the arrow flew harmlessly by. Before the Blackfoot could fit another arrow to the string, I was close to him and had sent him to join his companions.

We let the Shoshones do the hair-lifting, but we appropriated the plunder, which consisted of pipes, tobacco, and *pemmican*. The *pemmican* was pounced upon by all, as we were good and hungry. "Silver Tip" had received a glancing arrow in the ribs, but it was only a slight wound.

The trappers and Indians gave me the pinto pony, and it was a good one; it was very fast and had originally belonged to the Utes.

We then started for camp, having recovered one hundred and fifteen head of horses and mules.

The five Indians rode through their village with the scalps tied on *coup*-sticks, and there was great rejoicing. They had had no hand whatever in killing the Blackfeet, but that did not matter. They recounted their bravery in recapturing the ponies and taking each one a Blackfoot scalp. We came in for no praise whatever from the women, as they considered that we were only assisting their brave young warriors. The dancing and feasting over this affair lasted for several days.

The Utes, on hearing of my catching the pinto pony, crowded around to see my Runner and after looking him all over challenged me to a race. I was to ride against the owner of the pinto. Of course, I accepted and the bet was made, I on my part putting up a mule. The trappers and Shoshones all backed me and put up blankets, robes, and ponies. The track was selected, the word was given, and off we started.

Up to within one hundred feet of the finish we raced neck and neck, but I was holding my horse in and the little imp was mad. When I finally gave him his head, he distanced the Ute by twenty feet, much to his disgust. When Indians lose, they give up gracefully, and no exception was made in this case.

It was now time to lay in a supply of *depuyer* and *pemmican* for spring, and about thirty trappers went to North Park and secured all. the buffalo required. This kept all the outfits busy for some time.

CHAPTER 13

A Desperate Fight

In the early spring a trapper named Duranger, who had formerly been with the Hudson Bay Company, reached the rendezvous. He had come from the Walla Walla country, and reported that the streams flowing from the Blue Mountains contained large quantities of beaver. About the same time, March 15th, "Kentuck" returned, accompanied by ten trappers from St. Louis. They brought all the late papers.

Five days later Williams arrived from Santa Fé, and a council was held to select some new field for collecting furs. Williams said that he had many times contemplated a visit to the country described by Duranger, and he made a proposition that as the year was 1843, we should form a company of forty-three men and make all preparations for a two-years trip. This was agreed upon and the trip lasted a little over two years.

Williams, Perkins, and I packed five horses with Indian goods, and the expedition started on the 25th of March, with everything in prime condition.

We travelled to Snake River and thence to Blackfoot River, where we met a Bannock village, of whose chief, Tygee, so much has been written. He was acquainted with many in our outfit and was friendly. We traded with him for a few furs.

Our outfit consisted of four different parties, who collected furs in common, that is, each one had an equal share in all furs caught by their own party. We had thirteen in our mess—an unlucky number you will say; but in this instance it proved quite the reverse. For mutual protection we always pitched our tents and lodges together. Each mess furnished its quota of guards.

Before proceeding further, it will be necessary to explain about the northern Indians who were so troublesome to the old-time trappers. Three tribes, Blackfeet, Bloods, and Piegans, make up what has always been known as the Blackfoot nation. The Piegan and Blood Indians claimed and occupied the country from the British line, 49° north latitude, to the Musselshell River on the south; and west along the summit of the Rocky Mountains to a range enclosing what is now known as Prickly Pear Valley, where Helena, Montana, is now. This represented a large area, and was commonly called "Blackfoot country." In the aggregate these Indians were numerous, and they were constantly on the war-path against all other Indians and all whites.

The third branch of the Blackfeet resided in and claimed the country from the British line to Fort Edmonton on the Saskatchewan River. Hence when a war-party of these northern Indians were met with they were pronounced "Blackfeet."

Many people even to this day believe the Comanches to be a tribe distinct from others. It is not so, for they belong to the Shoshone family, as do also the Utahs, Pah Utes, and Water-rickers (Wata-tikka), who principally lived on the Great American Desert or its border.

It must not be thought that trappers are an idle set while at the rendezvous. The reverse is true. Many of them are constantly dressing buckskin, and their mode of dressing is far superior to that of the Indians, as the skin when prepared by them will not stretch nor shrink when wet. Others are hunting deer, to keep the camp supplied with meat, or putting arms and traps in perfect condition. Most trappers make their own buckskin clothes, although there were two tailors at Brown's Hole.

Tygee told us that there were two parties of Hudson Bay trappers on these streams near his village, and that another party had gone up Snake River.

We held a council and decided to take the Boisé River trail, as the Hudson Bay Company had a trading post in that section. We hurried along and reached the post with a few furs, which we traded to a gentlemanly old Scotchman who was in charge. He bought my pinto pony, paying me fifty dollars in cash. He told us that there were no trapping outfits in the Blue Mountains nor on the streams, but that the Howlack band of Bannocks were camped on Camas Prairie. This is known today, (1905), as Grande Ronde Valley in Oregon.

This band of Bannocks were not inclined to be friendly, and he advised us to cross the mountains to Walla Walla on the north side. This we did not care to do, as the streams between the post and Camas Prairie were full of beaver. We trapped all of them, and it was not until we reached Camas Prairie that we came in contact with the Bannocks. Here we ran on to their village of one hundred lodges.

The chief met us with a strong escort of painted and feathered warriors and commanded us to halt. This we did, not at his pleasure, but at our own. He asked us in signs what we were doing in his country, and in an insulting manner demanded several ponies. He also ordered us to unpack our goods, as he wished to see what we had. These demands we ignored.

The Bannocks were well up in sign-language and most of the chief's speech was understood by our men, all of it by myself. The chief was given to understand that he would receive no ponies, and that we would not unpack. If he wished to smoke and be friends, good. If not, he must get out of our way, as we were going on, and we claimed the right to trap in all streams either in the mountains or on the plains.

When the chief heard this, he appeared to be thunder-struck.

The Bannocks had a great many Hudson Bay flint-locks, bows and arrows, and a few lances, mostly carried for ornament, but used also to spear a fallen foe.

Our men were becoming impatient and would have opened fight then and there had not Williams, who had been chosen leader, restrained them.

The chief saw the action of our men and realised that he stood on delicate ground. He withdrew in a threatening manner. But it was plain to all that we would see more of these Bannocks. Heretofore they had stripped and robbed many small trapping outfits, but ours was the first large company that had travelled through that country.

We passed by the village and continued some twelve miles, camping in a commanding position on a Cottonwood creek. We built corrals and dug rifle-pits, as we felt positive that Howlack would resent what he considered an insult by following us with a strong war-party. All our band were old mountain veterans, with the exception of George Howard and myself. Howard was a brother of "Kentuck," and was over six feet tall.

A few traps were set, but not far from camp. Pickets kept a sharp lookout, and at sunset discovered a few Indians at a distance. They were locating our camp—a sure indication that mischief was intended.

Had Howlack seen the preparations we made to receive him he would have hesitated before attacking us. All our war-horses were saddled with pads. In fact, they were always saddled in readiness, but were never mounted except in case of emergency. Six men at a time stood guard, with three hours' relief.

At about four o'clock in the morning the guards fired several shots at wolves prowling in close vicinity to camp. Two of the wolves were shot in the head and proved to be Bannocks. Other wolves were seen departing.

Indians are very expert at this imitating the actions of wolves. Putting a large wolf hide on their backs and creeping on their hands and knees they imitate the wolf very closely. But mountain men are up to all such strategy, and many an Indian has come to grief while trying the game on trappers.

These warriors had been sent by the chief to ascertain the exact strength of our camp before he attacked in force.

When the guards shot, the rest of the men were all asleep with arms by their sides, ready for instant action. Before the smoke had cleared from the rifles all of us were at the breastworks.

For some time, nothing more was seen of the Bannocks. We were certain that the guards had made no mistake, for they dragged in two Indians who had played wolf, and "lifted topknots," as "Kentuck" said. The chief must have been waiting for these two men to return and report, although by this time he must have concluded that they were either killed or wounded.

Just at daylight a strong force of mounted warriors was seen approaching. When at about three hundred yards from camp they halted and held a consultation. We estimated that the Indians numbered three hundred.

After a little about one half of them dismounted and made a flank movement, crossing the creek so as to attack us from two sides. On the creek side, opposite camp, was an open country, and we were well fortified. Williams detailed ten men to watch this side, and arranged so that they could be reinforced in a moment if necessary.

Strict orders were given to make every shot count. It demoralises Indians when they see their comrades fall. A few determined men can stand off a great many Indians.

As soon as the foot Indians reached the opposite side of the creek, they opened fire. Immediately the mounted Indians with yells and war-whoops began the charge.

We held our fire until the enemy were within seventy-five yards and then opened up. Almost every shot counted. Many Indians fell from their horses, and ponies fell pinning their riders.

Then seven double-barrelled shotguns poured in their fire on the

Indians, who had halted and were somewhat clustered. The shots created havoc and with a yell, as of despair, they fell back, leaving many wounded.

Thirty-three of our men mounted their warhorses and charged, but the Indians were excited and bewildered and broke for cover.

Our men with their deadly Colts told with terrible effect. We kept up the chase for about a mile, losing one man, a Virginian named Albert Smith, a brave man in every respect, and one whom we could ill afford to lose.

We captured sixty ponies and many flintlock guns. Each trapper had one scalp and some two, but they were dearly bought. Of our men one was dead and there were eleven wounded—four seriously, but all recovered.

Perkins's favourite horse had a broken leg and had to be shot. My horse was shot in the fleshy part of the thigh, but the wound did not interfere with his part in the action. Many of the trappers' horses had wounds.

I have been in many an Indian charge since this one, but I have never been in one that was so savagely executed. What made this one so bitter was that when Howlack went from our meeting on Camas Prairie he said in signs, "You white dogs, I will wipe you out."

As soon as the Indians who had attacked from the creek side saw the tide of battle sweep away their companions, they left their position, leaving eleven wounded.

We buried Smith in one of our rifle-pits so that the Indians should not find him. They will dig down ten feet to get a white man's scalp. We fooled them this time, for they never discovered Smith's body.

I saw Howlack in the lead of the retreating Bannocks and told Williams that I thought my horse could catch his, but he said to "Let him go."

This was the same band of Bannocks who, a few years later, annoyed the emigrants in Oregon. It was an unfriendly tribe and is not to be trusted even today, (1905).

CHAPTER 14

Vicissitudes of the Trapper's Life

We raised our traps and packed up to move camp, constructing four *travois* for those who were wounded. Duranger said we could reach the Umatilla River by sundown, and we did so.

In this section were to be found a tribe of Umatillas who had friendly inclinations toward trappers, and who were enemies of the Bannocks. We were soon discovered, and the chief, accompanied by a few braves, paid us a visit. He was over six feet tall and was a fine-looking Indian. The Hudson Bay men had christened him William Snook.

When we returned to Green River in 1845 the report of our fight with Howlack had spread all over that country, and we were asked many times why we had charged these Indians. They claimed that we had the Indians whipped before the charge and that we were secure in our camp. Our answer was that if we had not charged them, they would have annoyed us constantly, and we wanted to stop that and force them to respect the white men. The trappers felt confident of their ability to rout them, with little loss to themselves.

The after-results confirmed the wisdom of our course, for ever after that fight these Bannocks dreaded trappers. I have heard Hudson Bay men relate that when these Indians acted arrogantly, they would scare them by saying, "We will bring those trappers if you don't behave." The threat always had the effect of restraining them. Indians will not stand a white man's charge. They dread close quarters and get bewildered. I have heard it claimed that the Indians can hold their own in hand-to-hand conflicts. The experiences of old mountain men do not show this to be the case. Fifty determined white men of experience can rout almost any number of Indians. I know that this is so.

Duranger could converse with the Umatillas in Chinook, and he told them of our fight with Howlack, showing the scalps and the bows and arrows. The chief became greatly excited and dispatched a runner to his village, and in a short while every Umatilla in the country appeared at our camp. They were the most excited lot of Indians I ever saw, and wanted us to move our camp to their village, as they were sure that Howlack would follow us to seek revenge for the loss of so many warriors.

We refused his kindness, declaring that we considered Howlack and his warriors as so many "old women." This was "big talk," but it had its effect.

These Indians had never seen so many scalps taken at one time, and they had never heard of such a thing.

They brought us an abundance of dried salmon and fresh deer meat and were very friendly.

The chief was a fair sign-talker, but he was somewhat astonished to see a smooth-faced boy who could excel him. He asked me what tribe I belonged to, or if I was a half-breed. Our men understood all this, and rallied me plenty about being a half-breed.

The chief had a fine horse which we wanted for Perkins, so we brought scalps and other things and laid them in a heap at the chief's feet, pointing to his horse. He understood in a moment and, taking the horse by the rope, passed it over to Williams, who in turn led it to Perkins. The old veteran was greatly pleased with the act, and the trappers were happy to be able to show the esteem in which he was held.

George Perkins, a native of Louisiana, merited all he received. He was brave and generous to a fault, and was ever on the alert for the interest of all.

We remained in this camp eight days and collected lots of furs, the Umatillas meanwhile keeping a sharp lookout for Bannocks, but seeing none.

On the ninth day our wounded men were able to ride, and we moved down the river to the base of the mountains. From a high knoll we could see the entire Walla Walla Valley, and it was a most beautiful panorama. The Umatillas also moved their village and camped three miles below us.

The fur season was now over and we took advantage of this opportunity to explore the country, remaining here two weeks.

Cayuse and Walla Walla Indians visited us. They were clean and somewhat proud, and very little addicted to begging. All these tribes were enemies to the Bannocks, who were constantly stealing their horses. The tribes owned large numbers of horses, and I have been asked where they got them from. Many years prior to this, the Indians had learned that there were great numbers of horses in southern California. Thereupon the Nez Percés, Yakimas, Cayuses, and others made up a strong war-party and went to the Sacramento Valley and returned with a vast herd. In later years, when I asked them, the Nez Percés confirmed this story.

The two weeks passed very pleasantly. Our time was spent in exploring, hunting, and fishing. Game was abundant on every side— deer, elk, mountain sheep; and we had all the fresh meat we wanted. The streams were full of trout.

The Indians were enjoying themselves to their hearts' content with their nightly scalp-dances. Williams and I remained in their village one night and I visited most of their lodges. They were neat, clean, and well furnished. The Indians were hospitable to friends. They had an abundance to eat, such as camas root, none of which is produced far east of the Rocky Mountains, dried fish, meats, and berries.

They occupied a rich and beautiful country, and Williams in commenting on it, said, "The time is not far distant when this country will teem with life and the Indian will pass away."

Our men had now fully recovered and we were ready to go. Duranger said that there was a beautiful valley situated about one hundred miles west, which the Hudson Bay men called Tygh Valley.

We bade the Umatillas goodbye and went to Tygh Valley, expecting to remain there until furs should come in season, which would be about September 15th.

We travelled slowly and made many camps, stopping three days at a beautiful stream called John Day River to hunt and fish. We next moved to Des Chutes River, the fountain-head of which is the summit of the Sierra Range.

We crossed the river below the falls, which must have been about thirty feet in height. Here the Indians secure large quantities of salmon by spearing. Their spears are made of light pine, and are from seven to nine feet in length and about an inch and a half in diameter. The lower end is tapering, and is wrapped with linen. A spike about five inches in length, sharpened at the points and wrapped in the centre with cloth, is fixed in a cavity of the shaft. The fisherman launches the shaft at the salmon, having a cord fastened at the upper end of the shaft and around his wrist. When the spike enters the fish, the shaft is withdrawn, leaving the spike in the fish. They never fail to bring the fish to shore. They split the salmon open at the back and spread them on racks to dry in the sun for future use.

At the falls was camped a village of Indians, whom Duranger pronounced to be the Dog Creek tribe; they were friendly.

About seventy miles north of this place was a Hudson Bay trading-post, situated on the Columbia River. As we had collected a considerable stock of furs, we concluded to visit the trader and dispose of them. It was my first sight of the Columbia River, with its scenery beautiful beyond description. The trader was Dr. McLaughlin, a formal but courteous gentleman, who owned a large share in the Hudson Bay Company's lucrative business. We traded all our furs for cash and goods, and had to wait three days while a runner went to Vancouver, the Company's headquarters, for the cash.

The head men of the Hudson Bay Company did not look favourably on American trappers and traders. They claimed the right to collect all furs in a given area on the American side, having a charter to hold their forts and trading stations up to 1861 or 1862. We held some interesting arguments on the subject, and Williams, who was better posted than the doctor, told him that their exclusive right was past and that in the near future all Oregon and the country up to the forty-ninth degree would be settled by Americans. Then, he said, they would have to move all their forts to the British side of the line. Dr. McLaughlin was somewhat surprised when Williams gave him the whole history of the country, and said he had not expected so much information from a trapper. All in all, we passed a very pleasant time with him, and he presented us with five gallons of port wine, inviting us to call again if we ever revisited this section.

We returned to Des Chutes River and camped about four miles above the Dog Indian village. They visited us daily, bringing fresh salmon. It was June and the fish were coming up the river.

In the meantime, everything was being put in condition for fall trapping. George Howard remarked one day: "The people back in the States have no conception of the life of a trapper." One day it would be all peace and harmony, with the trappers enjoying life as few could even in civilization. The next day just the reverse, among hostile Indians.

CHAPTER 15

In the Modoc Country

On September 16th we broke camp, knowing very little of our intended route, and not knowing whether the Indians we might meet would be friendly or hostile, but thoroughly prepared for every emergency.

We travelled over a rolling country, passing a warm spring where we saw a village. They were Warm Spring Indians, belonging, I think, to the Dog family. They did not appear very industrious, having poor lodges, very few ponies, and nothing to trade.

For several days we were busy trapping, and large quantities of beaver and otter were being caught. The country was beautiful. In every direction the scenery was grand and the region was a hunter's paradise for all kinds of game, particularly bear.

On Rush River we found the richest place for beaver we had yet come across, and it took us forty days to clean that section.

At one of our camps Howard made another of his characteristic remarks:

> If people in the States could see this camp, with the immense number of beaver stretched on hoops and hanging on every available limb, they would go wild. When I return and tell them about it, they will not believe me. Neither will they believe an account of the life of the trappers who appear to be perfectly at home in a country that none of them has ever heard of or seen.

It was now towards the last of October, and the weather looked stormy. We moved to a valley about ten miles from the Sierra Range of mountains, and by the time we had a corral built it was storming. By noon the next day there was over a foot of snow on the ground. Blacktail deer were seen in every direction, and we secured plenty of fresh meat.

We held a council and decided to cross the mountains before the snow got too deep.

From the summit of this range was the grandest view I ever beheld. To the westward lay a large valley, dotted with pine, alder, and Cottonwood. Beyond, a large and beautiful lake sparkled in the sun as if dotted with diamonds. At this body of water, known afterwards as the Great Klamath Lake, was the scene of the Klamath and Modoc war in 1856, in which I was a participant.

We moved rapidly down the valley, sending six men in advance to select a winter camp. They chose a spot on a beautiful stream about a half mile from the lake.

Here we built our corral in the centre of a grove of pine, and put up four lodges and three tents. We had an abundance of dry timber and pure water. Game and fish were on every side.

Since leaving the Warm Springs on Des Chutes River we had not come in contact with Indians, but an abundance of signs indicated that they were in close proximity.

On the third morning a party of fifteen appeared in camp, somewhat astonished at finding so large a body of whites. They saw at a glance that we were trappers. After they dismounted, we invited them into our largest lodge, and feasted and smoked. They were well versed in sign-language, and Duranger could talk with them in Chinook. Lalick, their chief, asked all manner of questions. He was of medium size, dark complexioned, and with rather pleasant features. After our telling him that we intended to winter in this place, he was satisfied and assured us that we would not be molested by his people.

Their village was about ten miles distant, on upper main Klamath River, and these Indians were on a hunt after elk, needing hides to repair their lodges. We unpacked some Indian goods and told them we would trade with them for any furs they might bring to camp. Martin were very plentiful in this section, and these Indians were adepts in taking them. A martin hide weighs about two ounces, and was worth in those days $6 per skin. The reason I mention this is to give some idea of the amount in value that could be packed on a horse. The average pack weighs one hundred and fifty pounds, which, if packed with martins, would mean in value $7200.

These Indians sometimes cross the Cascade Mountains to Willamette Valley to trade with the Hudson Bay Company. A few of the Hudson Bay trappers had passed through the country, but no such an outfit as ours. They knew that there was another class of white men called "Boston Men" (Americans). The Hudson Bay men were called "King George's Men," and are so called today, (1905), when speaking to Indians in Chinook. East of the Rocky Mountains these Hudson Bay men were called "Redcoats" by the Indians.

Lalick told us that there was another tribe below this lake, on a smaller lake, and they were known as *Cultus Siwash*—bad Indians. These were the Modocs, whom we almost annihilated in 1856.

We passed the winter very profitably, many of the men learning the Chinook jargon, which was easily acquired. About every tribe of Indians west of the Rocky Mountains can converse in this language.

Here was the greatest contrast between two tribes, living in close proximity to each other. One was exceedingly friendly and very happy to have whites in their country. The other had a hatred against both whites and Indians. Up to this time neither tribe could have met with many whites.

We asked Lalick how many warriors the *Cultus Siwash* could muster, and he counted on his fingers several hundred.

We also found out that they had a few flintlock guns and many bows and arrows, the points of which were poisoned. Williams was always supplied with ammonia, which was considered an antidote for poison; it was used by scarifying the wound with the point of a knife and applying the ammonia, as well as freely inhaling its fumes.

That winter we enjoyed ourselves as few mountain men ever had, and before leaving this camp we invited to a final feast the head men of the village. Among these was the noted war chief, Comtucknay, a noble-looking Indian. After the feast we presented each one with some article, giving to Lalick and to Comtucknay each a Bannock pony.

Highly pleased with their entertainment, they shook hands and bade us farewell, and invited us to come again. Lalick advised us to keep along the base of the mountains to avoid meeting the Modocs. The advice was good, but was not heeded, as after results will show. The next morning, we packed up and reached the lower end of the lake and remained there two days on account of rain. Beaver were scarce, and the time was spent in reading and looking after stock.

On the third day we started for Lost River, which empties into Tule Lake in the Modoc country, and explored it to its source, travelling through a beautiful valley, but found no beaver.

On our return trip down the valley, we met a party of thirty Indians, who approached us at a rapid gait. They came up boldly and in an insulting manner ordered us to halt. They wanted to know what we were doing in their country. We told them our business and also produced pipes, saying, "We are friends."

They scornfully refused the proffered pipes, saying, "We do not smoke with white dogs." This was dangerous talk, for our men understood every word and could have made short work of them.

Their demand for horses was, of course, refused, and the manner in which they left indicated that trouble was ahead. These Indians talked Chinook and were good in sign-language.

We travelled east about six miles to a patch of timber, and were fortunate to find a good spring. A corral was built and rifle-pits dug, the men jokingly saying, "We are going to have another Bannock rupture with these devils." Just before sundown several Indians hovered around, taking in our situation, but did not come close enough to discover the preparations made for their reception.

Our war-horses were placed in the centre of the corral, surrounded as much as possible by the pack-horses, so as to protect them from bullets and arrows. In the Bannock fight we had lost eleven pack-horses. On the north side of camp were some scattering pines, and should the Indians attack us in force this would be the danger point, although we had put up strong rifle-pits. These pits are constructed in the following manner. A long hole is dug to extend completely around the camp, the dirt being thrown up on the outside.

On the top of the loose dirt we placed logs, making port-holes under the logs. When shooting through these holes the logs protected our heads. Our arms were, as usual, in prime condition. Rifles in those days were muzzle-loaders and so were pistols. Trappers were very expert in making cartridges for both arms and could load and shoot a rifle four times in a minute. I have seen some experts shoot five times a minute.

It was full moon, and this was greatly in our favour, as we did not know what tactics the Modocs would pursue.

Fifteen men were put on guard at a time, but nothing occurred in the night. At daylight we could see the Indians collecting on a high knoll about a mile and a half distant. Their every action was watched by Williams and others with spy-glasses.

All stock was watered and put back in corral, and we all ate breakfast. As these Indians used poisoned arrows the trappers prepared what they called their "coat of mail." All the men had heavy blacktail deer skins, which they wore over their shirts or coats, tied or buttoned up to the chin and reaching down to the thighs. Just prior to an engagement these were all soaked in water and wrung out. It is impossible for any arrow, whether iron or flint-pointed, to penetrate buckskin so prepared. I have heard many people express doubts as to this, and I have always advised them to wet a piece of buckskin and try to penetrate it with a needle.

By eight o'clock fully two hundred Indians had assembled on the knoll and were holding a great council. I told Williams that I would give one hundred dollars to be there and hear their comments on the easy manner in which they were going to "capture these few white dogs" and all their horses. The thirty Indians whom we had met the day previous had counted our exact number, and had taken note of our fine horses and the many packs. All this would be magnified, whetting to a high degree the cupidity of the whole tribe.

CHAPTER 16

Modoc Slaughter

The Modocs at length mounted, and in a leisurely manner, approached to within three hundred yards of camp and halted. Two of their number dismounted and came towards camp holding up both hands, which was the sign for "we have no arms."

Williams and I met them, but we went thoroughly armed, as we noticed bows and arrows slung on their backs.

They were chiefs and asked us many insulting questions, calling us "dogs," demanding all our horses, guns, and, in fact, everything we had. In return for all this, they said that if we complied with their demands, they would let us go. If we did not comply, they would rub us out, rubbing the palm of one hand over the other, signifying that they would annihilate us. Williams replied in a calm manner, and told them that they could have none of our goods. If they wished to smoke and make friends, good, and we would leave their country. I think, judging by their looks, that they thought we were afraid of them, for they told us to "go, dogs." Williams's eyes flashed fire, and I felt like making the Modocs eat their words. They stepped backwards for some distance, and we also.

The Indians now held a long council, after which about half of their number dismounted. Their intention was to rush camp and take it by assault. The footmen made a detour and reached the scattering pines. The horsemen divided, and we understood we would be attacked from all sides.

Fifteen men were detailed on the north side facing the scattered pines, with every preparation made for a hand-to-hand conflict. Each man had his tooth-pick or large knife in his belt, besides a trapping hatchet. The latter contained two pounds of steel, a sharp and dangerous weapon in the hands of determined men who were contending for their lives.

When the footmen reached the timber they gave a signal for the attack, which was responded to by the horsemen, who sent forth yell after yell, thinking, no doubt, it would paralyze us with fear, but it had the opposite effect. On the south and west the battle opened, and the war-whoops and yells sounded to us on the north as if pandemonium had broken loose.

The footmen began a charge, firing a few guns and sending a flight of arrows. We reserved our fire until they had come within forty yards of the rifle-pits. The Modocs could not see us and, having noticed that no shots came from that side, they must have thought that we were all contending against the horsemen, for they came on a run and in close body.

We emptied our rifles and completely surprised them, for they halted and looked bewildered. Then the shotguns and Colts were brought into play with terrible effect, almost every shot bringing down an Indian.

Seventeen of their bravest warriors made a charge to the east of us and almost reached the corral, when ten of our party met them at close quarters. It was a furious hand-to-hand conflict and showed the great superiority of palefaces over Indians. Pistols, knives and hatchets did terrible work, and in less time than it takes to tell it fifteen of the Indians were dead, two of the attacking party making their escape. There were no casualties among the trappers, except a few scratches.

While the hand-to-hand fight was going on, the five men in the rifle-pits kept the rest of the Indians at bay. The ground in front of our breastwork was literally covered with sprawling Indians, many of whom crawled to the trees and were helped away by their comrades.

After this repulse it was simply a tree fight on our side.

On the south side of the camp a hot fight was raging, and some of us rushed over just in time to assist in repelling a furious charge. Three of our men were down and several others wounded, but the latter were not disabled. On this charge the Modocs came up to within fifty feet of the rifle-pits, but with all their bravery they could not withstand the steady fire of the trappers, and they soon withdrew to a safe distance.

Many women arrived and rendered assistance, taking the dead and wounded back to their village amid the most dismal howls that I have ever heard.

At a signal from the chief, the Indians collected in a body to hold council.

We had lost three good and brave men who had been in many a desperate engagement. These we buried while the Indians were holding council.

A single Indian was soon seen approaching and he was met by Williams and myself, and we asked him what he wanted. He said he wanted us to stop fighting and to let them take off the dead and wounded. We told him to send for the women and pack them off. He returned to the main body, and in a short time the women appeared leading ponies. They packed two bodies on a pony, and acted as if they were frightened to death, not knowing what manner of men we were. We dragged out the fifteen who had been killed in the hand-to-hand struggle, and they soon had them all packed off.

Many of our men were in favour of making a charge, knowing that we could rout them with ease. Ours was certainly the first large party that they had come in contact with. They had, no doubt, met with smaller outfits, for we found on them several trappers' knives. At all events, they knew our exact numbers and they made sure of having overwhelming odds in their favour, expecting to win easily. Where their calculations failed was in their ignorance of the trappers' arms. They did not know that each one was armed with two six-shooters, and that we had seven double-barrelled shotguns besides the rifles. Had they known these things I doubt very much if they would have attacked us in the manner in which they did.

After collecting all their dead and wounded the Indians withdrew.

An incident occurred in this same grove during the Modoc war of 1856, which will well illustrate the difference between the whites and Indians in attack and defence.

General Crosby was commander of the whites, and in his command was a company of sixty rangers, the original California Rangers of which I was a member. The Modocs were in possession of this grove, with the rangers on the outside, just the reverse of our present fight. The Indians outnumbered the rangers two to one, but in just one half hour's fighting the rangers routed the Indians, inflicting considerable loss, and secured possession of the grove.

After the Indians had retired, we turned out our horses to graze, protected by a guard of ten men, mounted on their war-horses.

Some of the men climbed to the tops of high knolls, so as to get the lay of the land. As yet we had collected no furs this spring, and as there was no possibility of a trade with the Modocs, we determined to break camp the next day, Indians permitting.

Our intention was to travel eastward to the base of the Sierra Nevada. During the day we strengthened our position somewhat to prepare for another defence, as Lalick had claimed that the Modocs numbered several hundred.

Stock was left out until dark, and all kept a sharp lookout. A few scattering Indians could be seen towards the lake, but none seemed inclined to make our acquaintance. The Indians must have called together all their medicine men to explain the cause of the disastrous defeat at the hands of a few "white dogs." At all events they did not bother us during the night.

At daybreak all our belongings were packed and, mounting our war-horses, we started. Ten men acted as an advance guard. Ten brought up the rear, and five on each flank. At every point we were prepared to repel an attack. We proceeded south for about three miles and struck a lodge pole trail leading from the lake, going east. We followed this trail to the foot of a bluff having a rise of some three hundred feet.

It was on top of this bluff that the massacre of twenty-nine emigrants by the Modocs occurred in 1852. Only three men made their escape to Yreka, Cal., and reported the occurrence.

Ben Wright, an old mountain man, collected a company of his acquaintances to avenge this slaughter of men, women, and children. He met the Modocs on Lost River at Natural Rocky Ford, about twelve miles from our battle ground, and after a hand-to-hand conflict routed the Indians with considerable loss. That was the second defeat for the Modocs.

Emigrants taking the Saunders cut-off to Northern California and Southern Oregon used to pass over this trail, but after the massacre they travelled by other routes. The place where the massacre occurred is called today, (1905), "Bloody Point."

CHAPTER 17

A Big Catch of Fur

We travelled east for about ten miles and reached Clear Lake, a beautiful body of water. Plenty of Indian signs were in evidence, but no Indians.

For camp we selected a small point of land which extended out into the lake, and dug a few rifle-pits. Deer and antelope were plenty and we secured quantities of fresh meat. By this time, we had come to the conclusion that the Modocs were not as numerous as Lalick had reported, or they surely would have given us another battle.

Next day we continued east to a fair-sized stream running south, a branch of the noted Pitt River, but not known to us at that time.

In July, 1844, we reached a beautiful valley called today (1905), Honey Lake Valley, but at that time without a name. We remained here three months, enjoying ourselves as only men can who love the grandeur of nature. Our time was spent in exploring, hunting, fishing, reading, and practising with all arms.

Many Indians came to camp bringing furs, for which we traded. They appeared to be very poor and were very indifferent sign-talkers, although we got along with them for a time. Towards the last they commenced stealing, and when caught doing this we let them feel the weight of whips applied by "Kentucky George," who understood his business. At this the Indians ceased their visits, which was a sign to look out for some devilment. We always kept guard both night and day. By experienced mountain men that practice is never omitted.

Early one morning shots were fired by the guards, and we rushed out just as an Indian ran by the lodge. One shot put an end to him. The guards had killed four others with shotguns. As it was break of day we scouted the valley for some distance, but discovered no more Indians.

We had treated these Indians with all kindness, and their acts in trying to steal offended the men. Some were in favour of attacking the village.

We held a council and determined to set an example by cremating the five whom we had killed.

This was done in an "approved manner," as Perkins said. There was plenty of pitch pine and other dry material close at hand, and the dead Indians were carefully placed in the centre of a big pile. By noon only ashes were left, which brought forth Perkins's remark.

I have been told by intelligent men that it was cruel in us to cremate these Indians. Wherein the cruelty? Do not our leading scientists advocate cremation as the proper mode of disposing of the dead? It was practised in both ancient and modern times. Bear in mind that ninety-eight *per cent*, of mountain men were pronounced free-thinkers, and as a rule they were more humane, more generous, truer to friends, with less deception than those in civilization, with few exceptions.

We held several councils as to our future route. Some who had been in southern California advocated returning by way of Los Angeles. Others wanted to take the eastern route by way of Carson City. This route was finally decided on, as the prospect for collecting furs was better; and about the 10th of October we broke camp and moved in a southerly direction along the base of the mountains.

On leaving camp we noticed a few Indians watching our movements, no doubt glad of our departure, as they would be able to recover their five friends. They probably found the ashes. It would be a lesson for them to leave white men's horses alone, and it would be commented on for many a moon in their councils.

We trapped all the streams leading from the mountains, and reached Pyramid Lake in what is now the State of Nevada. Here we met a village of Pah Utes, who were able to converse in the Shoshone language. I noticed that a few of them had flint and steel such as trappers used for making fire, but the majority used sticks.

They thought we were a new tribe of white men because we used pads on our runners and were bronzed like Indians. Here we traded for a few furs, but we offended the Indians when we refused to let them have our best horses.

Our next stop was on the Truckee River, and during the journey we saw more blacktail deer than I have ever seen before or since. It was a hunter's paradise, with the streams full of fish and blue grouse in every direction. A blue grouse is the daintiest of food and has no equal among fowl.

At the upper end of this river is a large lake and beautiful valley, which in 1853 were called Biglow's Lake and Valley, but later on, I am told, were renamed Strawberry Lake and Valley. In 1844 the lake had no name, the Indians in signs calling it "Upper Lake."

A small band of Indians had their village about a half mile from our camp. They were a miserable and degraded set. I doubt if our ancestors of a million years back could have been more so. They could properly be classed with the savages of the flint age, as they used flint for the points of arrows and spears, of indifferent manufacture. Game was readily approached and they were easily able to supply themselves with meat, while they were expert in catching fish. They were notorious beggars and thieves.

As we left this camp dark clouds began to gather, foreboding heavy snow, and we started to cross the mountains. At noon it began to snow, and when on the summit the trail was completely obliterated. Any but experienced mountain men would have been bewildered, and as it was it put us all on our mettle. Imagine yourselves driving two hundred and fifty horses, and with the snowflakes falling so fast and thick that all view was obliterated, and you will have some idea of our condition. To extricate ourselves without the loss of some of the livestock in this strange country, among dense forests of pine, cool and practical judgment was required.

In such an instance there must be no bewilderment or everything is lost. I observed in the features of all the men a coolness and determination which would have been commendable in any general in a desperate battle, where victory or defeat hung in the balance. Ten men rode in advance, two abreast; all loose stock following. The remainder of the trappers rode on each side of the loose stock to keep them from straggling.

We followed a given course, taking the light breeze for a guide. Soon we found ourselves going down a steep ridge, floundering through deep snow, not knowing where we should bring up, and finally reached a plateau.

We could not see any distance, but as it would not do to camp here, we journeyed on, keeping to the right, as we thought, and hurrying along, for it was getting late. The old saying is "*fortune favours the brave.*" In this case it favoured us.

For half an hour we continued our course, descending all the time, and at length came to a level bottom. To our left we heard a fall of water, and found there a small creek fringed with Cottonwood. We soon had our lodges and tents up and all packs secure in a large tent. The horses were turned out to graze with six men as guards. The snow was now fully twelve inches deep. Here our spades came well into play; while some shovelled snow, others collected a quantity of dry wood, and none too soon, for when the last load of wood was brought in it was dark. There was no time to build a corral, so the horses were tied to trees. The snow was still falling, and it looked gloomy.

We did not know what kind of a country we were in. All we were certain of was water and timber on our left and the level we were camped on. Whether there were any Indians in the neighbourhood we had no time to ascertain, but we kept a guard—two men at a time—with one hour reliefs. I have been in many a dismal place, but none more so than this. Several of the men had watches, and when daylight should have appeared it was still dark and the snow was still falling. At seven o'clock the snow was two feet deep, with no sign of abating. We untied the horses and sent a strong guard with them in case of a stampede, although a hundred of them had chains on their fore-fetlocks.

It stopped snowing at two o'clock, but continued cloudy. The next morning the sun made its appearance. A white shroud covered the country as far as the eye could see, but on one point we were satisfied, and that was that we were out of the mountains. We remained in this camp four days, by which time most of the snow had disappeared. On the morning of the fifth day, we moved along the base of the mountains, crossing several high ridges, until we came to a small valley and creek. From a high promontory we had a fair view of the surrounding country. To the south was an open low-lying valley, which some of our men pronounced Carson Valley, and declared that the shining looking country beyond was the Great American Desert.

Our next camp was on Carson River, and we selected a strong position, as Indian signs were abundant. A sight which gave us much encouragement was the many beaver signs.

We had just finished putting up our tents and lodges when a dozen mounted Indians rode into camp. They were Pah Utes and very intelligent, and told us their village was some distance below our camp. They asked us where we had come from, and seemed pleased when we told them that we intended remaining all winter to trap the streams. They next asked us to give them some of the beaver meat which they relished highly.

All the beaver they secured was what they shot with arrows. A few of these Indians understood a little Spanish, which showed that they had come in contact with that people. Besides, they had a few Spanish flintlock guns, but no ammunition. They had to depend for meat wholly on bows and arrows. Antelope were plentiful, but notwithstanding their expertness in the use of bows, they often suffered from lack of food. They caught a great many fish, such as suckers and whitefish, but these are poor eating.

We invited the Indians to sup with us, and the quantity of food they devoured would have astonished a gourmand from the East. I suppose it was the first square meal they had partaken of for years. After supper the Indians departed, notifying us that they would see us the next day.

That night we set traps and put only one man on guard. Our sleep was undisturbed—a rare thing in a trapper's life.

The next morning at daylight the stock was turned out with two herders, and all the others went after beaver, returning with a good catch. After breakfast the skinners went at the beaver, and had the hides off when the Indians made their appearance. They were astonished at the number of beaver we had caught. When we told the women they could take the skinned beaver with them, they were pleased beyond expression, and insisted on shaking every one of us by the hand.

For the next six weeks we were busy handling furs, and experienced no difficulty with these Indians. Peace and harmony prevailed, and the general routine of a trapper's life was unbroken.

On the 25th of February, 1845, we parted from our Indian friends, the whole village having assembled to see us off, and all united in cordially inviting us to come again to their country.

From the camp on Carson River, we took the Indian trail to what is now called Humboldt Lake, fifty miles across the desert, reaching there at five o'clock with all our horses in prime condition.

We trapped up the river to a rocky point, when a war-party of fifty Indians intercepted us and wanted to know what we were doing in their country. In an arrogant manner they demanded some of our horses and many other things. These Indians were a branch of the Pah Utes, and we plainly saw that unless we were very careful, we should have trouble with them. With all Williams's diplomatic tricks, he could not induce them to smoke the pipe of peace, and they departed looking daggers at us. As there were plenty of beaver signs we determined to trap here, even if we had to fight. We constructed corrals and prepared for every emergency.

That night we set our traps and were not disturbed, but we suspected that the Indians were up to some deviltry.

Next morning the trappers all returned, with the exception of Frederick Crawford, who had set traps some distance from camp. As he failed to return at ten o'clock, ten of us mounted and went to see what had become of him.

Docket, who was next outside trapper, had seen Crawford setting traps at a bend in the river at some distance, and to that point we went.

Scouting to some Cottonwood groves to make sure there was no ambush, we went in and soon discovered where traps had been set and also Indian tracks. Then we were satisfied that Crawford had gone under. We saw where his horse had stood and, going to a thick bunch of willows, we found the ground saturated with blood. The Indians had lain hidden in this bunch of willows, knowing that the trapper would come in the morning to look after his traps. By the signs the Indians had made there must have been six or eight of them. They had thrown Crawford in the river, which was four feet deep. We could easily see him and soon had him out.

When we had poor Crawford out on the bank, I would have liked to have present one of those sensitive beings who hold up their hands in horror when they hear of a trapper scalping an Indian.

He was scalped, his eyes were gouged out, his face was slashed with a knife, and he was otherwise mutilated in a way too horrible to describe.

Crawford, who came from Texas, was a handsome man, six feet tall, well educated, brave, kind, and generous. We found five of Crawford's traps and four beaver. The Indians got the remainder, with his rifle, two pistols, and a horse.

We were soon back in camp with the body of our comrade. When our men saw Crawford, it was plain that death would be the penalty to any of those Indians should they be caught.

We dug a secret grave and, wrapping Crawford up in his blankets, put him carefully away. No monument marks the grave where this kind and brave man was laid to rest. Such too often was the fate of trappers, many of them not even receiving burial.

At two in the afternoon our pickets signalled, "Indians coming on horseback." We soon had all our stock in corral and were prepared at every point. The pickets now came in and reported having counted sixty Indians. They soon made their appearance on a ridge, about three hundred yards from camp. They delivered one shot, which came so close that some of the trappers said, "That is Crawford's rifle; we will recapture it."

The Indians now challenged us to come out and fight. Crawford's death had cut our number down to thirty-eight, but that did not matter. It was impossible to hold the men in. Leaving three men to take care of camp, the others mounted and started out.

When the Indians saw us mount, they gave yell after yell, thinking, no doubt, that we would become paralyzed with fear. They divided and charged us from two sides. We let them get to within one hundred yards, when we halted and brought our rifles into play. Dropping rifles on the ground, we charged them pistols in hand. Fully twenty-five Indians fell from the rifle shots. This bewildered them, and before they could recover, we were amongst them.

A fight like this lasts only a few minutes, and very few Indians made their escape. One tall Indian was riding Crawford's horse and he tried to get away, but delayed too long. One of our men caught him and recovered horse, rifle, and pistols.

We captured forty-three ponies and collected all such plunder as we cared for, besides ridding the earth of a lot of insulting Indians. Crawford was fully avenged.

A few of our men received arrow wounds, but none were serious. We lost but two horses, shot in the breast.

This was undoubtedly the first fight these Indians had made against an outfit like ours, otherwise they would have exercised better generalship. The main secret of the trappers' success was in making every shot count in the first volley. This bewildered the Indians, and before they could collect their thoughts, we rushed in among them.

There was no question that our outfit was the most effective fighting body of trappers on the plains. It contained men who, I firmly believe, would have been able to command an army. It is a question in my mind if any soldiers of any nation were as well drilled in the use of rifles and pistols as this body of trappers.

The horses also were drilled to stand fire and to be quick in evolutions. The war-whoops and yells of Indians did not affect them. They simply pricked up their ears or looked unconcerned.

After the fight we held a council and decided that it would be best to move from this place, as we did not know how many warriors these Indians could muster. At any rate, it would not be safe for one or two men to go any distance from camp after furs.

We now raised all our traps and by three o'clock started up the river. A few Indians could be seen riding swiftly along the base of the mountains, for what purpose we could not tell, nor did we care. We were aware of one thing, and that was that they would be anxious to find out about those Indians who failed to return to the village. The reader may be certain that when they found that their invincible warriors had gone to their happy hunting-grounds without their scalp-locks, there would be much wailing, gashing of flesh, and cutting off of fingers.

They would be occupied for some time to come with the laying away of their braves, and also in calling on all their medicine-men for an explanation. Poor Crawford's scalp at this time would suffer untold indignities.

CHAPTER 18

Expedition to the Big Horn Mountains

We reached what is called Thousand Spring Valley after dark and unpacked, but kept all stock close. We built no fires and put up no lodges.

By daylight we had packed and at two o'clock we reached Raft River. A short distance below smoke was discernible, which on investigation proved to be from a camp of seven Hudson Bay men, who were trapping.

We soon had a feast prepared and invited these men to join us, for they looked hungry and crestfallen. Duranger, who was acquainted with them, asked the cause, and they replied that the Indians had stolen seven head of horses from them, leaving three, a number insufficient to pack their furs.

These big companies treated their men like *peons*. They were poorly armed, and had but a scant supply of food. They had to depend on their own resources and live on what the country produced, which to them meant beaver meat and berries in season. The story of the Hudson Bay Company's treatment of their employees is too well known to be commented on, although I will say that if I had my choice between being a slave with some masters in Missouri or being a Hudson Bay employee, I would prefer the former.

We gave each one of them an Indian pony, giving them a bill of sale, so that they could show their title to the "*busware*" (*bourgeois* = boss). We also traded seven more of the Indian ponies for furs, and advised them to leave this section, as the Indians would most likely follow us. And what chance would these men have, armed with a few old Hudson Bay flint-lock guns? They took our advice and accompanied us to Goose Creek, west of the Goose Mountains. Here we separated, the Canadians going down Goose Creek and we continuing on to Bear River.

We trapped Bear River and crossed over to Green River, picking up considerable fur. We then crossed over to Warm Land *via* the Big Wind River Valley and visited the hot springs, remaining there three days.

We met four trappers coming from the lower country, where they had lost all their horses and one companion, killed by Blackfeet. These men were strangers to all of us and stated that they were employed by the Northwestern Fur Company. We presented each one of these with a pony and advised them to get out of this section, as Blackfeet war-parties were numerous. They took our advice, but they did not seem aware of the danger. It was a sin for these companies to send out a few men, poorly armed, on these trapping expeditions. They cared nothing for the lives of their employees. All they wanted was furs.

We held a general council as to what route we should take, as the trapping season was over. Many of the men had decided to take a trip East to visit relations. All of them, except Duranger and "Scotty," came from three States, Missouri, Kentucky, and Virginia. We finally decided to cut across country and go to the North Platte River to pick up a few buffalo. We arrived at the mouth of the Laramie River without mishap, and there met an emigrant train going to Oregon. This occurrence brought home the truth of Williams's prediction to Dr. McLaughlin. It was also our first intimation of the Mormon migration to Salt Lake Valley.

Twenty-five of our men concluded to go to St. Louis and take their furs with them. Our party or mess sold our furs to buyers who were present, and settled up everything among ourselves. The original thirteen all returned.

Thus, more than a band of brothers parted company, few of them to meet again. Many remained in the East and settled down. Williams went to Santa Fé, accompanied by Perkins and six others. It was the only sad parting I have ever experienced.

An exploring party desired to visit the Big Horn Mountains, and engaged Docket, Noble, Evans, Russell and myself to accompany them. This party was sent out by the Northwestern Fur Company, as we afterwards found out, to ascertain if there were a favourable location to establish a trading-post in that section. Had we been aware of this we would not have gone, although they paid us well.

On Powder River we had to take to timber in order to stand off a war-party of thirty Blackfeet. There were ten in our party, but only five armed as prairie men should be in those days. The Indians shot several times at long range, and we emptied three of their saddles, and to our disgust were blamed by our employer. None of his party had ever been in a battle, and they knew very little about Indians. The head of the party was named Overstall, and he was an arrogant sort of a fellow, who thought we were like the remainder of the Northwestern Fur Company's employees. We took pleasure in informing him that we belonged to the free traders and trappers, and held all the big companies in contempt. We also told him to let up with his arrogance or we would leave him and let him get out of the country as best he could.

An imbecile proposition that he made was for us to go and have a talk with the Indians, and let them know we were their friends. The idea of meeting Blackfeet Indians, after having been run into the timber and shot at, was preposterous—not to be thought of for a moment.

It was about ten o'clock in the morning when the Indians forced us to take to timber, and they hovered around until three, occasionally throwing a shot at us at long range. We wasted no more ammunition, though had they come within range it would have been different.

The old man thought that this point would make a very desirable location for a trading-post. We were within one mile of where Fort Reno was established years afterwards.

Finally, the Indians disappeared, and Docket, Noble and myself mounted our horses and scouted the country for two miles, taking the Indian trail, which led towards the south end of the Big Horn Mountains. On our return we reported that these Indians were either Blood or Piegans, as those two branches of the Blackfeet often went to war mounted.

The old man just then remembered that he had pressing and important business on Platte River and at St. Louis, and that there was not a moment to spare in getting there. He and his four companions had an attack of the ague. They asked if we could find our way back in the night? If so, they would make it worth our while to reach Laramie River as soon as possible. It was disgusting to see such cowardice. We ate, mounted, and started, and travelled at a lively gait. They asked us many times if we thought the Indians would follow us. To these questions we answered "No, but we might come across others," which was true, although we did not expect to.

About midnight we halted and made coffee and lunched. We told the old man to eat and then sleep for two or three hours, for he ap-

Free Traders

peared exhausted. His men spread blankets for him and he lay down, but not to sleep, for every few minutes he would rise and ask if there were any danger yet. We told him to sleep, that we would look out for him.

After two hours he could stand it no longer, and begged us to saddle up as soon as possible, as he had a premonition that the Indians were upon us. His thoughts dwelt on nothing but Indians.

We started and reached Rush Creek on North Platte River, opposite where Fort Fetterman now stands, at seven in the morning. Some Mormons were camped there. The old man and his men were completely worn out. There was not much force or snap in any of them. We cooked breakfast and called the old man, but he could not eat, though he emptied a flask of brandy, with which he was well supplied. He invited us to partake of it, but we declined with thanks, saying that he would require all he had for himself and friends. We remained there overnight, the old man evidently forgetting that his presence was urgently needed in St. Louis.

We reached Laramie on the second day, depositing Overstall and his four men at Tebeau's, all five of them being in a condition fit for the hospital.

Overstall settled with us and said he would get his company to give us employment. We thanked him and told him his company had not sufficient means to employ us, and then added that we were free trappers and would not be employed by anyone.

Docket, Noble, Evans, Russell, and myself remained together for many years, and were known as the "Tartar outfit."

CHAPTER 19

The Mexican War

We had a few things stored at Green River, so we returned there and settled up.

Washakie was preparing to start on his fall hunt in the Big Horn country and we mentioned to him that we would like to accompany the village. Besides wishing to explore that section, we were desirous of studying more accurately the habits and characteristics of the Shoshones. Washakie was delighted, and we bought one thousand dollars' worth of choice Indian goods to trade, as the opportunity might occur.

We started on the first day of October, travelling by easy stages. At night the young folks would keep the village awake until midnight with their singing and dancing. They enjoyed life for all it was worth, giving no heed to the morrow. A happy aggregation on the whole, one to be envied by many. The older members of the camp would hold councils and would speculate on what tribes were most likely to be met with on the journey.

In eight days, we crossed the Snake Range of mountains and found our first buffalo, a small herd of about two hundred. About seventy-five Indians mounted their best horses and started after them. It was a sight worth going hundreds of miles to see, and only the pen of Mark Twain could describe the ridiculous mishaps which occurred—ponies falling, riders going heels over head, getting up with a yell, remounting, and off again in pursuit of some wounded buffalo.

They secured over two hundred head, which was an abundance, although large quantities of meat were required to supply a village of one hundred lodges.

We crossed the Big Horn River and proceeded to the noted Stinking Water. Washakie pointed out the hot springs, and on the west side of the main Stinking Water we saw several sulphur springs which were apparently dying out. The main spring is in the *cañon* at the base of the mountain, and its fumes can be smelled for miles. I have heard it said that there were sulphur springs on the north and south forks of Stinking Water; but we did not see them, nor did Washakie mention the fact.

We had been in this camp seven days when a party of Crow Indians arrived on a visit to the Shoshones. They said their village was on another river called Sun Dance (Clark's Fork), and that they had come over to see their friends. They brought three good-looking ponies and wanted to race. The Crows are not as intelligent as the Shoshones, and are not to be compared with them in independence and cleanliness. They are noted beggars and pilferers, and it is the reverse with Shoshones. You can, with perfect safety, trust them with everything you possess. I was not much acquainted with the Crows at this time, having met them only once before on the Sweetwater River, and then only a war-party.

On the second day the racing commenced, and the Shoshones ran their second-class ponies so as to let the Crows win. The Crows went wild and thought they had invincible ponies.

In the afternoon the Shoshones brought out their race-horses, and they were an indifferent-looking outfit. The Crows were positive that they had a sure thing and they bet everything they had, and on being bantered by the Shoshones to bet their race-horses, jumped at the opportunity.

It was a sure thing on the Shoshones' side, for in the previous races they had gauged the speed of the Crow ponies.

The distance was one mile over prairie. They do not prepare a smooth track. Such an idea never enters the Indian mind. Young Indian boys, stripped naked, are mounted on the ponies and led to the starting point. There is no jockeying such as white men indulge in, and no foolishness either. The order is given to go, and the first horse passing the winning post wins the race. It makes no difference what becomes of the other horses. Falling down or flying the track cuts no figure. This system is the same amongst all Indians, and the same rule applies in foot-racing. Ninety-nine times out of a hundred the best horse wins in an Indian race.

After the races the Crows departed, crestfallen, but promising to come again and bring other horses.

It was now a busy time with the Indians, who were hard at work curing meat and making *pemmican*. We were also busy and caught many beaver, otter, mink, and martin, and killed six fine black bears. Buffalo were more plentiful than usual and Washakie told us that the medicine-men gave us the credit for their abundance.

We had only one difficulty with war-parties, and that of minor importance. A few Blackfeet stole some of our ponies and drove them into the mountains. A small party started after them one morning, and by three o'clock were back in the village with the ponies and one scalp.

In the latter part of November, the Indians having all the meat and robes they required, we started on our return trip to Green River.

On the 15th of December we reached Green River and sold all our furs to traders. We set up our lodge next to Washakie's, and had many interesting conversations with him. He had heard of our fight at Rocky Point with the Pah Utes, and gave us credit for having inflicted the punishment they merited, for they were bad Indians. He thought that they would not soon forget this lesson.

We asked Washakie if these Humboldts or Pah Utes were not Shoshone Indians, and he answered that they were, but that they did not recognise them or any of the Pah Utes or Utahs, though they met sometimes and traded.

We also asked Washakie if the Shoshone had occupied and claimed this section of the country, and his answer was that they claimed the country to the Elk River (Yellowstone), and had done so as far back as they and their fathers could recollect. He said the Crows, Flatheads, and Nez Percys hunted upon their land. In fact, it was held by other tribes as neutral ground, claiming the right to hunt thereon.

I asked the chief if he had any idea whence sign-language originated, and he answered as many other old Indians have, that he did not know. It was handed down from father to son. Don Alvares, a Chilian, once told me that the Indians who occupied the base of the Andes Mountains used almost the same signs as the North American Indians.

After disposing of our furs, we went south to the Arkansas. The next two years and a half of my life had no bearing on prairie life, and I will pass it over. In 1846 the Mexican War commenced, and almost all the trappers joined General Price's forces.

In the spring of 1848, I returned to St. Louis promising to meet my four companions at Green River in the fall.

I went home and remained there six weeks. Everything had changed. Many of my schoolmates had married and settled down or departed to new pastures. My people were anxious for me to remain and settle down, but after tasting the free life of the prairie it was now too late. Both of my parents passed away within a year afterwards and our family scattered to the four winds, many of them never to meet again. "Westward, Ho!" appeared to take possession of everyone. Rumour spread that gold had been discovered in California, which by the treaty with Mexico now belonged to the United States. Emigrants were moving to Oregon by the hundreds. Salt Lake was being rapidly settled by the Mormons, and the whole country was assuming a new aspect. By the whole country I mean California, Oregon, and Salt Lake.

On the 25th of July I took steamboat for Council Bluffs and visited old Sarpee, who had a trading-post at a place called Plattsburg. The old man was anxious to have me remain and do the trading with the Indians who frequently visited there.

An Oregon emigrant train came to the post, intending to travel on the north side of the Platte River, crossing the Missouri at Kanesville, which was a new Mormon town. The captain wanted to get an experienced man to pilot the train, and I offered to take it as far as Green River and find him some one there to take it over the remainder of the trip. After consulting with his outfit, he offered me $250 and a fine five-year-old horse, which I accepted.

The train consisted of twenty-five wagons drawn by mules and oxen, and the people had with them a number of milch cows. In the party were fifteen women and several children. They came chiefly from Kentucky and Indiana. The captain's name was Reeves. He was a fine gentleman of about fifty years of age.

We crossed the ferry without mishap and moved steadily along until we reached the left fork of Platte River, where we came in contact with a party of Pawnee Indians.

They wanted to trade their ponies for some of the blooded Kentucky horses in our train, and were angry when we refused, saying that the Sioux would steal them all.

They would have made a dash for the horses right then if I had not placed well-armed guards around them.

We made a corral of the wagons, fastening them together with chains, and at night placed the stock inside.

Four men went on guard at a time, the captain and I going on at two a.m. We had not been on guard an hour when I heard the hooting of an owl. I told the captain to get more men out quietly.

The hooting ceased, and when the Indians had crawled close to the corral they gave their war-whoop, thinking they could stampede the stock. These were tied by halters to the inside wagon wheels, and although the yells did create, some disturbance among the stock, none got away.

After the first yell they made a rush for the corral with furious war-whoops, expecting to paralyze these strangers. They were met by a murderous fire. Ten men had been placed in front of the tents with orders to lie low. About six Indians made a dash for the tents and were met by a volley from the shotguns, which killed four of them. The Indians now disappeared, leaving nine of their number on the field. I told the captain that it was customary for mountain men to scalp Indians. He laughed and advised me to let it go, as it might shock the ladies. These ladies showed remarkable presence of mind and nerve. They had rolled up their bedding, placing it on the outside so as to form a breastwork, and had lain down behind it with the children.

At daylight we pulled out and travelled about fifteen miles and camped on a bend of the river, making a corral of the wagons. The ladies asked me if I thought the Indians would try to revenge themselves on us, and I answered that as they were unsuccessful in getting our outfit, they might decide to leave us alone and try to get even on some other train. This very often happened and the fault lay with emigrants themselves who did not take proper precautions. All emigrants had been warned time and time again to be very careful, but they seemed indifferent to their surroundings and neglected taking precaution. The result was that their stock was run off, leaving them helpless on the prairie with their families and wagons. Soldiers had to come to their assistance.

The Pawnees did not follow us nor did we see anything more of them.

We passed many small parties of Mormons, who appeared poor and miserable. Some of them were afoot and were pulling or pushing small hand-carts.

We saw no more Indians until we reached Ash Hollow, which was on the opposite side of the river. This is a noted place, where General Harney had a fight with the Sioux. About seventy-five Cheyennes visited the camp, many of whom I was acquainted with, but had not met them since 1842, when trading on Cherry Creek. They asked me many questions: Where had I been? Where was I going? Who were these people?

The ladies prepared a feast and invited the Indians, who were led

Pawnee horse thieves

by White Antelope, a noted chief and a proud and fine-looking warrior. They behaved remarkably well for Indians, not begging and only once offering to trade horses.

We moved steadily along, day after day, without obstruction or annoyance of any kind. Antelope and grouse were plentiful, and there was always an abundance of fresh meat in camp.

We reached Fort Hall October first, and I parted from one of the most accomplished emigrant outfits that ever crossed the plains.

I remained at Fort Hall for three days at the request of Captain H. Grant, who was employed by the Hudson Bay Company. He was a tall Highland Scotchman, and had been in the employ of the company for thirty years, and his reminiscences of the great Mackenzie and Frazer Rivers would fill volumes of most interesting matter.

One thing struck me forcibly, and that was the manner in which his company recruited their forces. Every year their agents in Scotland would get recruits from the Shetland and Orkney Islands, who would sign agreements to serve the company for from three to five years at twenty-five pounds a year and to live on what the country produced.

On their arrival in Canada the men were induced to take upon themselves a wife, an Indian woman. Calico in those days was fifty cents a yard, other things in proportion, and at the end of their term of service they were overwhelmingly in debt to the company. They were then kept in service to work out this indebtedness. Mexican *peons* and Hudson Bay employees were in much the same condition.

The Northwestern Fur Company differed very little from the Hudson Bay Company in the treatment of its employees. These companies did not like to be interfered with in collecting furs and robes from the Indians, and endeavoured to have a law passed making it a felony for any except themselves to do this trading; also, to compel all trappers to be in their employ.

Mountain men had more influence with the Indians than they, and they were aware of it, and from this sprang the feeling of antagonism which I retain to this day, (1905.)

CHAPTER 20

Hunting and Trapping in the Big Horns

On the road to Fort Bridger, I passed two trains bound for Oregon, which contained many women and children, and one Mormon outfit.

There were several Mormons at the Fort and a visible change had taken place. We were all aware that in a very few years a great emigration would take place, but we had not looked for the Mormons migrating to Salt Lake.

In every direction rumours were afloat of large gold discoveries in California, and all the trappers were discussing the possibility of making fortunes.

Two days before I reached Bridger a war-party of Indians had run off thirty horses belonging to the men at the Fort, who followed them for a day without success. They were a poor lot of men, who eked out an existence by just hanging around trading-posts. We trappers called them "doby men."

I continued on to Brown's Hole rendezvous and found there my four partners, as well as fifteen of our old companions.

The next day a couple of wagons arrived from Weston, Missouri, laden with goods for trading purposes. They brought news of great excitement throughout the East over the California gold discoveries; and that a great many people were taking ship, some going around Cape Horn and others by the Panama route. The news created much excitement at the rendezvous, as the majority had not heard of it before. A council was held by the trappers on the advisability of starting at once for California, taking the southern trail. Our party decided to wait until spring and take the Humboldt trail, striking middle California. We believed that if any gold were there, it would probably be in that section of the country.

Among the arrivals were three gentlemen, two from St. Louis and one from Kentucky, who were anxious to have a hunt in the Big Horn Mountains. They had heard and read a great deal about that romantic country, and of the wild and free life of the American trapper and mountaineer, and they were desirous of investigating in person with a view of publishing an account of their trip.

We warned them that it was a dangerous country at all seasons of the year, but that ten trappers would see them through. They were eager to go and offered to engage ten trappers for two months, furnish the outfit, and pay each trapper $100 a month. Besides this, the trappers could take their traps and retain all furs caught, as they were anxious to see in what manner beaver and otter were caught.

While these gentlemen were making their offer, Perkins arrived from Las Vegas, bringing a letter to me from Williams, who wanted me to come there and go into partnership with him in trading. I should certainly have gone had I not decided on the California trip. I never saw Williams again. A few years afterwards the Southern Utes killed him by mistake in Apache Pass. They were great friends of old Bill, and they packed him to their village and gave him a chief's burial, mourning for him as for one of their own. The Utes themselves told me this.

Perkins and I accepted the offer of these eastern men and made up a party of ten trappers. There were several Indians at the rendezvous who had ponies for trade, and our outfit was soon furnished. The trip was a most enjoyable one for all concerned, game of every description was abundant, and the easterners became good hunters. They were highly pleased at their success and paid each man double what they had agreed to.

The Shoshones discovered our camp on Nine Blackfeet Sleep Creek, so called because nine Blackfeet Indians were caught asleep by the Shoshones, who forced them to continue their sleep indefinitely.

The day the Shoshones found us, "Silver Tip" was on duty as picket. He could almost scent an Indian a mile off, and his eyes were as keen and penetrating as an eagle's. He was never known to give a false alarm. We were bear hunting at the time, and we saw his signal and hurried to camp. He said that Indians were not far off, as a few buffalo had been raised and antelope were scampering in every direction. These signs were significant to mountain men, though, of course, the game might have been raised by friendly Indians. The stock was all corralled and everything prepared for the reception of a war-party. At sunset fifteen Indians were seen advancing, one riding in advance at full speed, firing a rifle, which meant "friends."

He came boldly into camp and we soon recognised him as "Humpy," a most remarkable Indian of about twenty-five years of age. His height was only five feet two inches, and he had a large lump on his shoulders. He was a leader of war-parties, fearless and cautious, with many "*coups*" to his credit. These Indians had been after a war-party of Cheyennes who had stolen some Shoshone ponies. Overtaking them on the North Platte River they recovered the ponies.

They had heard shots from our party and could not understand who could be in that country with such guns, the report being much louder than theirs. They scouted and discovered boot-tracks, which mystified them even more. Finally, they discovered a trapper's *moccasin* track and they no longer hesitated in approaching camp. We invited them to supper and conversed until past midnight, interpreting every word to the three eastern men. They took a keen interest in the conversation, and said they had not expected such intelligence from wild Indians. We told these gentlemen that the Shoshones ranked for acumen with the most advanced Indians in America.

"Humpy" told us that Washakie's village was on a creek called Graybull, but would soon move to the south fork of Stinking Water, and he advised us to go there on account of the many war-parties in the country. This we concluded to do, and it was while *en route* that we gave the gentlemen a practical illustration of Indian warfare.

We were camped on Shell Creek, and Docket, who had been out scouting, reported having seen smoke, presumably from an Indian camp. The next day, about two o'clock in the afternoon, "Silver Tip" signalled "Indians." The stock was immediately corralled, and "Silver Tip" reported having seen a small band of Indians, some on horseback, travelling direct towards camp, though he was certain they had not discovered us as yet. The men put on all arms, which, in fact, were seldom off, and the easterners began to get a little uneasy, asking if these were hostile Indians. We answered that it was a sure thing that such a party were after scalps or horses, not being particular which.

We hid in a thicket to observe their movements, and did not have long to wait before they came in sight on a rise about three hundred yards away.

They could not see camp from that side, but they had discovered our horse tracks. They approached very carefully and looked over, but could discover nothing. We counted nine on horseback and ten on foot. The Indians now consulted for some time and then the horsemen made a detour, looking closely for tracks. After crossing the creek, they saw our lodge, and at once returned to the footmen on the rise. Another consultation was held, its object most likely to estimate how many men would be there with only one lodge. "Must be a trappers' lodge."

At all events, after some time passed, the footmen divided, five going above camp and five below. The nature of this movement was well, understood by the trappers, for the Indians intended to crawl through the timber and underbrush to the lodge and find out who was there.

Should they find no one they would conceal themselves until the return of the occupants and take them by surprise; then kill, scalp, and plunder. These are Indian tactics; but this time these red men were circumvented.

Three men were sent up the creek to conceal themselves about seventy-five yards from camp, and three below. They had not long to wait. The Indians approached in a careless manner without suspicion. Above camp the trappers let the Indians get within ten feet, when they jumped out, pistols in hand. Before the Indians realised what was happening, they were dead.

A moment afterwards a scattering fire was heard below camp, and two Indians were seen running towards their mounted companions on the ridge.

The trappers rushed to the corral and mounted, bidding the eastern men do likewise and see an Indian fight, as it might be their only chance. The Indians on the ridge were somewhat mystified, and remained there until we were out of the timber. At the sight of us they beat a hasty retreat, but it was too late. In order to escape they should have started as soon as they heard the shots. Their horses were indifferent ones, while ours were the very pick of the plains, and could not be excelled in any country for either endurance or speed. The two footmen mounted behind the horsemen.

When we reached the ridge the Indians were about four hundred yards away and going for "all that was out," as "Silver Tip" said. They were making for the Big Horn River, about three quarters of a mile distant.

Before they had covered half the distance, we were amongst them, passing in single file. By the time the last trapper passed they were all on their way to their happy hunting-grounds. As the last Indian fell the three easterners rode up, greatly surprised at the sudden termination of the fight. They had expected to see the Indians make some resistance and then they would have taken a hand.

"But you trappers do not give a person time to do a thing except follow."

They had heard just such fights described, but could not believe it possible.

We collected all the plunder the Indians had, besides scalping them, to the amusement of the gentlemen. We asked them to lift some of the hair, but could not prevail on them to do so; although after we had the scalps stretched on hoops and dried, they took half a dozen to show to their friends in the east.

That night they asked why the Indians had not used the bows and arrows which they carried in their hands. We answered that the Indians had their minds set on getting to the timber, and they did not know the quality of the men who were after them. We rode passing them on their right, because they could not use their bows and arrows on that side without turning around.

They did not know which side we would come up on, for we did not fire a shot until within ten feet, then passing in single file we delivered shots as we passed. They had no time to turn, as we passed like a whirlwind. When the last man passed the Indians were most of them dead.

Had we passed them on the left side some of us might have been hurt, though that is very doubtful, as men and horses alike were quick and active. And another thing, the closer you are to an Indian the less danger there is of getting hurt. You confuse him and he does not seem able to collect his thoughts.

These Indians were strange to us, but when shown the scalps Washakie told us that they were Pend Oreilles.

We spent a very pleasant time at the Shoshone village, especially the first evening, when we recounted to Washakie how we had trapped the Indians. He was highly pleased and said "Old trappers are wolves," meaning in Indian way of speech, hard to take in or always on the alert. He thought the Pend Oreilles were fools to think that there were no trappers at the lodge.

We gave the rest of the scalps to the Shoshones, and the young folks had a merry scalp dance, which kept up until past midnight.

We went on buffalo hunts, on bear hunts, and, in fact, gave our employers an opportunity to try their hand on every variety of game to be found in that section, much to their satisfaction.

When we reached Green River and bade our three gentlemen *adieu*, we were all well satisfied with the trip.

CHAPTER 21

We Trappers Turn Miners, and Stake Our Claims

We moved to Henry's Fork of Green River, intending to complete preparations for our California trip at this place. Many mountain men had already congregated there.

A fearful storm set in and lasted three weeks. Our whole time was taken up in looking after stock, so as to keep them up in flesh. We cut the bark of young cottonwoods, which is very nutritious and will keep stock in good shape for a short time. We also kept a close guard both night and day, for we knew that war-parties were about. Fortune favoured us, as we were not visited by any horse-stealing parties while we remained in this camp. Parties on Black and Ham Forks of Green River did not come off so well, but lost several ponies through negligence and were constantly bothered by the Indians.

Several of the men at this rendezvous had relations in Oregon and decided to go that way, visit them, and pass on to California. Others decided to take the southern route, passing through Utah. Our party selected the middle route, *via* Humboldt River and through the Carson Valley.

Some of the men had heard of our difficulty with the Pah Utes at Rocky Point, and thought that we might come in contact with our former antagonists. "Yes," I said; "but they have not forgotten the reception we gave them, and may conclude to give us a wide berth." We thought that nine trappers were sufficient for those Indians. We had another motive in going by this route, namely, to see if Crawford's grave had been molested. If so, those Pah Utes would better keep a long distance from us, as in that case a few more of them would be likely to suffer.

We intended to start on the 15th of February, travel by easy stages, and collect furs. We had been told that we could find a good market in San Francisco. We did not rely altogether on being able to pick up gold on the top of the ground. Newspapers telling of fabulous finds had been brought out by the fur-buyers. The news set half of the men wild, but for all that they did not credit the report in the papers. They reasoned that if gold could be found in such quantities, the Spaniards would have overrun that country centuries ago.

Parties we came in contact with urged us to throw our traps in the creek and go with them, declaring that by the time we reached California with our furs they, simply by looking for it, would have gold enough to buy our furs, horses, and everything we had.

We went to the trading-post and bought $250 worth of trinkets to trade with Carson Indians, and on the day set, packed up, intending to strike Bear River and collect furs. We reached there without any mishap and trapped down to the mouth of Malade River, securing many furs. At Malade River we were joined by several young Mormons, who camped with us that night. They were on their way to California, excited, as many others, by the gold reports. Next morning they were off by daylight.

We made quite a catch of furs here in three days, crossed Goose Creek range, trapped that stream, Raft River, and other creeks, and did remarkably well. Having as yet come across no Indians, we proceeded to the head of Humboldt River. A few Indians showed themselves, but kept clear of us. We continued down to Rocky Point and camped on our old ground. We examined Crawford's grave and found it had not been disturbed.

The Indians hovered around us, but did not approach. It was manifest they had not forgotten the merited chastisement we had administered or they would have paid us a visit. We did not set any traps, but pulled out early the next morning and made some thirty miles. Here we camped and set our traps and made a good catch. As soon as the hides were off, we packed up, and made twenty miles over the same old route. We saw a few Indians at a distance, but whether they were following us or belonged to some other village, we did not know. At all events, we did not give them an opportunity to raid us or our stock. We took extraordinary precautions, catching only a few furs close to camp. The next morning, we were off early and reached Humboldt Lake, but caught no beaver. The next day we reached the lower end of the lake and spent two days stretching and drying furs. Here some more Mormons arrived and camped with us over night.

Here is the starting point of the two routes across the Great American Desert, one leading to Truckee and another to Carson. We advised the Mormons to take the latter, which they did the next morning.

The next day we crossed, getting to Carson River early, and found our friends the Mormons in a sorry plight. It had been exceedingly warm the day they crossed the desert. As a result of their having urged their horses beyond endurance, they had to lay up for a week to recruit their stock. Hundreds suffered the same way when crossing this desert by not exercising proper judgment. We traded with our former friendly Indians, who were really glad to see us. They had considerable fur, all of which we got, besides collecting much ourselves.

The snow being exceedingly deep in the Sierras we camped at the base. Here some of the Mormons returned, saying that it was impossible to cross the mountains at this time. They had an Indian with them as guide. We engaged this same Indian and another volunteered to go also. As I stated before, we had treated those Indians with the greatest kindness and they were ready to do anything for us, so we accepted this last Indian's offer. These Indians guided us through the night as easily as by daylight, for they had crossed the mountains many times. We started at nine o'clock in the evening, with forty-five head of stock, the Indians having two. On this route there are two high divides. The Indians thought we could cross the first by sun-up and get Cottonwood bark for the horses.

We strung out our horses single file, the Indians in advance. When we first struck snow, it was not very deep, and consequently there was considerable floundering. As the snow deepened travel became easier. The deeper the snow the more compact it is. At daylight we came to a creek with the snow eight feet deep. Before unpacking we tramped upon the snow to make it more solid. We cut down a lot of fir limbs, spread them upon the snow, and unpacked. The horses seemed to have human intelligence and would not leave the place we had tramped for them. Leaving two men to prepare breakfast, the remainder got large quantities of young Cottonwood limbs, which the horses, being very hungry, relished greatly.

After breakfast all but one man rolled up in blankets and took a good six-hour slumber. This refreshed us greatly and we awoke as hungry as wolves. A meal fit for the gods was soon prepared, and we spent the afternoon in prospecting for a place to cross the creek. The water had made a tunnel under the snow, and it was some time before we could find a place to bridge. We cut fir limbs, laying them thick enough to cross on without stepping on the snow. The reader can imagine it would be no easy trick to extricate a horse should he fall through eight feet of snow into the creek below. We did not intend to take any chances, but piled the limbs thickly across the dangerous place.

It must have been 80° in the shade. The snow was settling rapidly, and the horses trampling around kept it comparatively solid. They were well supplied with bark, so they did not suffer for lack of food. The Indians thought we could make the west side of the main divide by daylight and would find grass. On the south side of the ridge, we made some hoops and stretched rawhide over them, using them as snow-shoes. At two-thirty in the afternoon, when the snow was at its softest, Russell and "Scotty," accompanied by the Indians, donned temporary snow-shoes and took the supposed trail, going some three miles. This trail assisted us in the fore part of the night. Russell and "Scotty" said these Indians could excel them on snow-shoes, for the trappers were fagged out on their return to camp.

We packed up about nine o'clock, crossed the bridge, carefully leading each animal over, then mounted, stringing them out in single file. You could not get a horse to step one inch out of the trail. They would step into each other's foot-tracks. We experienced no difficulty *en route*. Each mount would lead an animal, a certain number of loose ones following, they in turn being followed by a mount. One hour before daylight we crossed the divide, made good time, and reached the place designated by the Indians, and we found everything just as described. We camped on a bare spot, cooked and feasted; the horses nibbling green grass much to their delight. Grass grows under the snow in this region.

According to our reckoning this was the third day of July. As far as the snow was concerned our difficulties were over, though we still had some snow to cross. The Indians advised us to pack up at midnight, while the snow was the hardest, and we would be out of it by daylight. At eleven o'clock the next day we reached Hangtown.

Some miners—Americans and Mexicans—were located on the creek. Of the Americans all but two had come to California by the Panama route. The two mentioned were trappers who had come with Fremont. Thousands must have come by water in 1848, as these miners spoke of a town on Sacramento River called Georgetown where considerable mining was going on.

A small town was starting up here with one small store. After staying here three days we learned how to mine and save gold by a rocker and a pan. The dirt is stripped away to a depth of three or four feet, then the gold is panned out from what they call the pay dirt. This is quite different from picking up gold on top of the ground;

On the 9th of July we arrived at Sacramento, a small town then, but full of life. We put up our lodge outside of town and had many visitors; for, being dressed in fringed buckskin, a custom among free trappers, we were quite a curiosity.

Three of our men could speak Spanish, and the Mexicans gave them all the news about the mines. They claimed that the best mining section was towards the north, on the Yuba. We remained here ten days, and in the meantime disposed of our furs to a Mexican *Don*, who paid us our price.

After we had settled everything, we bought picks, pans, rockers, crevice spoons, rubber boots, slickers, and flannel overshirts. We were transformed from trappers into miners. Packing up our mining outfit we started north, not knowing whither we were going and not caring. One thing was certain, we had set out to see some mining. None of us relished pick and shovel work, having never used these implements except to dig a few rifle-pits. However, we went cheerfully along, visiting several places where mining was in progress. We set up our lodges, taking turn about looking after the stock and cooking, the others staking off mining claims. We continued thus until the spring of 1853 with indifferent success. I saw as many men out of funds in California in those days as I have seen anywhere, in spite of the fact that work was plentiful. But the country was overrun with gamblers and rounders, generally hard characters. Many of them died with their boots on, while many who merited the same fate escaped.

At this time, we were at Little York, and some of the miners who had interests in the claims had gone to prospect some other creeks, promising to be back in a few days. They had left their clothing, and some of them considerable money. Their friends became uneasy at their long-continued absence, when news was brought to town that Lawyer Lewis had been horribly butchered at Auburn. Lewis had his tent pitched outside the village, not far from an Indian camp. The morning following the murder the Indians disappeared.

Lewis was a great favourite with the miners, and when his fate became known a council was held by the miners and business men, who decided the Indians guilty.

There were very few arms among the miners. Those who had crossed the plains had rifles, but they had made crowbars of them.

CHAPTER 22

More Indian Outrages

The news brought in of miners being found stripped, scalped, and otherwise mutilated created almost a panic among the prospectors. These generally travelled either alone or with one or two companions, and seldom carried arms to defend themselves with.

A general rumour was afloat that the Indians from the Colorado River west, and from the Mexican line to the British-American border, had united against all the white men.

News came that Governor Joe Lane of Oregon was fighting Indians on Rogue River and that the Indians in the Walla Walla country had declared war. Everything looked gloomy and desperate to the many miners, and daily councils were held, especially by the business men.

Our outfit was almost everywhere known among the miners as the "Mountaineer Miners." We had retained all our arms and horses and had each two suits of buckskins, one as a Sunday suit, so Noble said.

Six of us had traded our Hawkins rifles for Sharps rifles, brought in by emigrants. The barrels of the Hawkins rifles made good substitutes for crowbars. These were the first Sharps rifles we had seen and we found them most effective weapons, our only criticism being that the triggers pulled too hard. We had a gunsmith resight them and fix the triggers, and securing a lot of tape caps and ammunition, we practised for several days. They were equal in accuracy to our old rifles and far superior in effectiveness.

A dispatch was received from the business men of Nevada City asking us to come there at once and attend a council relative to the Indian problem. We dressed in our buckskins and mounted our war-horses, as Docket insisted on calling them. "Scotty" was left to take care of camp. At three in the afternoon, we reached Nevada City and found the place full of miners. A person looking on as we rode down the street would have imagined a circus in town. Every man, woman, and child in the town rushed out of the houses, and many of them looked as if they thought we had come to capture the city.

We rode to the California Hotel, where we were met by the leading business men and city officials. Here we dismounted and our horses were put in the stable, with orders to take the best of care of them. We were then escorted to the reception room, where a tempting repast awaited us.

After feasting to our hearts' content, we advised the citizens to hold council at once. Mr. A. L. Graham, a banker, presided, and he said that the object of the council was to consider the ways and means of putting a stop to the slaughtering of prospectors and miners by the Indians. He read a paper recounting the number of miners who had been found scalped and otherwise mutilated, and dwelt upon the barbarous manner in which Lawyer Lewis had been treated. When through with the paper, he called the attention of the assemblage to our party, remarking that these mountaineers were the ones to take a leading part in deciding what to do in the disposition of the Indians. All were satisfied that these murders had been committed by the Indians.

We were called upon to address the meeting. As Perkins was the oldest, we selected him to do the talking. In a few terse remarks he informed the meeting that he thought there should be no time wasted in following these Auburn Indians, as this tribe had done most of the killing. To his question as to how many lodges there were in the Auburn village, he was answered sixty. Perkins thought this signified from one hundred and twenty to one hundred and forty warriors. He also thought that fifty men armed with rifles would be sufficient to punish the Indians.

A runner was dispatched to Grass Valley, three miles distant, and one to Auburn, calling for fifty volunteers who had rifles to meet at Grass Valley that evening. There were but twelve men in Nevada City who owned rifles, although several had pistols. Horses were plenty, but there was a scarcity of saddles, blankets being used as a substitute.

We deposited most of our funds with Wells Fargo Company's bank. Up to this time we had always packed our funds, having little confidence in banks. Supper was furnished at the city's expense, and we were not allowed to pay for anything. Immediately after supper we mounted and proceeded to Grass Valley, where fifteen men had already assembled. By eight o'clock we mustered sixty-three mounted and fairly well-armed men.

Perkins was elected captain and, by order of that dare-devil Russell, I was elected first lieutenant, Evans second lieutenant, and Russell first sergeant, to his great disgust, as he said that all he knew was "how to shoot." Four pack-horses were loaded with supplies, as it was uncertain how long we would be absent, and game was not over plenty. Many of the mountains in California are grassy, with open timber, and clear of underbrush.

The best information to be had was that the Indians had gone towards the mountains, passing a small mining camp called Cold Spring. We made for this place and soon struck the Indian trail. We followed the trail, crossing a creek called Blue Canon. Here the Indians had killed three miners and burnt their cabins. The miners, who were horribly cut up, were known to several in our party. We gave them decent burial. The Indians had camped one night at this place.

We now followed the trail at a gallop wherever the ground permitted. The Indians had remained together, as we kept a sharp lookout to ascertain if they divided their village. About noon we came to a lake, and the signs showed that they had camped there that morning, as the ashes in the fires were still hot. We were certain that up to this time they had no idea that we were following. We remained at the lake one hour for lunch and then took up the trail, which led up a long ridge towards a high mountain. From the ridge the Indians must have discovered us, for we now saw signs that they had been hurrying forward.

We soon overtook their rear lookouts, who made for their outfit. The village had just reached a creek when we came in sight of it. The Indians soon had their packs off and formed a breastwork. Perkins remarked, "There is a chief who understands how to prepare for a fight." We had not looked for this from these Indians. They were armed with a few good rifles, obtained, no doubt, from miners, and had many Mexican rifles and bows and arrows.

We now divided our forces. Perkins ordered me to take twenty-five men and cross the creek, so as to make a flank movement. This was done with considerable difficulty, as the banks of the creek were very steep. When we got opposite the Indians we tied our horses behind trees for protection. Meantime the Indians were sending forth yells of defiance and firing a few shots from long range. They had no protection from our side, as the creek bank was fully six feet higher than it was on the Indian side.

Perkins had deployed his men and opened the engagement, and

was gradually drawing nearer the Indians, until he was within one hundred yards of their breastwork.

About forty Indians were facing us. The women were rolling up lodges so as to make temporary breastworks against our shots. We kept creeping closer and closer, taking cover behind trees, until we got within fifty yards of the creek.

The chief was brave, and if all his warriors had been likewise, Perkins would have had a hand-to-hand combat, as the chief with eighty warriors charged him. They had covered half the distance to Perkins when the chief fell. This disheartened the others and they beat a hasty retreat to the breastworks. Here the Sharps rifles proved their superiority over the muzzle-loaders, and the rapidity of their fire astonished the Indians.

From our side we had the Indians at a great disadvantage. The edge of the bank was fringed with trees, and we were able to keep creeping nearer and nearer. The women and children soon became panic-stricken and before long the warriors also, and it was now that they suffered the most; the warriors running about within their enclosure and getting mixed up with the women and children. Almost every shot we fired took effect.

Perkins was now almost at the breastwork and we had reached the very edge of the bank. One miner in my command had an arm broken by a shot and another was shot in the ribs. "Silver Tip" had his ear split by an arrow.

The Indians now became frantic and they jumped into the creek *en masse*, women, men, and children all mixed up. Perkins's force charged over the breastwork and, amid the greatest screaming, howling, and yelling one ever heard, killed what few Indians were there.

About thirty of the men escaped. We captured the women and children who remained. Many of the latter had fallen, which could not be avoided, for they were mingled with the men, and the miners shot at anything that looked like an Indian.

Perkins had six wounded in his command, two quite seriously, but by careful nursing they all recovered. Russell had a close call, getting a bullet through his hat.

We captured seventy-four horses; many in the bunch had been stolen from miners. We also found seventeen white men's scalps which we took with us to show, so as to teach a lesson to those sceptics who believed in the innocence of the Indians. Besides the horses we found saddles, blankets, clothing, and about five hundred dollars in gold dust in buckskin purses.

We destroyed everything in the shape of lodges and scalped all the men. Every miner had one scalp and some two, besides a quantity of bows and arrows and guns. After the fight a council was held and many of the miners were in favour of wiping out the women and children whom we had captured, but the trappers persuaded them not to do so. We considered for some time taking the women prisoners, but concluded they would be a burden. The men who had escaped would return soon after our departure, and there was no danger that they would starve, as berries and roots were plentiful.

We constructed three *travois* for the worst wounded and returned to the lake at the foot of the ridge, reaching it about midnight.

At daylight six miners were dispatched to settlements to have doctors and wagons meet us at Blue Cañon. We travelled slowly on account of the wounded, and reached the *cañon* on the second day. Fully one hundred men were there to meet us, and they were wild with elation over our victory. The miners made it appear that we trappers were more than heroes, and "Silver Tip" said it made us blush to hear such flattery. The doctors took charge of the wounded, putting them in spring wagons. We arrived at Cold Spring Hotel by sundown, and the people there would not let us cook, but made us dine at the hotel.

Next morning we prepared to start for our camp at Little York, but the citizens all protested. We must go to Nevada City and let the people see a true American mountaineer. I suppose we did look strange to them with our two big Colt revolvers, rifle, and a two-pound tooth-pick, besides our fringed buckskin suits and *moccasins*. When we arrived in Nevada City the whole population turned out to greet us. They were no longer depressed in spirits over all the murders, as they were satisfied the mysteries were solved and the guilty detected and punished. Even the mayor got beyond himself in a public speech, giving the trappers credit for being the "avengers of all this slaying of prospectors." He held up to view the seventeen white men's scalps, and one man in the crowd rose and pointed to a certain one, saying, "That is Lawyer Lewis's scalp."

The miners who were with us overdid the killing, saying we had wiped out over two hundred men and women. We heard afterwards that some of the ministers gave us credit for being savages and fit only to dwell among such.

Next day we brought in the seventy-four horses, twenty of which had belonged to prospectors. They were turned over to the city au-

119

thorities and sold at auction, bringing in about fifty dollars per head. This money, at our request, was given to the wounded men.

The citizens offered to raise a purse for us but the offer was rejected, as we stood in no need of money. They prevailed upon us to spend the day with them, and when the stage arrived in the evening the papers were full of accounts of massacre. One large pack-train had been taken and all the packers killed except one Mexican, who had escaped and brought the news. This took place at Biglow's Lake, at the head of Truckee River. Volunteers were called for to chastise the Indians who had committed the crime.

CHAPTER 23

I Go as Scout

The next day we returned to Little York, where the news of our victory over the Auburns had spread like wildfire. A letter came to the mayor requesting us to go to Hangtown (now Placerville), where volunteers would be enrolled, and we went as requested. Great excitement prevailed there, and sixty men were mustered under the command of Bob Williams. We came in contact with the Indians at Biglow's Lake, where there is a prairie of some extent. The Indians were armed with lances, bows and arrows, and some Spanish flintlock guns. When we deployed on the prairie, Indians to the number of one hundred and fifty charged us. We passed through them, wheeled, and recharged, attacking the Indians in the flank.

At this they became bewildered, for they had not expected to be charged in turn. There happened to be twenty-five men in the company who had served as cavalrymen in the Mexican War. But for that fact we would have met with disastrous defeat. The volunteers' horses became unmanageable in the yelling and firing that ensued. Through it all the trappers, who had right flank in charge, remained together, striking the Indians on their left, where the Indians were three to one. Led by two chiefs and armed in part with lances they charged us, but the chiefs went down when within fifty yards of us.

The Indians, seeing their chiefs fall, halted for a moment, which was fatal to them. The trappers passed through them with their Colt revolvers playing before they had recovered their presence of mind. It was a slaughter. The trappers wheeled and charged the main body of Indians and struck them on the left flank, doubling them up. At this instant the Mexican War veterans had wheeled and charged with a yell. They were brave men, and if their horses had been trained as ours were they would have done three times the execution they did. As it was, the charge they made saved the day to us.

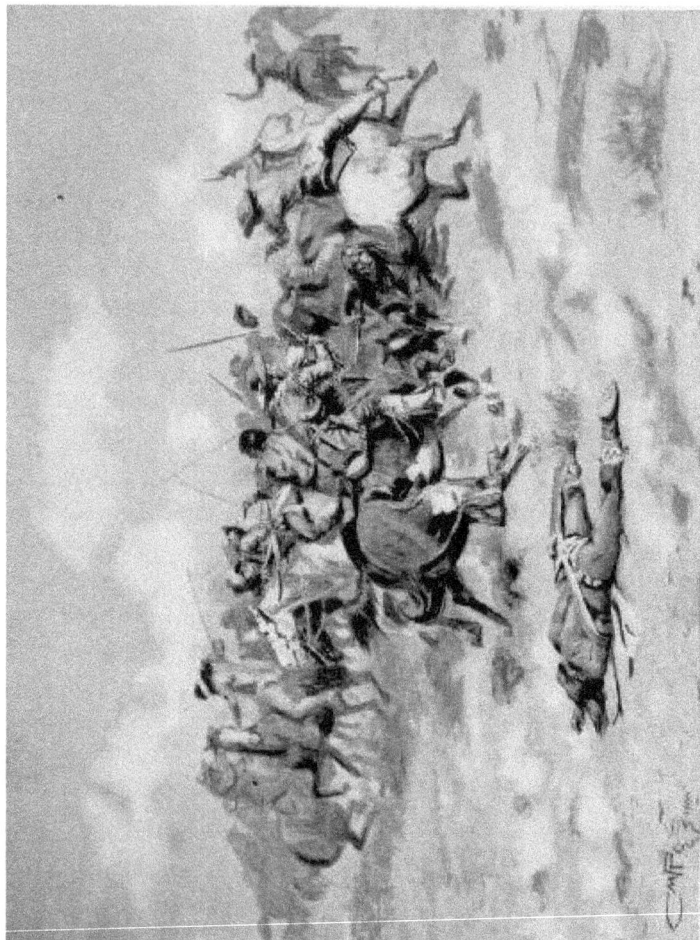

THE TRAPPERS PASSED THROUGH THEM WITH THEIR COLT'S REVOLVERS

There was one tall Indian decorated with all the barbaric splendour of war-bonnet and feathers on a fine horse, who was endeavouring to rally the Indians. The trappers saw at a glance that this chief must be gotten rid of if we were to gain the victory, and we made for the cluster of Indians he was rallying, scattered them, and killed the chief and several lesser ones. When you put a quietus on a chief you have a battle won. The Indians beat a hasty retreat up the valley, where their village was located. Russell's horse went down in this charge, but he secured the Indian's horse and soon overtook us.

In rounding a bend, we came upon the packtrain of mules. About sixty-five Indians who had passed through the village were at their heels. The old men and women who had witnessed the battle and its results had abandoned the village and taken to the mountains.

We burned the village and everything it contained, collected the mules and ponies, and returned to the battlefield. Only forty of us followed the Indians to their village, and in this running fight the superiority of our Sharps rifles became again apparent. When we began fighting, we had forty rounds of ammunition, and we came out with from three to seven. Captain Williams gave them the credit for gaining the victory, but there is no doubt in my mind that it was due to the Colt revolvers.

The captain remarked that he had seen lots of cavalry service, but had never seen such well-trained horses as ours. I rode my Kentucky horse "*Otto*," and came near losing him, for a bullet passed through his ear. Perkins's horse died from wounds. "Scotty's" horse fell at the first charge, but he quickly found another mount. "Scotty" was a hero in a fight, quick as a flash, cool and collected under the most trying circumstances.

Six of the Mexican veterans and two miners fell in the fight. Many of these volunteers were poor horsemen and had never fired a pistol before. They were brave enough, but they could not control their horses. For such an engagement as we had just had, constant drill in the use of arms and in horseback riding was required.

We had buried the eight men who had fallen when thirty men arrived as a reinforcement. It was amusing to see these new arrivals scalping the Indians. The trappers showed them how to accomplish it and they were apt scholars.

Some of the trappers had received slight wounds. The only thing that annoyed them was getting blood on their buckskin suits. Buckskin is hard to clean.

A council was held to consider whether to follow up the Indians or not. Finally, the captain concluded that this chastisement would prevent them from molesting any more whites.

We started on our return trip and reached Hangtown without further trouble. The owner of the mules, who lived in Marysville, was notified to come and get his property.

News had arrived that the Indians in Shasta and Trinity counties were hostile, and while we were absent had committed what is known as the Trinity massacre, slaughtering right and left, men, women, and children. Volunteers had been called for, and the captain, with his old soldiers as well as we trappers, joined the forces. When we reached Shasta City, we found everyone scared nearly to death, and there were many families there.

Those Indians are known as "Tar-heads," and they received a just chastisement when, in less than thirty days, more than half of them were placed *hors-de-combat*, which put a quietus on any further devilment on their part. The Indian Commissioners gathered the remnant of them and they became wards of Uncle Sam.

We remained in this section until 1855, when we took part in the wind-up of the Rogue River war. The volunteers were commanded by General Lamrick, who received his appointment through political influence. He understood nothing about military tactics and less about Indian fighting.

In 1856 the Modoc war broke out. Three companies were called out, and we belonged to what was known as the "Buckskin Rangers." Our commander was General Crosby, a third-rate lawyer, who also received his appointment by a political pull. He was a counterpart of Lamrick in knowledge of Indian fighting. Neither of them ever went into an engagement.

At the close of the Modoc war the Pitt River Indians committed the Pitt River massacre and the three companies went after them. After annihilating about half, the remainder surrendered and were placed on a reservation. The volunteers were disbanded, but we trappers remained together, mining a little until 1858.

In the spring of that year Perkins, Noble, Docket, Evans, and "Scotty" concluded to go to New Mexico. Russell remained with me. We all promised to meet again, but never did, although we often corresponded.

About this time there was great excitement over the discovery of gold on Fraser River in British Columbia, and for a while it looked as if the stampede would deplete California of her mining population. Pack-trains were rushing to Dallas, Oregon, to pack supplies to the miners on the river. Don Alvares, a Chilian, engaged Russell and myself to guide him and his two pack-trains from Yreka to Dallas. We took the east side of the Cascade range, as grass was reported scarce on the west side. This route took us through the Modoc country by Klamath lakes, but we experienced no difficulty and it was evident that the Indians had cooled down, for a while at least.

When we arrived at Dallas we met some officers from Walla Walla, who told us the commander wished to employ some experienced scouts. We were offered good pay to accompany a pack-train to Fraser River, but declined, preferring to visit Fort Walla Walla.

When we reached the fort, we saw a number of Nez Percés Indians on the parade ground surrounded by officers. We attracted considerable attention owing to our fringed buckskin and *moccasins*. The Indians immediately asked us in sign-language where we had come from? We answered in signs, much to the astonishment of both officers and Indians, who did not expect such proficiency from us. Colonel Wright, the commanding officer, invited us to his office and asked us many questions, which we answered truthfully, after which he engaged us as scouts.

Some little time before we reached the fort the Yakimas, Spokane, Colville, and other tribes had declared war. Colonel Steptoe met the Palonse and Spokane tribes and was defeated. Lieutenant Caston, a nephew of General Scott, lost his life in this battle. The Nez Percés came between the hostiles and troops and saved the latter from being slaughtered. (*The Nez Percé Campaign, 1877* by G. O. Shields & Edmond Stephen Meany also published by Leonaur.)

Colonel Wright had succeeded Colonel Steptoe by order of General Harney, who in turn had succeeded General Wool as commander of the Pacific Coast. There had been a lull in Indian affairs, and Colonel Wright was anxious to find out, if possible, what the Indians were doing and how many warriors they could muster. This was a difficult problem for us to solve, as we were strangers in the country.

CHAPTER 24

I am Left Alone

Russell bought a fine unbroken horse and saddled and mounted him outside of the parade grounds, where there were rock-piles. He was an expert and fearless rider, but the moment he was in the saddle the horse began pitching furiously. The officers asked me if he would be able to "stick," and I answered "Yes, if nothing breaks."

I had no sooner spoken when the cinch broke and Russell landed on his head on one of the rock-piles. We rushed to him and found him unconscious. The doctor was immediately called and ordered to have him conveyed to the hospital. His skull was badly fractured and he never regained consciousness. On the second day he died, and I lost one of my closest friends. He was one of the bravest men I had ever known, kind and generous to a fault and a man of infinite resource. He had been in more desperate engagements than fell to the lot of many who followed prairie life for a calling. I was left alone.

I had lost my horse "*Otto*," which had received a poisoned arrow in one of the engagements on Pitt River. Another one of my trained horses was crippled by stepping in a badger hole while in pursuit of Indians. I had purchased a thoroughbred in Yreka, calling him "*Hickory*."

This horse I retained for many years, and he was well broken. He would lie down on a blanket and he seemed to have human intelligence. The officers wanted to buy him, but I told them he was not for sale. He would come at a gallop when I whistled, expecting sugar and some petting. The ladies said, "Hamilton, you love your horse and we don't wonder at your not parting with him."

Soon after Russell's death I was introduced to a Scotch half-breed named McKay, who was well acquainted with the country and could speak two or three Indian languages. The officers told me he was brave and could be trusted.

We held a consultation about the best way of penetrating into Indian villages. McKay had found out that the Indians were in need of ammunition and tobacco, so I proposed to the officers that we take two pack-horses loaded with the articles named, and make the Indians believe we were their friends. We would also tell them that if the officers found out that we traded ammunition they would hang us.

The council of officers approved this plan, and we began at once to prepare for the expedition.

I concluded to leave my horse "*Hickory*" and take Russell's horse, which was a good one. We secured two gentle ponies to pack the ammunition and tobacco, and left the fort after dark. We made about forty miles before daylight and hunted up a spring which McKay knew of. We remained here until sundown, and that night reached the Columbia River about ten miles below the mouth of Umatilla River.

On the opposite side was a Klick-a-tat village which had joined the hostile tribes. It was about one o'clock in the morning when McKay called to them. They asked, "What's wanted?" and we answered friends, and to come over with canoes, as we wanted to cross. They came over with two and we crossed, swimming our horses.

On reaching the village we found the whole tribe assembled to see who could possibly come at that time of night. They were acquainted with McKay, but they sized me up. I was dressed in a Hudson Bay *shacto* coat, with a Scotch cap. These Indians were friendly with Hudson Bay employees. They feasted us with dried salmon and we told the chief what we had. After this we slept till daylight, when a council was held. The chief informed us that the Palouse and other tribes would assemble on McNatchee River that day, as the Yakimas with their great chief Kan-a-yak-a wanted to see how many warriors each tribe could furnish. He further said that they would be glad to see us with ammunition and tobacco. We traded a little with these Indians, and as a blind had to take in exchange two good ponies.

We reached the rendezvous after dark, accompanied by a delegation of Klick-a-tats, and were taken direct to the chief's lodge.

Our arrival created quite a disturbance in the village and the chief eyed us closely for some time, in fact until the Klick-a-tats told him how they crossed us after midnight and traded for some ammunition. This lulled the chief's suspicion, my Hudson Bay dress assisting.

I had acquired quite a knowledge of Chinook jargon and we conversed in this language. They asked me many questions, all of which I answered, telling them that Hudson Bay men were their friends, and that I had been sent with this ammunition and tobacco to trade with them for a few ponies. It came near choking me to tell such outrageous falsehoods.

Next day about four thousand warriors assembled, and they were a gay and proud lot of Indians, who looked with disdain on both McKay and myself. We found out all that Colonel Wright required— the approximate number of warriors, and also that the lull was caused on account of waiting for the different tribes to gather all their outside Indians and then to hold a council. They decided to assemble all their warriors on the Spokane River and draw the soldiers on, when they would kill all the cavalry and take "walk-a-heap" (infantry) prisoners and make slaves of them.

We traded all our ammunition and tobacco, and such a trade was never made before or since. We gave all our stuff to the chief and told him to give us what ponies he thought proper. He called up the Indians who had no ammunition and issued some to each, for which we received a few ponies and not very good ones either.

That afternoon at five we started as if going west, but when out of sight of the Indians we turned south, so as to strike the Columbia opposite Wallula, at the mouth of Walla Walla River. We rode the best ponies, leading our horses. The poor ponies we left on the prairie, having no use for them. When the ponies gave out, we rested for half an hour and then saddled our horses, which were, comparatively speaking, fresh. We made excellent time and at sun-up were opposite Wallula.

McKay knew where the Indians always kept canoes "*cached*," but we rested an hour before attempting to cross. The river is wide at this place and it takes a good horse to swim it.

We crossed without mishap and let the horses feed for two hours, after which we proceeded towards the Fort, where we arrived at ten o'clock that night. It was thirty miles from Wallula to the Fort. We reported our arrival to the officer on guard and he sent an orderly to Colonel Wright. This orderly soon returned with orders to report immediately at headquarters.

A council was in progress and we made our report. Colonel Wright was well pleased at the news that the Indians were collecting on Spokane River, and he said the campaign would be a short one. His predictions proved true. The Indians, in force estimated at five thousand strong and fairly well armed, were met by Colonel Wright with one thousand soldiers, forty Nez Percés Indians, and two howitzers, which, when the shells burst among them, doing considerable execution, frightened the Indians very badly. They beat a hasty retreat to St. Joe Mission, and the chiefs pleaded with the fathers to intercede for them. Nine chiefs were taken prisoners and held as hostages for the Indians' good behaviour. We then returned to the Fort, having been absent but six weeks.

An Indian rumour had it that all tribes east of the Rocky Mountains were forming a combine against whites. The United States was getting tired of these continual outbreaks of the Indians, so I volunteered to find out whether there was any truth in the Indian rumour. I took McKay with me, also a trading outfit. We passed through recent hostile tribes, going by St. Joe Mission, and found the Indians surly, but on their good behaviour.

We camped one night where Missoula, Montana, now stands, and I noticed many Indian trails converging. It struck me as an ideal spot for a trading-post, and I told McKay that if we got back from this trip with our lives I would return and establish a trading-post there, which I did late that fall.

We made the trip and found the Indian rumour false. Returning, we reported the news to Colonel Wright. I received great credit for that trip. Settling with the government, I purchased some goods and started back to Montana, establishing a trading-post at the aforesaid place. I remained there until 1864, when I sold out and moved to Fort Benton, and opened up a business at that place. I was elected Sheriff and appointed Deputy United States Marshal. In 1869 I sold out at Fort Benton and moved to the Yellowstone Valley, intending to open a trading-post.

About this time the Sioux, Arapahoes, and Cheyennes became very hostile, even making raids on the farmers in the Gallatin Valley.

In 1874 an expedition was organised, consisting of one hundred and forty-eight men. We started in midwinter, going down the Yellowstone River, crossing at lower Porcupine Creek. We then travelled over a broken country to East Rosebud, having two small engagements *en route*.

On East Rosebud we had two rifle-pit engagements, repulsing the Indians in every instance with heavy loss. We then went to the Little Big Horn and had two more fights, one on Grass Lodge, where fifteen hundred Indians charged us, but we repulsed them with heavy loss. The people in Bozeman having had no tidings, concluded we were all lost.

This was the expedition which brought on the war of 1876, that was so disastrous to General Custer and his command. In that year I joined General Crook on Goose Creek, engaging as scout along with nine others. (*Custer: The Civil War Years Volume 1* by Frederick Whittaker and Whitelaw Reid & *Custer: The Frontier Years Volume 2* by Frederick Whittaker & Lawrence Barrett also published by Leonaur.)

The general took his troops to Wolf Mountains and had a fight with the Sioux and Cheyennes, losing thirteen soldiers besides having several wounded. We beat a retreat back to Goose Creek and remained there until joined by General Merritt with reinforcements. Meanwhile General Custer had been annihilated while we rested with eighteen hundred soldiers. When General Merritt joined us, we moved down Rosebud to Tongue River without meeting any hostile Indians, and then to Powder River. General Terry arrived on a steamboat.

A council was held which lasted several days. In the meantime, the Indians had divided, Sitting Bull crossing the Yellowstone and Crazy Horse going east until he crossed the Little Missouri, then southeast to Slim Buttes.

Our command followed Crazy Horse. We struck a Sioux village, with American Horse as chief. We captured the village and took American Horse prisoner. The chief had received a wound in the fight, from which he died that night.

The troops had been living on horse-meat and were anxiously looking for supplies. The command proceeded to White Wood Creek, where supplies arrived from Deadwood. The troops were given a week to recruit up in and then proceeded to Custer City, remaining there a few days.

From Custer City we went to Camp Robinson, capturing a few Indians on the road.

At Fort Laramie I resigned and returned to the Yellowstone Valley, locating at Columbus, Montana, then known as Stillwater. At eighty-two years I am hale and hearty and always spend a part of each year in the mountains trapping; thankful that I can still enjoy and appreciate the wonderful beauties of nature.

A Trapping Expedition, 1848-9

The winter of 1848-9 I was in camp with twenty-four other free trappers in a small basin in the Pryor Mountains. This was in a section of country afterwards set apart for the Crow Indians in the southern part of what is now Montana. In those days it was frequented only by the Indians.

We had been trapping the previous fall on the various streams from Wind River to Pryor Creek, and when the streams froze up the several parties of trappers collected and made a camp in this basin where with our numbers, we would be comparatively safe from the Indians and where the essentials of the mountaineer—grass, water, fuel and game—were abundant. We intended to stay here until spring and then trap back along the stream to market at Green River.

Shortly after we had gone into camp five of our number had been sent to Green River for ammunition, salt and camp supplies and these men were expected back by the 15th of December. On Christmas day they had not returned and we were fearful that they had encountered some war party of Indians. In the afternoon of this day the lookouts from a prominent *butte* discovered seven men coming rapidly across the plains towards camp with six pack animals. They signalled to camp that a party was coming, evidently white men, but whether comprised of our absent comrades, they were not able to say. All doubts, however, were soon set aside as the party came riding into camp, and the well filled packs were evidences of a safe journey for the supplies. The party was comprised of our five comrades and two gentlemen from New York who had come out to spend the winter with us in camp.

The reason our trappers were overdue was because of a delay back at Green River occasioned by these gentlemen in getting their outfit together. They had arrived at Green River the same day the trappers reached there and had brought a letter from some wholesale merchants in the east to Francis Bovey (I am not sure about the spelling), stating that they wanted to spend the winter with some reliable trappers and have a chance to study the life and habits of mountaineers.

The merchant at once informed them of the arrival of our men for supplies and recommended our camp. It was accordingly arranged that they should provide their own horses and outfit and return with our comrades to the winter rendezvous. They were assisted by Mr. Bovey in getting suitable horses and an outfit which was very complete, and thus equipped they had set out for our camp in the wilderness.

This camp had been carefully selected. We were very particular to select a place which afforded an opportunity for noting the approach of enemies and warding off their attacks.

We had constructed a winter corral for the horses and built a high rail fence around the lodges. We had three good lodges, each large enough to contain ten or more persons with comfort. Four of the trappers had their Ute wives with them. These squaws were very expert in setting up lodges, and helped us all in cooking, and repairing moccasins and in dressing skins for clothing. All of us dressed in buckskin in those days and had as much dislike for store clothes as for a house. We preferred a lodge, and I will here remark for the benefit of those who are inexperienced, that a lodge properly made and set up is a very comfortable abode, certainly giving much more comfort than many habitations in settled communities.

That night a terrible snow storm set in. When the fire in the centre of the lodge had declined to a large bed of coals, we closed the flap at the top and wrapped up in our blankets. Our guests told us about many things which had happened in the civilized world since we had left it. Our companions narrated the details of their trip and how they traded the furs for camp supplies.

It snowed for three days, about eighteen inches of snow falling, but on the 30th of the month it had cleared up and we organised a hunt for the benefit of our guests, and at the same time to replenish our supply of meat. Elk, deer, buffalo and some bear tracks had been discovered at no great distance from camp. Five of the trappers and the New York gentlemen saddled up for the hunt. Those who remained in camp cleared away the snow from around the lodges and prepared buffalo meat for *pemmican*.

The hunters came across some deer and antelope about a mile from camp. The New York gentlemen wanted to take a shot at them, but were advised not to do so since buffalo and elk were not far distant, and shooting would probably alarm them. They proceeded about half a mile from the ridge and discovered a small band of buffalo browsing. Crouching around the summit of the ridge the two gentlemen and one of the trappers were motioned to follow up a small draw so as to get the advantage of a flank fire. When all were in place they fired close together and had the satisfaction of seeing two fat cows down and another wounded. The rest of the band stampeded.

Four of the trappers were mounted on their choicest runners and were sent among them. Each selected a fat cow and giving chase soon brought her down. As this gave them all the buffalo meat they wanted, two of the trappers remained to carry the choice parts to camp and the rest of the party went after other game. They had not gone far when they came across the track of the bears which they had discovered previously. Following them for a mile or more we found their course ran down a canyon toward a cotton wood grove.

As it was not possible to take the horses down, we here left them with one man in charge and the rest of us advanced down the canyon to the grove. More we stationed the New York men on a knoll about fifty yards from the grove, cautioning them to make a shoulder shot, if possible, while the rest of us circled the grove. The bear had not passed through the grove down the canyon. The men then examined their guns and entered the brush. We were armed with old Hawkins rifles and Colt's revolvers. We advanced about two-thirds of the distance through the grove, which was about one acre in area, when we discovered that the snow was trodden down at the upper end of a large fallen tree, which was evidence that there was the bear den.

After consulting a moment it was determined to fire one shot from a pistol at what we thought was the bear den in order to stir them up and drive them out, if possible, towards our friends on the knoll, as we wanted them to get a shot. No sooner was the pistol fired than out came three bears with terrible growls. Another pistol shot in unison with our loud yells drove them to flight and they rushed for the upper end of the grove beyond which our friends were stationed. Before the rear bear, however, could clear the timber we brought our guns into play and dropped him. He was a large brown fellow, a proud prize for even experienced hunters. Hallooing to our friends to look out for the other two we followed in pursuit and soon heard shots in close succession.

We rushed out of the brush to learn results and there, not over fifty feet from the rocks where the two gentlemen had been stationed, a bear badly wounded was rolling and tossing in the snow. The other bear had got off about one hundred yards when he was hit and was now coming back to take vengeance. Our guests had forgotten to reload their guns and two of the trappers hurried to them and offered their guns. They were soon able to place their enemies *hors de combat*. We quickly had the hides stripped, returned to our horses, and made our way to camp, which we reached late in the afternoon.

We found the squaws in high glee, surrounded by the choice buffalo meat which our companions had brought in. The best meat of all was the *depuyer*. It may not be out of place for me to describe this *depuyer*. It is a substitute for bread, but much more nutritious. It lies on each side of the back bone next to the hide, running from the shoulder blade to the last rib. The upper edge, according to the condition of the animal, being from one to two inches thick, decreasing to the lower edge from one half to one quarter of an inch thick, and averaging in width from twelve to fourteen inches, and being from eighteen to twenty-two inches long.

The average weight is about nine pounds. It is cured by dipping in hot grease and then exposed to the air to dry. If properly cured it will keep indefinitely without taint. This *depuyer*, together with the hump and the tongue, are the choicest parts of the buffalo.

All hands are now busy cutting up meat into strips for drying and thus making ready to be packed up in *parfleches* for future use, while the other meat was prepared to be made into *pemmican*.

This was the season when experienced trappers laid in their spring and fall supplies, for when the trapping season begins, they have enough to do looking after their traps and horses and keeping an eye out for Indians. Our guests set to work fleshing their bear hides until the squaws called us in to supper. These squaws were clean and tidy and under the direction of the trappers had learned how to prepare a meal which would have pleased an epicure. With fresh supplies of meat and the delicacies lately brought from Green River, we had a feast fit for kings.

That night we held a council. The trappers, being well acquainted with Indian tactics, agreed that if any Indians were in the country and heard any shots during the day, they would likely pay us a visit that night. Our trails through the snow would be plainly seen and it behoved us to be on guard. We accordingly rolled up in our blankets, dressed for action, with pistols buckled on, and loaded guns ready to hand. It was a bright, frosty, starlit night. About one o'clock the growling of the dogs startled us, but upon looking out we could discover nothing wrong. The horses in the corral were quiet, and we turned in again thinking it might have been a coyote or wolf which caused the disturbance.

About half past two the dogs rushed for the corral, giving mouth, and the trappers were at once in pursuit. We discovered seven Indians trying to get at the horses. As we approached, they scattered and beat a hasty retreat, but not soon enough to escape our bullets, for two of them were mortally wounded and the dogs had them by the throat. We chased the others some distance and then returned to camp. Some of the men had made the two dead Indians "bald-headed." We discovered that two of our comrades had received arrow wounds—Russell, a wound in the cheek, and Nelson, one in the thigh. These wounds were soon dressed.

We then held a council. It was decided that none of these Indians should escape to bear the news of the location of our camp and the loss of the two who were killed to their camp, for then we were certain to be visited by a large force. We kept a close lookout until morning and at daybreak ten men with the two guests started on their trail.

About a quarter of a mile from camp we discovered considerable blood on the trail of one of the Indians and saw where he had evidently staggered in the snow. It was plain he had received a bad wound during the attack the previous night and could not have gone much farther. We therefore kept a sharp lookout, for an Indian, like a coyote, will fight when cornered, and many a brave white man has been killed by rash approach to an Indian so near expiring as to be unable to walk.

A short distance forward we found the tracks of the other four Indians coming from the right and joining the trail of the one wounded. They followed the ridge where the snow was not so deep. Soon we saw where the wounded one had fallen down and had been assisted by the others to rise and move one. It was broad daylight at this time, the snow about one foot deep, our horses in prime condition, and we were able to press on at a rapid gait. After going on about a mile we came upon a spring which flowed into Pryor Creek. The Indians had left the ridge and turned down this branch. We followed their trail and saw it enter a patch of willows, which we circled, and found four tracks coming out at the lower edge of the willows. They had gone on, leading the wounded one behind, probably expecting to return for him after they had signalled their band.

We then agreed to get the Indian without shooting, if possible, as the noise might be heard by the four Indians ahead and warn them that they were pursued. Two men dismounted and went into the willows. In about five minutes we heard a rustling, then an imprecation, when all was still. In a few moments the men made their appearance, carrying a war bonnet, fancy blanket, pipe, and a bow and arrows. They had discovered the Indian as expected, with bow and arrows fitted for use, but had sprung upon him before he could use it and put him to sleep with his own weapon.

By this time the sun was shining in all his glory. Deer and elk were feeding at no great distance. We were thinking, however, of something else than scenery. Self-preservation is said to be the first law of nature. We understood well that if those four Indians were permitted to escape our camp would be continually annoyed, and the probable result would be that we would lose some of our horses, and perhaps our own lives, for the Blackfeet, to which tribe it was manifest that these Indians belonged, when they leave their village on a war expedition, go in large numbers and when they arrive in the country of their enemies they separate into small bands, with an agreed system of signals to be given when enemies are discovered and concentration is desirable. It is therefore necessary, knowing Indian character and methods as we did, to exterminate these horse thieves and camp spies if it lay in our power to do so.

Tying behind our saddles the personal effects taken from the Indian in the willows, we followed on down the trail at a rapid gait, and soon learned that the Indians were making for Pryor Gap. They had turned to the left, keeping along the base of the southwest end of the mountain; and here reaching a small spring creek we saw where they had stopped to build a fire and roast some meat. They must have remained here sometime, and as the fire was still burning, they evidently had gone on only a short time before our arrival.

The snow at this point was sixteen inches deep, making it very laborious traveling for them, while we with our horses were making good time. Keeping a sharp lookout, we saw that the trail was making towards a ridge leading up the southwest corner of the mountain. If the Indians had suspected that we were on their trail they might have discovered us as they ascended this ridge, and give us trouble, for the north side of the mountain was much broken and cut up into narrow canyons affording excellent cover.

As we approached the apex of the ridge we sent two men ahead, cautioning them to proceed very carefully. They advanced to the apex, keeping some stunted trees directly in their front, and soon returned, saying they had discovered the Indians clearing away the snow on a cone *butte* not more than three hundred yards distant. This *butte* had a small grove of pines on its summit affording them fuel for their signal smoke which would soon bring reinforcements, and they were evidently clearing off the snow for this purpose. The only thing to do was to surround the *butte* and make the attack before they could signal. We accordingly doffed our coats, blankets, and everything not needed in the tight, and then mounted.

Dividing into two equal parties we slowly approached the top of the *butte* from opposite directions. We had no sooner reached the top than the Indians discovered us, and before they could descend into any of the ravines or canyons, we had them surrounded and drove them back into the pines. One Indian with a gun crept to the edge of the pines and shot, the bullet coming very close to one of our number. He received two bullets as soon as he shot and fell face downward just outside the grove. Another Indian crawled in the snow to recover the dead Indian's gun and he also was immediately dispatched to the happy hunting ground.

This left two others to be disposed of, and in short order, for if there were other Indians in the vicinity, they would hear the shooting and give us trouble. We tied the horses out of range and approached the timber from opposite sides. Evidently, they had discovered only one of our parties in the former advance and were not expecting to be approached from different directions, for when the men from the east had crawled to the edge of the grove, they discovered the Indians looking keenly to the west, and not forty yards distance.

These were soon dispatched and we congratulated ourselves that we were free from the danger of an attack from the larger band to which they belonged, which would certainly have happened if they could have signalled their comrades. The effects of these Indians consisted of three war bonnets, three prime Hudson Bay blankets, four bows and arrows, two pistols, a fine curiously curved pipe, besides knives and tomahawks. Their gun we broke to pieces as we had no use for it.

It was eleven o'clock in the forenoon when we returned to our horses, packed on the plunder, and started to camp, on our back trail. Four of the men, however, did not return with the party, but intent on exploration, crossed the north end of the mountain around its base on the east side, and there struck an Indian trail going south. It was evidently the track of the band which had attacked our camp. It crossed Pryor Creek, kept along the base of the mountain to its middle fork, after crossing which it turned abruptly to the right, and began the ascent of the steep ridge.

At this abrupt turn they had evidently heard our shots when we were hunting the previous day, and had mounted the ridge. From the summit of this ridge, they had stood and viewed our camp and horses nearly a mile away. They afterward turned down a draw where they saw water and camped, waiting for night before they made the attack. They then approached the camp with results previously narrated. The scouts who went around the mountain reached camp about three o'clock in the afternoon, and found that the rest of the party had already arrived, reporting no other signs of Indians.

What we wanted now was a snow or high wind to obliterate the trails made by the Indians and ourselves, and we had our wish, for before we had retired that night a light snow was falling. Selecting one of the men who had remained in camp the previous day as guard we turned in and were not disturbed during the night. The next morning it was still snowing. We soon had half a dozen men to scout around camp, and afterwards turned out the horses, with two guards. In the afternoon a strong wind sprung up which was most desirable, as it cleared the snow from the south side of the hills and gave our horses a chance at the nutritious grass, which in this country cures on the stalk and affords the best of provender.

Our guests expressed a desire to have buckskin suits similar to those the rest of us were wearing, and as one of our men, Ned Williams, a Kentuckian, had learned the tailor trade, we arranged to gratify their desire. The best suits are made from the skins of mountain sheep, and as there were plenty of sheep on Pryor Mountain, not three miles from camp, we planned a hunt a few days after our expedition with the Indians. Early in the afternoon six trappers with the two New York men saddled their horses and started, taking some pack animals and the two dogs. These dogs were well trained after sheep. They would run them up on the high rocks and hold them there until the hunter could get within range.

We had quite a time in places wallowing through the deep snow, and about nine o'clock made the ascent of some lofty *buttes* and found tracks, whether of deer or sheep we were unable to decide. Here we dismounted and divided our number into two parties, each party taking a dog. Continuing the ascent but a short distance, one party went to the right, the other to the left, and approached the summit of one of the highest *buttes*, from opposite sides. Our dog was very keen to go but we did not permit it until we were farther up and close to an abrupt, rocky eminence. We soon heard the bark of the dog with the other party and in a moment a band of sheep made its appearance some two hundred yards above us, rushing for the rocky eminence.

Our dog now raised a small band which also struggled up the steep mountain side to join the main band above. The snow was too deep for rapid climbing and we took our time, feeling quite certain that the dogs would keep the sheep corralled on the rocks at the peak. We soon came out from behind the rocks with the band plainly in view. There must have been sixty or seventy of them. When we arrived within one hundred yards of the highest rocks, we heard shots from our companions in quick succession which caused a commotion among the sheep, but the dogs still held them. When we reached a point within seventy-five yards of them we commenced action, selecting large does because their skin was thinner and their meat better than that of the rams.

Taking careful aim, we dropped three and wounded another. The band then disappeared over the apex, but only for a moment, as shots were heard on the other side and back, they came pell-mell all in a bunch. We delivered our shots this time into the band generally, as the sheep were panic stricken, jumping over each other, striking at the dogs, and generally so lively as to preclude aim at any one animal. As the result of the onslaught, we got twelve fine does, three rams and two yearlings.

We ought to have done better at the distance we were shooting. We at once set to work skinning them and soon had the pelts off. In these we packed the brains, the tongues and sinew. The last is a substitute for thread. The brains were used by the squaws in dressing the skins. We also packed into pelts about two hundred pounds of the choicest meat, tied the legs, thus making our trophies secure, and dragged them down to the horses. We fastened the pelts to the pack horses, and getting down the mountain safely reached camp about three o'clock in the afternoon. As soon as we could get something to eat, we went to work on the sheep pelts and soon had them nicely fleshed and grained (freed from the hair). When hides are first taken off, they are easily grained. We then turned them over to the squaws to be oil-dressed and thoroughly smoked.

We had planned all along to move our camp on or about February 15th to the south fork of the Stinking Water, and there to commence our spring trapping. But, before breaking camp, some of our number wanted to go on a hunt to Wolf Mountains, a place famous for bear and mountain lions. As this region was distant a journey of three days there was no time to spare.

Accordingly, on the morning of the 6th, eight trappers with the two gentlemen started on this hunt. They took our best saddle horses and four pack animals. On the afternoon of the third day, they arrived at the southwest end of Wolf Mountains, where two of the trappers ascended a high peak, from which were plainly seen the valleys of Tongue River and Goose Creek.

The object of this scouting was to ascertain whether there were any Indian villages in the vicinity. Herds of Indian ponies were reported quietly grazing in the valley, and a dense smoke from a village showed conclusively the presence of Indians. The Arapahoes, Cheyennes and Sioux were in the habit of hunting buffalo in this region at this season. It was therefore determined by the party to abandon the hunt. The shooting' would soon bring the Indians to them.

They at once began their return to camp, and on coming back to the Big Horn River had the satisfaction of running across a small band of buffalo. As we had what meat we wanted in camp, the trappers did not engage in the run. The two gentlemen, however, gave chase, being mounted on horses which showed that they had been well trained by the Snake Indians, from whom Mr. Bovey had procured them. They returned on the 11th, much to the surprise of those at the camp, but there was no division of opinion that they had adopted a wise course by avoiding any conflict with the Indians.

The next few days we were busy getting ready to move. The usual February thaw showed signs, and we hastened our preparations to start to our spring trapping as originally planned. The sheepskins were all dressed, thoroughly smoked and all ready for the tailor, the *pemmican* and dried meats packed away in the *parfleches*, and the girths of our saddles and packs inspected and repaired. Our *moccasins* were all mended or replaced by new ones and the guns carefully cleaned and oiled.

On the morning of the 15th, the weather continuing favourable, we were ready for the start. First sending out the scouts and hearing that no Indians were around, we began our journey. We travelled fast and by sundown reached Stinking Water. The lodges were up in short order, our runners picketed and the balance of the herd turned out with two guards. Scouts went up the river for some distance and reported the country free from Indians. We guarded the horses, however, all night, and the camp was not disturbed.

On the morning of the 16th, we were off early, and ascending the South Fork, reached Beaver Swamp, a distance of thirty miles. The ground was clear of snow in many places and there were appearances of plenty of game. Selecting a suitable place for camp, we soon had the packs down and the lodges up and plenty of wood gathered for the women. Four scouts viewed the country for a considerable distance and reported no signs of Indians.

Before daylight the next morning, we sent guards out to the horses and by nine o'clock had constructed a strong corral. This was the Shoshone or Snake country, a tribe friendly to the whites, but as the upper basin of the river abounded with game of all kinds, it was often invaded by hostile tribes and was considered a dangerous country, and we therefore trusted nothing to chance.

Scouts went down the river on our back track to ascertain whether any Indians were following us. Another scout kept a lookout from a lofty hill. The river was open in places and the beaver and otter signs were abundant. Some of the men went out along the banks and set seventy traps, and others went out for bear. The scouts returned from down the river and reported no Indians in sight, but inferred that they would be on hand before many days, as herds of buffalo were coming up the bottom and likely would be followed. The hunters returned with four bear skins.

Nothing unusual occurred until the 22nd. Up to this time we had succeeded in collecting a large number of beaver and several otter, and the hunters had shot twelve bear and four mountain lions. In the afternoon of the 22nd, the scouts reported Indians coming.

We corralled the horses and summoned all the trappers to camp, our forces being all present except the hunters. About twenty Crow Indians rode up. We halted them at some distance from the lodges. Several of us were acquainted with the chief, Iron Bull. He personally was friendly enough but the tribe generally was a notorious set of beggars and thieves. The chief with two other head Indians were invited into the lodges. Three of us trappers could speak the Crow language and all of us could converse in the sign language, which was universally used in those days. The Indians in reply to the inquiry from whence they came replied, "Grey Bull Creek," and said they were on their way to Elk Water (Yellowstone River).

Upon their informing us that they had lost a great many ponies by the Blackfeet, we exposed for their inspection seven scalps and asked if they knew to what tribe they belonged. After examining them carefully they pronounced them scalps from the Blackfeet and wanted to know where we got them. We informed them that we ordained them at Pryor Mountain and that the Indians were trying to steal our horses, and gave them to understand that any Indians attempting to steal our stock would lose their scalps, even if we had to go into their villages to get them. This was brave talk, but it had the effect upon those Indians.

Iron Bull then said his people were very poor; no tobacco, no sugar, no ammunition, no blankets, no meat. This was the Indian method of begging. We gave the chief a pound of tobacco, but refused the ammunition, which he wanted very much. We also gave him two scalps and warned him to keep his people from our camp. The chief replied that the Crows were great friends of the whites and that they would not steal from us. All this we took for what it was worth. We knew the rascals would steal anything whenever they had a chance.

Just at this juncture our hunters returned, making our number twenty-seven. We observed one of the Indians counting our company. As they had only twenty-five lodges, with about fifty warriors, we had no fear of them in an open attack. Before returning the Indians wanted to trade horses. We informed them that we had no horses to trade, but would trade for any good beaver and otter. The chief said they had several of these furs and would bring them the following day.

On the following morning a number of the trappers visited the traps and returned about nine o'clock with a fair catch. About noon Iron Bull with six squaws and a few bucks arrived with twelve beaver and two otter pelts. Some of these our guests traded for and the remainder the trappers took in exchange for sugar, salt, tobacco, two knives, one scalp and a few notions. I think the Indians would have given all their furs for the scalp. The chief said his young men and women had danced all night over the ones we had given them the previous day, and "this one makes our hearts glad and strong." It makes little difference to an Indian whether he takes the scalp or not, so it belongs to an enemy.

The Ute squaws soon had a feast prepared for the Indians and after the feast the usual smoke followed. It was very interesting to note the conduct of the squaws. There was a wide contrast between those of our camp and those belonging to the Crows. Ours were neat and cleanly. We could see at once there was a mutual contempt between them. On the part of the Ute squaws because the Crow women were filthy and ugly; on the part of the Crow squaws, I presume, because the Utes were more handsome, and cleanly and tastily attired. Very little conversation and a few courtesies passed between them.

It was a relief to us all when Iron Bull finally withdrew. It was likely our treatment of him upon this and the previous day induced him afterwards to call off his warriors from obstructing our advance on the trial when next we moved camp, as hereafter narrated.

As we wanted to move soon, we were very busy these days stretching the pelts and getting our furs in condition for packing. We would select two beaver hides of the same size and stretch them on one hoop, so that even if they were not dry, they would be convenient to pack, and the pelts that were dry we were carefully baling, which is an art in itself.

On the morning of the 24th the traps were all brought in and after skinning what beaver and otter were caught the night previous, we got everything packed up and by ten o'clock started. We had gone about eight miles when we discovered about forty mounted Indians standing in line across our trail. There were about ten of us in front, the rest of the company being in the flanks and in the rear. The Indians held their ground on the trail. It never would have done to go around them, for that would only have made them bolder.

We rode forward to where they obstructed the trail and requested them to move aside. They refused and our outfit stopped. The man behind seeing the difficulty rushed to the front. There stood the Indians clustered in the trail, with hands on their guns and bows and arrows. Just at this moment Iron Bull, the Crow chief, arrived and ordered them out of the trail, a fortunate act, for the eyes of many of our men were flashing with anger, and a shot on either side would have brought on a battle. Fortune thus favoured us and we passed on without further delay. We travelled fast and camped on Grey Bull Creek by four o'clock, and by sun down had lodges up and everything in good shape.

I remember on the way over we met Washakie, the chief of the Shoshones, on a buffalo hunt. We informed him of the Crow camp and where he could find the buffalo. He did not approve of the Crows being on his hunting ground. These Shoshones were friendly to the trappers for needed assistance rendered them in their fights with hostile tribes. We crossed the Owl Creek mountains and camped on a small tributary of the Big Wind River.

We remained here several days, finding plenty of fur, and then moved about sixteen miles to the west end of Bull Lake, where the beaver were very abundant and game plentiful. Our tailor, with the help of the squaws, who were very expert sewing with sinew, completed the sheepskin suits for the gentlemen. They were double fringed at the seams and a splendid fit and furnished their owners much pleasure. The trappers inspected the streams for miles around, going as far as Dinwiddy Lake.

In the afternoon of the 3rd of March, one of the squaws, who had been digging roots on a knoll not far from camp, rushed in giving the alarm of an attack from Indians, belonging she thought to the tribe of Arapahoes. We heard shots in the vicinity of where the herd were grazing. Seven of the runners were picketed, fortunately, and these were mounted in an instant. The rest of the men whose horses were in the herd rushed out with their guns. We observed the herd coming to camp with a rush. Our horses had been trained to run to camp when any shots were fired or yells given.

The seven horsemen hurried down like a whirlwind, meeting Jack Perkins, who was wounded, had one rib broken and was spitting blood. Five Indians had come up unperceived by the herders, and getting close to Perkins had shot him. Fred Douglas (Old Otter), the other herder, rushed up and gave a yell to the horses, which started for camp. But the Indians had cut out six head and were making off with them. Douglas dropped one Indian and the rest of the band, seeing the horsemen coming, made off with the six head as fast as possible.

It was a hard race as the thieves were well mounted, but then they were retarded somewhat by the loose horses and did not give them up until they knew our men were on faster mounts. They then let the horses go and tried to escape. But too late. It was a running fight for half a mile when the last of the Indians took his way to the happy hunting ground.

Our men had several close calls and two of the horses were wounded, one very seriously, a beautiful, speedy mare, which died the next morning. As soon as the herd reached camp, the other trappers mounted and came as fast as possible not knowing how large a band might be in waiting in the direction in which the thieves had fled, but before they arrived on the scene the work was over.

On arriving at camp, we found Perkins in a bad way with a shattered rib and a shot in the lung, but we doctored him as best we could and he finally recovered. We doubled the guards that night but heard nothing but the howl of the wolves and yelp of a few coyotes.

The next morning breakfast was over by daylight and the traps were brought in. By ten o'clock we were on the move. Early in the afternoon we camped on Dinwiddy lake. We intended to remain here for several days and then cross the mountains to the west fork of Green River. Here we were busy. The fur was abundant. Two of the most expert skinners remained in camp while the two herders were with the horses, and generally two scouts on the hills. The gentlemen took turns attending Perkins, who was having a hard time of it, while the squaws in intervals of cooking made and repaired moccasins. The trappers with their traps and the hunters in quest of bear and mountain lion filled the camp with green hides, and the drying and baling made things lively.

By the 10th of March Perkins had improved so rapidly that we thought he could stand the trip over the Wind River Mountains to the head waters of Green River. The snow was so soft that we knew we would have to make the crossing in the night. All the traps were collected and by sundown we commenced the journey. Several of the trappers were well acquainted with the trail. We placed Perkins on an easy, sure-footed saddle horse, and secretly appointed one of our number to attend and watch him carefully. We travelled in single file, a man behind every one or two pack animals, and two men in front leading a pack horse. The night, as we had hoped, was bright and frosty.

At midnight we reached the summit of the range without mishap. Perkins had never complained and was standing the trip well. By daybreak we had descended to the west fork of Green River, down which we followed five miles, where we found the ground clear of snow and sufficiently level for our lodges. Here we unpacked and the lodges were soon set up and the breakfast ready, all of us being as hungry as wolves. Perkins had stood the trip without a murmur, though evidently weak. We had a large amount of green hides which required immediate attention, and so, putting the two gentlemen to sleep in a lodge with Perkins, the rest of us went to work fleshing bear hides, putting the pelts on hoops and sampling the stream with traps. We knew we were reasonably free from Indians here, unless they followed us over the mountains, in revenge for the slain horse thieves, but we soon discovered that the beaver were few and the grass poor, and determined to move on in the morning.

About two o'clock the guests woke up and seemed much surprised at our industry after being up all night. We then had a lunch consisting of beaver tail, *pemmican* and *depuyer* and made some tea for Perkins, who was much improved after a good sleep. The squaws, who woke up about an hour after this, acted as though they were ashamed of their long sleep, and by five o'clock had a substantial supper ready. Early in the evening the trappers retired, leaving the two gentlemen guarding the horses and the camp.

The next morning breakfast was over by daybreak and we moved down to the mouth of the stream about twelve miles, where there was a large bottom and plenty of grass. We selected camp in a beautiful cottonwood grove. After dinner fifteen men, each with six traps, started out in different directions to inspect the streams and afterwards reported signs of plenty of beaver and good hunting for elk and bear. The clouds were threatening and we built a strong corral and packed in plenty of wood. We retired early, trusting the care of the camp to the dogs.

In the morning a heavy snow was falling. We remained in this camp till the 15th of March, collecting the beaver for ten miles from camp and bringing in many bear and several elk.

On the 16th we moved to the forks of Green River, and on the next day, after the men had gone out with their traps, were visited by five strangers who had come from Fort Bridger. These men had been trapping in the employ of fur companies, but had now set out on their own account. We advised them not to go up Green River, but to cross over to Snake, where beaver were abundant and where they would be comparatively safe from hostile Indians.

When our trappers came back in the afternoon, we gathered in one of the lodges and heard from these strangers the news of the outside world. They talked about the Mexican War, of the gold excitement in California and the growth of the recent settlement of Mormons down in Utah. We asked if any fur buyers had come to Bridger yet and learned that they were expected there in a few days. These buyers were the ones we wanted to meet and it was determined to go into market. The strangers left the following morning, and our company proceeded to make all arrangements to go in to Bridger. While the traps were being lifted from the streams, four of the trappers with the two gentlemen went out for their final hunt, and late in the afternoon returned to camp with the hides of three bears, two mountain lions and two very fine elk heads, the antlers being large and points uniform. The gentlemen requested us, if possible, to pack these heads to Bridger, as they wanted to take them back home with them.

On the 21st we packed up and arrived in Fort Bridger in four days, just in time to catch some parties who were on their way to

Independence, Missouri, with wagons. The gentlemen arranged to go through with these teams, taking their elk heads and other effects. We asked them to select what furs and hides they desired, but they would only take four bear hides, four beaver pelts and two otter. They asked for two Blackfeet scalps for their collection of curios. We gladly assented, and forced upon them two *parfleches* of *pemmican* and *depuyer*, feeling sure they would stand in need of them before they arrived at their destination. They in turn compelled us to take three times as much as all our services to them were worth, and the next morning, the wagons being ready, we parted. It was like parting with brothers.

The fur buyers had arrived at Bridger the day before we got there, and came over to camp to look over our outfit. We had a large and fine assortment, having accumulated both the fall and spring catch, and had no difficulty in disposing of all we had for a fair price in gold.

We remained two days at Bridger before breaking camp. Eight of us agreed to go to California, the four who had the squaws were going down Green River to Brown's Hole, where the Ute Indians came every spring to trade. And the remainder of the company determined to go to various parts of Oregon where they had families or relatives.

The day we broke camp the squaws rigged themselves up in their best trappings. They thanked us all for kind treatment and went away with their men to rejoin their tribe. They took with them the scalps of the Arapahoes. This tribe was a bitter enemy of the Utes.

The eight of us who had determined to go to California struck the trail with a good pack outfit and arrived at Hangtown on the morning of July 4th, 1849. We celebrated there.

A Trading Expedition Among the Indians in 1858 from Fort Walla Walla to the Blackfoot Country and Return

During the Spokane and Yakima War, which was brought to a close by Col. Wright, afterwards promoted to Brigadier General, I was employed as a scout by the government, in which capacity I had been acting for several previous years. Upon the conclusion of this war, in order to put a quietus upon any further hostile demonstrations by those turbulent tribes, the Yakima, Spokane, Palouse and their alles. Col. Wright took a number of their principal chiefs and head men as prisoners. He tried eleven of their number by drumhead court martial, found all of them guilty of murder at different times and places and ordered them hung, which order was happily executed in fifteen minutes after its issuance, on a tree, in the presence of twenty-five hundred Indians who had been ordered to be present at the trial.

The son of Col. Bell of Texas was appointed hangman, and the ordeal was witnessed by the surrounding Indians, who held their hands over their mouths as a sign of wonder and astonishment, while the squaws were howling and wailing. Col. Wright retained nine of their principal chiefs as prisoners for the good behaviour of the tribe to which they belonged. This was about the first of September, 1858.

Proclamation was then issued declaring the Walla Walla country open to settlement and the country was soon overrun with settlers from Oregon and Washington territories. There was a rumour received from the Indians who had been east of the Rocky Mountains that the tribes there were inclined to be hostile, and as the government was becoming tired of continual Indian wars, it was determined to investigate this rumour. So, a week after the closing of hostilities upon the conclusion of the Spokane and Yakima War, an orderly informed me that I was wanted at the officers' rooms. The meeting was held at Capt. Dent's quarters. (He was a relative of Gen. Grant's wife.) I accordingly reported and found some twenty officers present. It looked like a council of war.

They directed me to a chair in their midst, and I soon learned that they were discussing the possibility or probability of another Indian war east of the Rockies, by reason of the rumour received as above stated. They asked my opinion of the news received. I had been interviewing many Indians who had lately arrived from the buffalo country and learned that they were on friendly terms with all the tribes through which they sojourned, except the Blood Indians, and I had ascertained from them the section of country which each tribe inhabited, and the disposition of the same, in so far as they were able to give me information on this point. I accordingly imparted unto the officers the information I had thus received, and my opinion regarding the same.

The officers asked me if I had ever been in that country and I replied in the negative, but informed them that I had a great desire to visit and explore those sections as far as the Missouri River. I was acquainted with the country to the south of this river. Lieut. Sheridan and others thought it would be a fool-hardy undertaking at the present state of affairs. I replied "Yes for any person not acquainted with the Indians and who could not converse with them." I was then credited with being the most expert sign talker among the Indians. This knowledge came almost natural to me and therefore I do not give myself any particular credit for proficiency in that art.

The knowledge of the sign language is necessary to mountaineers and scouts. It assists them in extricating themselves from many difficult dilemmas. All wild tribes of Indians have great respect for a man who meets them boldly and can converse with them by signs. It is the reverse with them when they meet a man they cannot make understand. I informed the officer I apprehended no great difficulty in making the trip; that the greatest danger was in passing through the late subdued tribes, but if these chiefs were held as prisoner's until I returned I did not think there would be any danger; the Indians, being well aware that I represented the government should the trip be finally determined upon.

I informed the officers that I should visit the villages of the subdued tribes and would want an official envelope with some reading matter, and that I would interpret what would be necessary in order to set them thinking of something else besides taking my scalp. The officers all laughed at this mode of outwitting the Indians, and before the meeting broke up shook hands with me, Phil. Sheridan with others expressing great confidence in my ability to carry out the undertaking. They then informed me to hold myself in readiness for a few days and they would take the matter under advisement.

So, about the 20th of September 1858, I received an order from Col. Wright to report at headquarters at 2 p. m. I reported promptly on time, the reception room being crowded with officers and their wives with most of whom I was acquainted and was somewhat taken back by their presence in the council. With an array of maps and writing material spread out upon a large table, I surmised that some move was on tap different from what I anticipated, but in a moment was undeceived. I then received an appointment as secret Indian detective with pay as scout, and was ordered to proceed through the different tribes of Indians to the Blackfoot Nation, east of the Rocky Mountains and report on the condition and disposition of the different tribes visited, at the earliest possible moment.

It was ordered that the quartermaster would furnish me with anything I required for the trip. Col. Wright and the ladies advised me to be very careful of myself. I assured them I had undertaken more difficult propositions than this expedition would probably be, and said "Ladies and gentlemen I am not going simply as scout and Indian detective, but as an Indian trader, and will impress upon the minds of all the Indians I come across that I am their friend. Rest assured that I will bring back to these ladies many nice Indian trinkets." And I informed the commanding officer to look for me about the 15th of November.

When departing the ladies all jumped to their feet and in chorus exclaimed "Let us all shake hands with our favourite scout, for what we fear is the last time." I felt like kissing the whole outfit, they looked so lovely and expressed such sympathy for me in the undertaking. I told them they would see me again before the lovely plain was covered with snow the coming winter, and immediately commenced preparations for my departure. I was particularly favoured in the matter of my outfit from the quartermaster and the sutler, probably by reason of the following incident:

In one of my scouting expeditions among the Boise Bannack Indians on Burnt River as now called, I had captured a three-year-old Pinto pony, very small, gentle as a kitten, proud as Lucifer and the handsomest piece of horseflesh I ever saw. I got him to Walla Walla safe and without any serious damage excepting being very tired, but in a few days, he was as playful as a kitten. I had him trimmed up with fine trappings, a fancy saddle blanket etc., and on Saturday I got a fourteen-year-old Spanish boy to ride the pony through the parade grounds, when most of the ladies were promenading. The officers and ladies were taken by surprise and wonderment at the beauty of the pony and the quartermaster and his wife were the first to question the boy as to who owned the pony. He answered "Scout Hamilton".

Shortly afterwards I received a notice from the quartermaster stating he wished to see me, and going to his office he informed me that he wanted the pony and asked the price. I replied that money could not buy him, but that I would see him the following day. Upon reflection I determined that the pony would be of no special use to me and that I would make a present of him to the quartermaster for his beautiful little daughter.

I got some Spaniards to assist me in trimming up the pony. They are experts in making horses appear to the best advantage, and on the following day, the 4th of July, 1857, I placed the boy upon the pony with a note to the quartermaster, expressing my compliments and asking him to receive the pony with the trappings and present the same to his young daughter. That afternoon I saw the quartermaster who thanked me most sincerely for the gift.

Afterwards the quartermaster and family moved to Oakland, California, taking the pony with them by steamer from Portland. I heard of it afterwards. It was acknowledged by all who saw it to be the handsomest piece of horseflesh they had ever seen. This little incident placed me on most excellent terms with the quartermaster and serves to show that one at all times should be courteous and kind to his associates.

I went to my quarters and made out a list of articles I intended to take. The quartermaster's department contained many of the things wanted, while the sutler's store was well supplied with all manner of Indian goods, the character of which I was well acquainted with having traded with the Indians for several years. The quartermaster had received an order to outfit me with anything I desired, and thus assisted by this order and the kindly disposition of the quartermaster, we had no difficulty in picking out an excellent outfit.

The first item was five pack mules with saddles, panniers, etc., and two saddle mules; and having packed up what the quartermaster had in store suitable for my purpose, I then carried the order to the sutler who told me to step behind the counter and make my own selection, which I did to the sutler's delight, for he was sure of a large profit. He charged for what I got six hundred and fifty dollars, which was about one hundred and fifty dollars too much. The quartermaster thought I had a very insignificant outfit and wanted me to take more. I thanked him but declined. I then got Alex McKay, a one-eyed half breed, to accompany me. I used to take him with me when on a dangerous trip scouting. He was one of the bravest men I ever came across. I could trust him, as he had proven his fidelity to me more than a half dozen times.

On the 25th of September we were packed up and mounted, each leading our war horse. When the officers made their appearance, I thanked Lieut. Sheridan, Capt. Dent and others for procuring the commanding officer's consent to make the trip. I informed them I would bring each of them a beautiful buffalo robe, and they made reply not to count the chickens before they were hatched. I will here say our two horses were the swiftest in the country, thoroughly broken under fire and could not be stampeded, and I expect we were the two best armed men about the place. McKay carried his bow and arrows, being an expert in their use, and I was presented with two beautiful, long range, Derringers by Lieut. Howard of the Third Cavalry, a Virginian.

Bidding all present *au revoir* we started, making twenty-five miles and camped. Some Nez Perces camped with us that night. They tried to persuade us not to go through the St. Joe and Coeur d'Alene Indians, who had been in the late war, as it would be dangerous. We informed them we apprehended no danger as both of us were acquainted with both the Coeur d'Alene and St. Joe Mission Indians. They were not considered a brave Indian but were treacherous. Knowing the character of them, we knew the ground on which we stood when in their presence.

The hardest to deal with was the Palouse tribe, but their chief was held as a hostage. The Spokanes were a turbulent tribe, somewhat war-like, but their chief was also held as a hostage. They were a very intelligent tribe, having had more communication with the whites than the other tribes mentioned. In fact, we did not apprehend much annoyance from any of them, for they had received a severe whipping without doing any damage to the soldiers.

We were on the Colville trail to Snake, which place we reached on the second evening; saw Indians on opposite side of river; we made signs to some of them to come over, which they did. These were

Palouse Indians. They looked somewhat surly. I showed them my large official envelope informing them our business was with the chiefs and that we wanted them to cross us over in the morning. We gave them a few presents and some tobacco for their chiefs and asked them to meet us in the morning.

Early in the morning they came over in six canoes. We got across without any trouble and met their chiefs. They asked us many questions about their friends who were held as prisoners, and we notified them to be very careful that none of their young men committed any further depredations against the whites. We told them that Col. Wright was watching every move. They wanted to know where we were going. We informed them we were going to visit all the tribes to the Blackfoot Indians. They said "bad Indians east". I informed them they would very likely be good Indians after we visited them, showing them our large envelope and informing them that when the Great Father speaks, lighting strikes those who will not listen. They looked somewhat non-plussed. We informed them we would be back in about two moons.

We packed up leaving the Indians to digest what we had interpreted to them and two days brought us to Spokane River. We had travelled fast to get through the Palouse country. We pitched camp in the bend of the river and had no sooner got the camp in order than about one hundred bucks came charging down upon us, yelling like furies. When within about fifty yards of us we halted them. Most of them were acquainted with both of us as scouts for the United States. They wanted to know what we were doing there and where we were going. We told the chiefs to dismount and come into camp and we would inform them. We gave them to understand their young men must be kept back.

Five chiefs came in. I showed them the infallible envelope which always has a moral effect upon the Indian. After informing them of our intended visit to the Blackfoot Nation, they told us we were fools and would lose our scalps. They inquired about their friends who were held prisoners. I informed them they were well treated and seemed well contented. I also informed them it would please the commanding officer if some of them would take a trip to Walla Walla, and told them they would be well treated, and it appeared to please them much.

I then put up the magic envelope and made them a few presents and gave each of the chiefs a half plug of tobacco and informed them that our mules were afraid of Indians. They took the hint and all mounted and left. Their camp was about a mile distant, but they did not come nigh us anymore that night. I am satisfied the reason of our not being molested was the magic envelope and the government brand upon the mules.

Indians understood that brand, and they knew also if they made any signs of hostility some of their chiefs would bite the dust, for we were prepared at all points, keeping our saddle horses beside us. They knew also we were in the government employ or we would not have the mules. Several of the young bucks made signs they must have our saddle horses. We gave them to understand they could not have either of them and that they must leave, which they did.

We stood guard that night, in fact most every night. I omitted stating that after giving the chiefs the tobacco, when the young bucks wanted our saddle horses, we informed them if they did not leave, we would inform Col. Wright. That name struck terror to them every time they heard it. Of course they could have taken us in, but most likely we would have had company to the happy hunting grounds. We were not troubled by any of the Indians during the night and packed up early the next morning. The Indian village was direct on our route, and we had to pass by it or make a long detour, which I did not feel inclined to make. It would not have been policy for us to make any deviation from our course. It was necessary to put on a bold front, let the consequences be what they might.

As we passed in close vicinity to their village, they came out in full force. A surlier looking lot of savages I never beheld. There was no question in our minds but that they would like to take us in and would have done so if no hostages had been held. We both were mounted upon our horses that day and ready for a rupture with the Indians.

The second day from here we camped at St. Joe Mission. The Coeur d'Alenes and the St. Joe Indians were both camped close by the Mission. Father Joseph was the head of this institution. Both of us being acquainted with him, we went to the Mission and he met us at the gate and wanted to know our pleasure. We informed him we wished to camp inside of his enclosure and he admitted us. We also informed him we wanted him to take charge of the mules until morning and to provide stable for our horses. He demurred some, but finally conceded to our request. I had a letter from Col. Wright to him. After he perused the letter, a sudden change came over him, everything he had was at our disposal.

After supper a general council was held in his large reception room, the principal chiefs of both tribes being present. The priest showed the Indians the letter he had received and interpreted a small part to them. The chiefs asked us how their friends were getting on and when they were going to be set at liberty. We informed them that their friends were all right, but that their liberty depended upon the behaviour of all the tribes who had lately been at war. We said that Col. Wright had been informed that many of the late hostile tribes did not feel friendly toward the whites and that he had sent us to ascertain the truth.

They wanted to know where we were going with this big outfit of ours and we informed them that we contemplated a trip through the different tribes to the Blackfoot nation, to ascertain whether it was going to be peace or war with the Whites. If peace, good; if war, good also. Since Col. Wright was a great and good man, he was desirous of accommodating all Indians, either in peace or war. At this I showed them my magic envelope with a large seal attached. The priest opened his eyes somewhat at the sight of that seal, and the Indians put their hands over their mouths, a sign of astonishment.

The priest made a few remarks to them, when the principal chief got up and shook us by the hand, saying with a grunt "*How.*" Part of my statements to them as above given were false, but they accomplished their object. We could see by their countenances they believed our statements and felt uneasy. They invited us to visit their village and we accepted their invitation. The priest accompanied us and we remained in the village three hours. The principal conversation was about the late war and the hostages held, etc., and how good and friendly all the Indians were going to be from this time henceforth. We then returned to our quarters and conversed for some time with the priests and then turned in.

Up at daylight; attended to our horses; priests had breakfast ready; the mules being brought in we made the Indians a few presents, then packed up, bidding the priests farewell and started.

The country from here on was strange to both of us. The priest had informed us that it was seventy-five miles to St. Mary's River. This was a river which flowed into the Pend d'Oreille at White Horse Prairie. We camped that night on a prairie called Long Prairie twenty-five miles from the Mission. We killed a deer and had a feast for the first time. We had got through all the Indian tribes who had been in the late war. In two more days, we got to the St. Mary's River and crossed by rafting, finding no ford.

We had followed the Indian trail up St. Joseph and down St. Regis River, the route Lieut. Mullan constructed for his military road a year afterwards. We saw no Indians but plenty of signs. We followed up St. Mary's River three days, when we came upon an Indian camp of about forty lodges of Pend d'Oreille Indians. We camped in close vicinity to their village. They asked many questions as to where we came from and where we were going, all of which we answered. We made them a feast that evening and invited the chiefs to come. Conversation between them and ourselves was held in the sign language. I found they were proficient in that art.

After the feast we had a smoke. When once you get the chiefs to accept of some tobacco and smoke out of your pipe, peace and good fellowship is established for a time at least. We had a fancy pipe for such occasions, and found these Indians friends to some extent but very inquisitive. They informed us we must be very careful from now on, as Blackfeet, Piegans and Snake Indians were liable to steal our stock, if they did not take our scalps. I replied, putting on a big brave, informing them taking scalps was a two-handed game. They remarked we were only two, and I told them that I had fought Blackfeet many times, that they were cowardly in a fight, but expert horse thieves. We passed a pleasant time with these Indians, they making us a present of half a dozen buffalo tongues and we making presents in return. The magic envelope with the contents again served its purpose, we interpreting what suited us.

Next morning by sun up we were packed up and asking the chief the proper route to take, he pointed to a canyon some fourteen miles distant, stating we should follow up that stream three sleeps, then keep to the right of a certain *butte*, follow up a small stream and cross the mountains. The stream they mentioned is now called the Little Blackfoot. We crossed a rolling prairie, a beautiful country about 11 a. m., and arrived at a beautiful creek now called Rattlesnake, where we camped. We saw no Indians, but signs in abundance. We laid over one day and I explored this section for several miles, and informed McKay I would at some time in the future open a trading post at this place. It was manifest by the convergence of the trails that it would be a splendid place for trade on account of its centrality. All these trails showed signs of being constantly travelled by different bands of Indians.

We were aware of being in the Flathead country and thought we could not be over thirty or forty miles from Fort Owens. I was acquainted with many of the Flatheads. They were always looked upon by all mountaineers as being the bravest of Indians and mountain mens' friends in every circumstance. Flatheads never missed an opportunity to render assistance to the mountaineer, hence the great friendship between the two. I had met Major John Owens at Walla Walla. He was agent for the Flatheads. He invited me to pay him a visit at some time and I promised to do so, but on this occasion had not time.

Early the second morning we packed up and followed the trail up what is now called Hell Gate River: crossed a good-sized river call Big Blackfoot, as we afterwards ascertained. We then held council as to which of these two streams we should follow. We were aware both of them would take us to the summit of the Rockies, but finally decided to take the right hand one. We continued up what is now called Hell Gate River and camped on a beautiful prairie, where we killed a fat black tailed deer and had a feast. In looking around for a camp, we saw fresh Indian signs in every direction. Our packs were sufficient for good breast works.

I have before stated we were the best armed men on the prairie. I will now give an inventory: Each of us had a Sharp's rifle, abundance of cartridges and tape caps. They can be fired as rapidly as our present needle gun and are effective in execution. Besides this, we each had two Colts, twelve-inch barrel, six shooters, with skeleton stock; these pistols would kill two hundred yards. We also packed a heavy double barrelled shot gun, which we used for guard at night; in addition to these I had my Derringers and McKay had his bow and arrows, in the use of which he was the peer of any Indian I ever came across.

So, it will appear manifest to any one that if we retained our presence of mind and nerve, we were not easy to be taken by any usual number of Indians. Indians, as a rule, in making a raid on a camp of small numbers, avoid losing any warriors if possible. If any killing is to be done, they want to be the ones to do it. We trained our mules at the least alarm to break to camp. We had quite a time to break them in, but finally succeeded in getting them and the horses well trained. Nothing occurred during the night.

We got up early, this was the 10th of October, and noted as being the day we met a Mormon by the name of Van Eaton who was going to Fort Owen to buy ponies for the pony express. I sent my compliments to Major Owen by him, giving urgency of business as an excuse for not visiting him. Van Eaton informed us he had a trading post about seven miles beyond Flint Creek, the Indian name, which it still retains.

On the 12th we camped at the post. On the 13th while packing up, two Flatheads rode up and asked us where we came from and where we were going. After we answered them, they informed us they were going to the buffalo country and that their village was over the divide on Blackfoot River. This river also retains its Indian name. They informed us it was the shortest route to the Blackfoot country and that the Flatheads would be glad to see us in order to get the news from Walla Walla. We told the Indians to take the lead and we would follow and at sundown we came in sight of their village.

The Flatheads had discovered us coming and about fifty young bucks came like a whirlwind to see who it could be with a mule outfit. As soon as they got to us some ten of the oldest of them looked closely at me. It had been some years since I had seen any Flatheads and I did not recognise any of them at first, but they evidently recognised me and gave a war-whoop, a signal of gladness. We soon arrived at their village. Nothing would satisfy their head chief, Victor, but our entire outfit must be put inside of his lodge, which was done by the squaws. They would not allow us to either cook, or open our packs.

Victor's son took care of our packs. After supper we all took a smoke and all of the principal men of the village assembled in old Moese's lodge, which was a large one. Moese, as well as Victor, was an old acquaintance of mine and the second chief of the tribe. Their village was located in one of the most beautiful and romantic places to be found in the Rocky Mountains. They were anxious to hear all about the termination of the late war, known as the Spokane and Yakima War. The tribes engaged in that war, had tried hard to involve the Flatheads in it, but failed in their object, the Flatheads remaining firm friends of the whites and also keeping the majority of the Pend d'Oreilles from joining the hostiles. For this conduct alone on their part, the government ought to respect and treat the Flatheads justly in all dealings with them.

We remained up most of the night conversing on all matters of interest to an Indian, they being highly elated in receiving direct news from the seat of the late Indian war. The "Haranguer," as they call him, had to harangue the camp in order to let all those who could not get inside of the lodge have a place adjacent, so that the information could be imparted to them. Indians are just as keen, as whites, to hear the news from a distance.

I know that it will appear strange to very many that any person can hold counsel for hours with a tribe of Indians, who is not acquainted with a single word of their language. By the sign language thought can be communicated more rapidly, than by oral speech and with a certainty of being distinctly understood. A man who has a perfect knowledge of the sign language can converse readily with the Indians from Mexico to Alaska, and I never came across any Indians who did not prefer to hold conversation with a white man by signs, rather than in their own tongue. My knowledge of the sign language has assisted me many times in extricating myself and others from many tight places.

Just after sun-up Bear Track, another chief, called us to breakfast. After breakfast, another council was held, and we were requested to remain with them another day, and on the next day travel together as far as the buffalo country. We accordingly remained another day and spent the time in visiting the different lodges, making the chiefs daughters and wives presents of fancy calico and brass buttons, which at that time were held in high esteem, and with which we were well supplied. We compelled Victor to receive some flour, tea, coffee, sugar and tobacco, since we had to be his guests while we remained in camp and on the journey.

I informed Victor of my intention of locating on Rattlesnake Creek in the near future and opening a trading post and asked his opinion with reference to the matter. He and the other chiefs were highly pleased and pressed me not to delay, but as soon as I returned to Walla Walla to come back, advising me to return through the Nez Perces country, as it would be the safest route.

On the 15th at daylight, the village was all astir, and breakfast soon over. Forty young bucks were ordered as advance scouts and were requested to secure plenty of fresh meat and informed that the village would camp at a designated place. It will here be remembered that the Blackfeet were their ancient enemies. Indians move camp with something of a military system. It is necessary for them to do so, for they are likely at any time to be attacked by their enemies, if they are in their vicinity. In moving they not only have Hankers but front and rear guards. We had to go through about four miles of dense forest, a good place for an enemy to attack a moving village with hundreds of horses and *trevois*, with squaws and *papooses*, strung out for about two miles. We kept our outfit in the rear with a dozen picked warriors in company, stripped to their breech clouts and armed at all points.

About 3 p.m. we arrived at the place selected for camping without being annoyed by any enemies, though the scouts reported having seen Indian signs upon the top of a bald *butte* about a mile distant. They thought the sign was about two days old; at all events they kept guard out with their ponies. They had an abundance of fresh meat, there being plenty of deer and antelope in this section. At dark our stock was brought in and picketed. The young bucks and squaws kept the village alive until a late hour with the Indian drum, dancing and singing. Nothing occurred during the night except two false alarms.

On the 16th we were up early with scouts in advance moving across an open country and crossed the main range at Cadotte's Pass. Camped on Dearborn River and saw plenty of hostile signs, but no hostile Indians. The Flatheads scouted the surrounding country until sundown and reported that Indians were around and gave instructions to look out close for stock. This night another dance and song. The Indians stood guard all night.

On the 17th by 8 a. m. traveling north, keeping along the base of the mountains. Camped on the South Fork of Sun River; that is the Indian name for this stream The Flatheads were friendly with the Piegans and Blood Indians and expected to meet some of them at this place, and we also were greatly desirous of interviewing them. We concluded to remain here today at least. The Flatheads expected to remain here several days; their young men had seen a few buffalo at a distance.

On the 18th Victor invited me to accompany him and some others to the Piegan Agency, which was some twenty-five miles down the river. He requested me to ride one of his horses. As I had a long distance to travel, I accepted his offer. Fifty of us mounted, each armed to the teeth and arrived at the agency at 11 a. m. Some fifty Piegan and Blood Indian lodges were scattered around the agency. The agent came out when he heard that the Flatheads and one white man were there. He was a fine looking old man. It was Col. Vaughan from the State of Mississippi. He invited us in and held a short council with the Flatheads. After the council, he ordered the cook to prepare a feast for them and invited me to his office.

On this occasion I was first aware of the contents of one of the papers which I had in the envelope. It was simply a request to any Indian Agent, or any government officer to render any assistance which I might need in executing my orders. Col. Vaughan asked me what he could do for me. I asked him to give me a short statement, showing the condition of the Indians which he had in charge and their disposition towards the whites, and also what tribes were hostile, or were inclined to be hostile. He fully answered all my inquiries to my entire satisfaction and further informed me where Little Dog, the head chief of the Piegans was camped and advised me by all means to see him, as he might render great assistance, also informing me that the Piegans had very many fine robes.

After partaking of a lunch, I informed the colonel it was time to return to camp, as the Flathead chiefs had then assembled to bid the agent goodbye. The colonel invited us to remain all night, but his generous offer was declined. The agent and the Flatheads were old friends and he made them many presents. He made me promise if I ever passed through that section again not to fail to pay him a visit.

A few Piegans and Bloods returned with us to our camp, where we arrived at dusk. All the Flatheads were elated when shown the presents the agent had made to their friends, and when they heard of the reception they had received. Dancing and singing as usual until a late hour and enjoying a great feast, as some of the young bucks had killed a few very fat buffalo, the tongues of which, with some of the choicest of the meat they presented to Victor. We had a supper fit for a prince.

On the 19th up early, and presented chiefs with some ammunition, which they were short of, and some presents for their squaws. The mules and horses were then brought in, and turning to our packs we found six of the finest robes I had ever seen, presents to us from the Indians. When we were finally packed up and ready for starting-, the whole village surrounded us, each one wishing to shake hands and saying they were sorry at our leaving. I assured them they would see us again. They warned us, however, to be careful. The chiefs said they believed our medicine was stronger than any man's they had ever come across.

I presume it seemed to them a great venture to go through the late hostile tribes with such a big and rich outfit. If they had been thoroughly posted they would not have thought it so difficult after all. The hostages held by the government and the magic envelope which they could not comprehend was the secret.

We bid them "*How.*" Following along the base of the mountains, crossing the North Fork of the Sun River. Some ten miles beyond that stream while crossing a small divide we discovered some buffalo on the run; as we had a powerful glass we halted and made a careful inspection. Some five miles distant we discovered Indians running buffalo. These must be Little Dog's Indians we thought. We proved our conjecture to be true the next day. We followed down a draw out of sight of the Indians. They had not seen us yet. We came to a spring of water and good feed for horses and camped in a position strong enough for two men, armed as we were, to hold at bay any number of hostile Indians; had a feast on fat buffalo the Flatheads had given us, and the night passed without anything of note occurring.

On the 20th it was eight o'clock before we packed up. We wished to keep our stock in prime condition in case later we should have to travel fast and far. We travelled north, following lodge pole trails, taking it leisurely and keeping on the *qui vive* for either friendly or hostile Indians. We crossed one branch of the Teton River about 2 p. m. and while crossing a divide we discovered three Indians, distant about two miles. They discovered us at the same time and looked at us with their spyglasses, then wheeled and disappeared going north.

As we were aware that the Piegans were camped no great distance from this point we continued for about three miles further and found a good camping ground. Selecting a good place we soon had camp and breastworks in order. Both McKay and myself were certain if the Indians we had seen belonged to Little Dog's outfit that he would pay us a visit that evening, and expecting this visit we each put on our best rigs, *viz*: we changed our everyday buckskin suits for a caribou suit with double fringes at every seam. Both suits were tony and costly. Many might think no object could be gained by this change, but not so.

Imagine yourself appearing before some prominent person with a plain, dirty suit of clothes on. What would he think of your plebeian appearance? It has the same effect upon an Indian chief, or at all events I always found it so. I have appeared before many different tribes, and I always found that when I was dressed up in my fancy suit, both the chiefs and others received me as some person above the common order. The aged Col. Vaughan had informed me that Little Dog was considered one of the bravest and proudest Indians on the plains, hence the greater necessity of change in dress.

We kept our saddle horses saddled with the "Indian pad" and hackamore. With this rig they were ready for mounting at a moment's notice and for action in case of enemies. Mountaineers and scouts understand the value of time in Indian attacks. We had supper one at a time. I just got through and was looking north expecting to see Indians every moment, when sure enough about one mile distant, we discovered twenty-five Indians, splendidly mounted, coming rapidly. They saw that we had discovered them and when within one-fourth of a mile distant they pulled their guns and fired into the air, which is the sign of friends. We returned the salute. At that they came at a whirlwind speed.

It was a beautiful sight. When within fifty yards the chief gave an order and they halted at a jump, as trappers say. Sure, enough it was Little Dog, and he dismounted with a proud step and advanced. I met him half way. He scrutinised me from head to foot then reached out his hand with the customary remark of "*How.*" He was a fine-looking specimen of an Indian Chieftain. Many an artist would have been glad to have had this opportunity of taking his picture, just as he stood before me. He was over six feet in height, straight as an arrow with his implements of war on his person and a magnificent war bonnet upon his head. Three years after this I became the owner of this bonnet.

I invited him to camp. His warriors were approaching towards our horses and he noticed me looking at them. He spoke something to them, when they dismounted and came and sat in half circle around our camp. Little Dog walked around our outfit, examining the situation with a critical eye. He then smiled and coming toward us shook both of us by the hand and made sign "No fools." In the meantime, we had our fancy pipe out with the tobacco. I shook hands with the other Indians and invited them to smoke, saying we would talk afterwards. After we were through smoking, I remembered that the agent had given me a short note to be interpreted to Little Dog and also a beautiful blanket to be presented to him when we met.

These I now produced and gave to him. I could see he was highly pleased. He knew the blanket came from the agent. I had another one similar which the agent had made me a present of. Little Dog spoke to a splendid looking Indian, about nineteen years of age, to come and sit beside him and informed me that this was his oldest son. Well might the chief be proud of this son, a young man as handsome as an Apollo and as proud as Lucifer.

I made him a present of the blanket which was a counter part of the one his father had just received.

No sooner had he received the blanket than he jumped up and gave a ringing war whoop, which made all the horses prick up their ears, and then stepping proudly up to me took me by the hand and made sign to me "you are my friend." I observed his father's eyes sparkle with pleasure. Ever after father and son were as brothers to me and I to them, until their death, which occurred nine years after.

I then interpreted the note to them, the contents of which were to the effect that the Agent was my friend and that he wanted Little

Dog and all his people to be my friends also. All these Indians are expert sign talkers and they gave me credit to be their equal, if not their superior, hence the name "Sign-talking-White Man," which name I retain amongst the Piegans.

After answering all their questions as to where we came from and where going and all about the late Indian war, which they had heard of, we made the chief a present of provisions sufficient to feast all his principal head men of the village. Little Dog then held a short council with his warriors, when half of them mounted and took the provisions for the feast and also six plugs of tobacco.

After they left Little Dog asked me if Victor was with the Flatheads, and also what other chiefs, and many other questions, all of which I answered. McKay who had been cooking invited the outfit to eat and they accepted with evident relish. After this, followed the old time smoke; then as it was getting; sundown, the chief made sign he would go back to the village, but would leave his son and two other Indians to remain with us that night, as he believed there were Blackfeet Indians in the mountains, and if they came to our camp his son would make them leave.

After shaking hands they left for their village and we sat conversing with the Indians until a late hour. All our stock being picketed close, we then spread blankets and robes for our guests. McKay had been outside of the stock standing guard, and I called him in, taking the gun in hand to occupy his place, when Fringe, that being the name of the chief's son, stepped up to me saying that he himself would stand guard and let us two sleep. As we turned in, McKay asked if we could trust him. I was astonished at the question as McKay was an expert Indian man, and answered in the affirmative, but informed him we would sleep light in case of accident.

It was about 2 a. m. I happened to be awake when a loud challenge was given by Fringe. No sooner was the challenge given than McKay, myself and the two young Piegans were beside him. We could not discern anything, but Fringe pointed to the right. The two young bucks spoke to Fringe and he said something to them. They went swiftly to the left and disappeared in the gloom. It was dim starlight. In about three minutes we heard the Indians give a war whoop which Fringe answered in Piegan. It was then we could see dark objects moving rapidly to the right and disappear. In a moment the two young warriors returned smiling and making sign "Blackfeet." "They have gone, go to sleep."

165

I then told McKay to turn in and I would finish the night guard, but he would not allow it. When Fringe and his fellow Indians saw that one of us would stand guard, one of the young bucks joined Mc-Kay on guard and I took Fringe and the other Indian and turned in. We slept soundly and it was daylight when we woke up. Fringe smiled, saying in sign "Blackfeet gone to look for Flathead who would kill him." Fringe had two names, "Fringe"and "Never Tire." Now these two Indians, Little Dog and his son affected me as no other Indians ever had. An attachment sprung up in my breast for them that I could not understand and account for, since I was considered by all of my mountain friends to be very bitter and anything but friendly with Indians. I had lost many friends by them at different times. I intend at some future time to give a brief account of many thrilling experiences of Little Dog and his son.

After breakfast we packed up and continued in a northerly direction and had travelled about eight miles, when crossing over a divide we discerned some two miles distant a large number of mounted warriors approaching at a canter. Fringe informed me that they were his people coming to welcome us to their village. This welcome is always customary with any tribe of Indians when strangers are coming who are to be received as friends. When within a quarter of a mile they spread out in two wings and came like a whirlwind, yelling like furies, which came very near stampeding our mules. Fringe gave them a command and they ceased their yelling and we finally got our mules quieted. After shaking hands with some of the principal warriors, we continued our journey to their village, being some five miles distant, and located on what is called Marias River, but called Bear River by all Indians.

When we arrived at the village. Little Dog met us, being splendidly mounted and equipped and led us to the centre of the village, which numbered three hundred and fifty lodges, to a very large lodge finely decorated and there dismounted. Half dozen squaws took hold of the mules and unpacked everything and carried it into the lodge. We turned our stock over to Little Dog and he gave some orders and two Indians came forward and took the stock. I asked Little Dog to have good care taken of our horses, and he made sign "your stock will be well treated."

It was on the 21st, a day to be well remembered from the treatment we received by these wild prairie Indians. They surrounded us by hundreds and asked us all manner of questions, until Little Dog after letting the Indians exercise their curiosity for a time, spoke to them and they all fell back and we were invited into the lodge, where a feast was awaiting us. After the feast, all the leading head men being called into the lodge, we partook of the accustomed smoke and sat silent for some time, when Little Dog got up and made a short speech to them, as the result of which, they one at a time came and shook hands with both McKay and myself.

This was preliminary to a general council that was to follow. Little Dog then spoke to a large elderly Indian, who came and sat opposite to me. This Indian was very similar to our inquisitive newspaper reporters. He was the one who "harangued" the village, announcing by public outcry all the news received. As I have stated before, Indians are very keen to hear the news, as keen as any white man can possibly be. The first question asked was where we came from and what was our business in coming to this country, and how we got through the late hostile tribes, and then as to the result of the late war with the Spokanes and Yakimas; and if these Indians had made peace or were they going to war again and a hundred more minor questions.

All of these questions I answered in detail, all the Indians present understanding every sign and giving a grunt in the approved manner as the questions were answered. I did not omit to produce the "magic envelope" showing them the great seal with the eagle stamped upon it, at which they put their hands over their mouths, which is a sign of great astonishment at something great, and that the person having the same is no common person. I then interpreted some of its contents, such as was suitable to the occasion. They firmly believed I was an agent of the Great Father, which was true in a certain sense, since I was operating for the government.

Little Dog then asked me what we had in our packs, and if we were going to trade with them, and what it was we wanted to trade for, etc. I informed him that we had come a long distance and a great many white chiefs wished to get some very fine buffalo robes, and that we would want to trade also for some fat ponies and pack saddles. At this they gave a sign of approval, saying they had plenty of all of them. I informed him it was getting too late that day to trade and that we would trade tomorrow; that I wished to make a feast on that evening and that we had brought plenty for that purpose. Our supplies consisted of flour, crackers, rice, syrup which all Indians are very fond of sugar and coffee. We produced fifty pounds of flour and twenty of crackers, yeast powder and salt and other materials. Little Dog furnishing the meat.

About a dozen squaws set to preparing the feast. The "haranguer" was giving to the inhabitants of the village the news received and I made sign to Little Dog I should like to go through the village. He then spoke to Fringe who informed me to wait a short time and went out. In ten minutes, Fringe returned and called his father who motioned me and McKay to follow. Outside were four splendid ponies with fancy pads upon them. After mounting we promenaded all through the village and found it was rich in everything that goes to make Indians wealthy. We were received and greeted in every part of the village with acclamations of pleasure, which was pleasing both to McKay and myself. McKay swore they were the peers of any tribe of Indians he had ever been amongst and were the richest. Any person acquainted with this tribe at all at that date knows that his judgment was correct.

We returned to the chief's lodge and found the feast ready. All the leading Indians of the village were called into the lodge, the lesser set of head men being feasted outside of the lodge, mats being supplied for that purpose. Little Dog and Fringe proudly did the honours, being highly pleased to have the opportunity to give their people a feast such as this one was, an occasion which in those days did not often occur.

After the feast was over there was, I might say, a general tribal smoke and a general buzz of conversation amongst the Indians, some of the principal chiefs remaining in the lodge. I asked them where the Crow Indians and Gros Ventres were and whether they were at war with the Crows yet or not, they being the ancient enemies of the Piegans. They replied that they had made peace with the River Crows the previous spring and were looking for them to pay them a visit at any time. The Gros Ventres were a branch of the Arapahoe tribe, which was on friendly terms with the Piegans, but not with the Blackfeet. I was acquainted with the Crows, at least with many of them. They are turbulent and hostile at all times, never omitting to rob white men when opportunity served, frequently killing notwithstanding the declarations of many people to the contrary.

We remained up until a late hour answering and asking questions and at last turned in and slept soundly without any fear for stock or ourselves. Woke up about sun up. Little Dog and family were up and had breakfast ready. He smiled when we got up, making sign "sleep good." After breakfast we cleared one-half of the lodge and opened the packs and spread out our outfits in tasty order. As I was an old trader, I understood how to make things show to the best advantage.

We had almost everything wanted by these Indians. After everything was made ready, the crier was sent out to notify the Indians to bring in their best robes, and it was a busy time for three hours.

In an Indian camp where many desire to trade the ones who have traded have to step back and give room for the next until the rush is over. Fringe assisted me in trading, while McKay with an Indian was baling the robes. It was laughable to hear McKay get off some of his remarks at the rapidity with which the robes were thrown to him.

At 1 p. m. the rush was over, many of the robes being rejected as too common and not worth packing. I informed Little Dog of this and he explained to the Indians. To many of the squaws whose robes were rejected, I made presents in the shape of calico, buttons, etc., which pleased them highly and signified to them that we were not stingy and did not love our goods over much, which disposition an Indian is quick to observe in a trader. Many a trader has missed a good trade in not knowing how to humour Indians. We had one hundred and twenty robes baled and two *parfleches* full of dried tongues. Many of the robes were garnished beautifully and would bring from twenty-five to fifty dollars in any market in those days.

After dinner I informed Little Dog, I wished to trade for five good, fat pack ponies. Ponies were cheap in those days and I had some Colt's revolvers and ammunition, which were held in very high esteem by the Indians at that time. I was not in the habit, however, of trading them to any Indians who were not strictly friendly with the whites, and we considered Little Dog's outfit of the latter kind. We unpacked the revolvers and ammunition, this being their first knowledge of our possessing them.

I first presented Little Dog and Fringe each with first pick of the revolvers and plenty of ammunition. Their eyes sparkled with pleasure. Little Dog and Fringe then called me outside to look at the ponies with the pack saddles upon them. There were two long-maned mules on one side, one of them being a very handsome animal fifteen hands high and white in colour, the finest looking mule I have ever beheld. The chief presented this mule to me, making signs that it was a Sioux mule. The other mule was presented to me by Fringe. It was nearly as large as the white one; both of these mules were young.

I then examined the ponies and selected six, took my knife and cut the tips of their tails, the Indians understanding by this that I would trade only for them and they at once turned the remainder loose. We soon got through with the pony trade. Two old bucks each took a pistol. The squaws traded the remaining ponies for scarlet cloth, calico, buttons, knives, etc. I presented the second chief with a pistol and Little Dog's younger son with another. After the young boy got possession of it, he gave a yell and darted out of the lodge, which made all the other Indians laugh, an expression of amusement seldom indulged in by Indians.

In a short time Mountain Chief, that being the name of the chief second in rank, brought in eight fine head and tail robes, making sign that they were mine, and at this time, were brought into the lodge, two large parfleches full of dried tongues, and also twelve good robes, Little Dog informing me they were presented to me and said pack them up. I told Little Dog to inform his people that next time I came to their village I would make all their hearts glad. (I made my promise good one year afterwards.)

At this time there was a commotion in camp and in a short time six Crow Indian chiefs were brought into the lodge, where they were received with the customary greeting *"How!"* accompanied with a motion to take a seat, which was prepared for them out of robes. I was acquainted with two of these Crows, Old Yellow Bear and Rotten Tail, they being head chiefs of the River Crows. They were astonished to see me there and informed me that they had heard that "Crooked Nose," which was a term they had applied to me among the Crows, had been killed.

The Piegans then smoked the pipe of welcome with the Crows, myself and McKay being included in the company, and afterwards they partook of a feast and then a general council followed, the substance of which pertained to their visit, etc. They answered that their village was three bends below, that they came to see their friends (the Piegans), to have a buffalo hunt, trade and then move back to the Great River (Missouri). That is a synopsis of the council and covers all salient points. They asked me if I was not going to trade with them, and I replied by asking them what they wanted to trade, and if they had any robes like the best ones which I had just received. They answered "yes, and some finer." I asked Little Dog how many robes we were likely to get from the Blackfeet. He answered that he could not tell, but that we were likely to get some.

I made him a confidant, informing him of the number wanted and he said we had better trade for some with the Crows. This conversation was held outside of the lodge, as all conversation between the Indians and myself was held in the sign language. We returned to the lodge and I informed the Crows I would trade for thirty or forty good head and tail robes, but that they would have to come to this lodge to trade, as we had everything, they had named. They insisted on our going to their village, but we declined, I was not friendly with the Crows for good reason. Finally, they agreed to bring the robes on the following day and invited the Piegan chiefs to pay their village a visit that evening. About half a dozen accepted the invitation. Little Dog informed them that he would be at their village early in the morning and that I would accompany him.

They mounted with a "*How*" and disappeared singing. They were splendidly mounted, ponies being covered with trappings, while their riders were adorned with all the fancy regalia which goes to make an Indian vain and many of them as snobbish and foolish as our dudes. The evening passed off pleasantly. I informed the "crier" to proclaim that if any of the squaws had any fancy *moccasins* I would trade for them. The Piegans make very fine Indian work of all kinds and I thought some fancy little things would be acceptable and please the officers' wives and daughters. By bedtime I had a fine lot of *moccasins*, small and large and many interesting curios besides.

On the morning of the 23rd we ate breakfast before daylight. Fringe had his war horse saddled with trappings upon him which cast the rigging of the Crows in the shade. His father was equally well mounted. There were also two magnificent horses saddled for me and McKay. We mounted and arrived at the Crow village just as the sun was rising. The Crows had discovered our coming and met us in full force singing their songs of welcome. We were taken to Yellow Bear's lodge, our horses prancing about with pride. Many of the dusky maidens cast loving glances at Fringe. Well, they might, for he was the handsomest Indian youth on the plains, tall and graceful.

Entering the lodge, a feast was prepared for us of boiled buffalo meat and tongue. After the feast, followed the traditional smoke and then ensued a general council, the import of which was a fight the Crows had had with the Sioux, Cheyennes and Arapahoes, and how they, the Crows, after fighting awhile had turned their enemies to flight and taken many scalps, and captured many ponies and mules. They produced two scalps which were fresh and evidently all they had. I asked them to produce another fresh scalp and I would make them the present of a blanket. This they did not do but looked black at me. McKay then spoke to me in English, saying "better not tantalise them too much Bill."

The Crows were great boasters. They wished to impress Little Dog and the Piegans with the idea that they were terrible warriors. As a matter of fact, either the Cheyennes or the Arapahoes could whip them three to five. The Sioux could hold them in even numbers. Little Dog was well aware of these facts and so informed me on our way back to his village. He also remarked "you are not friendly with the Crows, and they do not like you very much. I saw many of them seemed to be acquainted with you. Have you ever had any difficulty with them?" I informed him that I did have some difficulty some years before.

We arrived at the village on our return followed by many Crows with squaws and bucks leading ponies to trade and two of their race horses, the Indians being very fond of racing. Having arrived at camp I opened for trade and by noon had traded for forty-two very good robes. They wished to unload a lot of trash, which we rejected. I then closed up our packs. The Crows are inveterate beggars and thieves, but they accomplished nothing in that line on this occasion.

After feasting and smoking it was about 2 p. m. when the crier harangued the village to the effect that the Crows wanted to run races with the Piegans. In a short time, there were fully five hundred assembled on the race grounds not over half a mile from the village. I took Little Dog to one side and told him to let the Crows win the first two races, that the Crows had one American horse they wanted to run about half a mile, and not to race any of their horses against this American horse, but for Piegans to bet all they could get on McKay's horse, which could almost fly for half a mile.

Little Dog secretly notified the Piegans of this program, and the Indians were quick to catch on. After three races had been run, all of which the Crows got away with, they became wild, having won several ponies and many robes. Fringe then led up McKay's horse, which was not so tall as the Indian horse. Fringe signed to the Crows he would run this horse against their American horse, and the Crows jumped at the offer, bringing all the ponies and robes they had won and twice as many more to bet on their horse, all of which bets were taken. I told Little Dog to inform his people to get all the bets they could and they certainly complied.

After leading up fully twenty-five more ponies and piling up the robes in abundance the Crows commenced to look carefully at McKay's horse, which they believed belonged to the Piegans, and they could see nothing extraordinary about him, but were somewhat taken back at the amount the Piegans were anxious to stake on the race; at all events they would only take a few more bets.

Little Dog's youngest son was called up by Fringe and told to prepare to ride the race, McKay having informed Fringe that any boy could ride the horse. The boy promptly complied with the order of his older brother by stripping naked. A Crow boy was also stripped, the track cleared and the horses led out to the starting point. An Indian race is started by the signal "go!" The first out wins the race no difference what may happen to either horse or rider. Little Dog and a Crow chief were judges. I had seen a great many races, but never saw one in which the Indians took such an interest as on this occasion. Neither myself or McKay could tell certainly what would be the result of this race, but one thing we were sure of: The Indian horse had to be a world-beater to beat McKay's that distance.

When the horses reached the starting place I turned round, everything was hushed (all the dogs being held by the squaws). I was looking at Fringe with a glass and could see him address his younger brother on the horse, and then both horses being turned Fringe let go of McKay's horse, which he was holding at the head, and the Crow let go of his horse at the same time. When the race was fairly commenced, I could see McKay's horse was being held, while the Crow was whipping. They ran together neck and neck to within one hundred yards of the coming out place, when the boy on McKay's horse gave him the whip. The horse fairly flew from the Crow horse and won the race by about sixty feet.

An Indian yell went up from five hundred throats. The Crows were the worst nonplussed I ever beheld. They appeared sullen and silent, having very little to say. In a short time, they departed for their own village. All the young Piegans had a great time dancing and singing that night until a late hour. A great many may say and think we played the Crows a mean trick by allowing McKay's horse to be used as if he belonged to the Piegans, but not so. We looked upon the Piegans as friends and the reverse with the Crows. I firmly believe the Crows had stolen the American horse from some white man on the emigrant road. I told the Crows as much and they did not deny it. At all events our action made the Piegans our firm friends ever afterwards.

The night passed off pleasantly. We had notified Little Dog we would move and go to the Blackfoot camp the following day; and on the 24th were up early, had breakfast by sun-up and packs all ready outside of the lodge. Little Dog then called me into his lodge and produced three arrows peculiarly marked, informing me not to lose them, but when at the Blackfoot village to show them to their chief. I am satisfied that by reason of those arrows we got clear of the Blackfeet, though Fringe and five other Indians accompanied us. As Little Dog had informed me the Blackfeet were not to be trusted at any time. He said he would send Fringe and five other young bucks with us to the camp, which was on the north fork of the Milk River—called Bear River also.

They were, as Little Dog had stated, a hard outfit and it was a difficult job to extricate ourselves from the difficulties we there met. If it had not been for those thick arrows and the assistance of Fringe, we never could have got clear of their village with our outfit. It was perhaps foolish in us to go to their camp, as we could have got all the robes we wanted and taken back track with comparative safety, but that idea did not suit either McKay or myself. It would not have looked well to have reported to Col. Wright that we had taken back track. The officers surely would have concluded we did not merit the reputation we had gained of being expert and fearless scouts and we certainly would have been laughed at, and neither of us cared to be ridiculed for lack of nerve.

We packed up, bidding goodbye to our Piegan friends. I told Fringe that we would like to camp within a few miles of the Blackfeet that night, if we could keep from being discovered. He informed us that he knew of a good camp and would try and get there without being discovered, if possible. He sent two Indians ahead to keep a lookout for the Blackfeet. About 3 p.m. we got to camp but made dry willow fire to cook by, the willow giving forth but little smoke. We kept our stock close and the night passed with no unusual incident, which was fortunate for us. We informed Fringe we would have to remain in the Blackfoot camp one night and asked him to have our stock looked after. He promised to see that the stock was not molested and said he would have his young men look after it.

After packing up, Fringe sent two of his warriors ahead to notify the Blackfeet of our coming. About a mile from the village, we were met by a large delegation of warriors. On the lead were two of their head chiefs. Calf Shirt and Father of all Children. We shook hands with the two chiefs and proceeded to the Father of all Children's lodge, a very large one. After unpacking, the stock was turned loose. Two Piegans remained mounted and would not allow the Blackfeet to take any of the stock. Many a mean sign was made behind their backs, all of which I understood.

After everything was placed in the lodge a short council was held and then the usual smoke. All of the men of the village being assembled they asked the object of our visit and where we came from. Having answered their questions, I produced those three arrows and passed them up to Father-of-all-Children. He scrutinised them closely and passed them around. After they were carefully examined by all they were handed back to me. At the same time, I informed them the object of our visit, brought out the magic envelope and interpreted to them the contents of one paper as coming from the Great White Chief.

At this they gave a grunt, sounding very much like a snarl, with a curl of contempt upon the lips of many, they having a dislike for anything American, they belonging to the Canadian side. Red Jacket's land as they called it. Not a glance, move or sign escaped either McKay or myself. McKay made a remark to me in English "Bill I believe we are in a tight fix and I believe some of these Indians know you from the way they eye you." They also asked me if I had not been with a party in the Big Horn country and also on Green River. The Blackfeet frequently visited those countries on their thieving expeditions, and never omitted attacking travellers. Invariably those travellers would make the Blackfeet that escaped the pruning knife, go back to their nation howling for the loss of their great and good warriors, as they called those whom they had lost by the "White dogs", that being the mildest term they had for the white men.

To these inquiries I evaded a direct answer. As a matter of fact, I had been previously in those countries and had fought them there. I was satisfied they thought they knew me, but they were not quite certain. By right, it was not they who had the right to complain, since they were always the attacking party upon the travellers and other white men in that country, which they visited.

We then got out some provisions for a feast, and the squaws busied themselves in making it ready. The head men of the tribe were then called in and after the feast the usual smoke followed. Fringe rendered valuable service, by informing them what we would and would not trade for. I will say here for the enlightenment of those who are not informed, that the Blackfeet, Bloods and Piegans are of common origin and hence speak the same language. We opened the stock and in two hours we traded for fifty-five garnished robes, more really than we wanted, and also two good packhorses and saddles, which they intended to steal back.

They said we would remain in camp a few days and let our stock rest, their design evidently being to get us to remain in their village until the Piegans would go back to Little Dog's village and then they would take in our entire outfit and get back to Red Jacket's land. They did not dare to attempt this outrage upon us while the Piegans were present, by whom we had been introduced as guests. We informed them we should leave in the morning.

They looked ugly when informed of our intended departure in the morning and scowled at Fringe. It was then I saw the spirit I had given Fringe credit of possessing, because when the Blackfeet scowled and spoke something to him, he jumped up, throwing his blanket off, drawing his revolver and pointing his finger at the head chief, his eyes flashing fire, and in a ringing voice addressed them in a tone which the Indians plainly understood. The Blackfeet chief looked down and appeared somewhat crestfallen, and not one of them looked Fringe in the eye while he addressed them.

The other three Piegans had thrown off their blankets and were standing by the side of Fringe leaning upon their guns; while McKay and myself stood with our backs against our packs, with arms ready for use. McKay was looking ugly. I cautioned him to keep cool and wait. If difficulty had started in that lodge many of their chiefs would have taken the trail to the "Happy Hunting Grounds" in short order. There is no question, however, but that they would have had our company, as there were two hundred lodges or more and our horses were in the herd; there would have been no chance for us to escape on horseback and perhaps not otherwise. If the Blackfeet, however had taken us in, Little Dog would have annihilated them in revenge for Fringe.

Finally Fringe got through addressing them, when the Father-of-all-Children and Calf Shirt arose and shook hands with Fringe and the other Piegans, but not with us. Many a wicked glance was cast at us. The lodge was crowded and a momentous calm prevailed. I produced a pound of tobacco and presented it to the chief asking him by sign to smoke. Many of them complied, but many left the lodge in order to avoid smoking, a true sign that their hearts were bad. I saw Fringe smile when several of the Indians left the lodge.

After supper myself and Fringe went outside of the village. When alone he asked me what route we intended to go from here. I informed him we would like to pass through the Kootenai country, as they were friendly. He wished us to return to his father's village, since these Blackfeet were bad. His counsel was good, but was not followed. He had found out from the Blackfeet that there was a Kootenai village camped by a lake (St. Mary's) which we could easily make in one day.

He also informed me that he and his warriors would go with us some distance, since we had too large an outfit to go from this camp unaccompanied. We had seventeen head of stock besides the two mules we had received from Little Dog and his son, which we did not intend to lose and we had in all fourteen packs. After this conversation with Fringe, we returned to the lodge. Fringe said something to the two young Piegans who went out and in about half an hour the two who had been herding our stock came into our lodge looking fierce, having heard of the previous rumpus. They sat down by the side of their young chief, who smiled, evidently reading the inward thoughts of his young tribesmen.

The evening was passed, by answering and asking questions, the Blackfeet asking us which road we were going to take. We evaded the question by answering we had not decided. If we had told them they would have the opportunity to dispatch a party of their warriors to intercept us and would have made it very unpleasant for us.

On the 26th we had breakfast by daylight, our outfit being outside of the Lodge and the young Piegans bringing in our stock. We soon had the mules and horses saddled and saddled very carefully, for we did not know what might happen that day, and we intended to be prepared for any emergency. We put our war rigs on our horses, which we intended to ride that day and by the time the three young Piegans had eaten we were ready to pack up. Fringe rendered valuable service to us by holding our saddle horses and keeping the Blackfeet back on one side, and the other Piegans keeping the stock surrounded and the Blackfeet back.

McKay and myself worked like beavers in getting packed up, and were getting rather angry at the Blackfeet at the manner in which they tried to retard us in getting off. The Blackfeet wanted among other things to trade for our horses and I gave them to understand in short order they were not for trade. They smiled a satanic smile and stepped back.

When the last pack was on, Fringe made a sign "ready" and we answered by springing upon our horses. No sooner was I in the pad than my horse let drive with both hind feet at a group of Blackfeet, who barely escaped being doubled up. This war horse of mine was a famous one. I called him "*Hickory*" and he would come to me as far as he could hear me call his name. He appeared all at once to be inspired with the very devil, pawing and tossing his head as if he knew the strain the Blackfeet had put upon us. At this time, I was afraid of McKay doing something which would bring on a fight, for his eyes were ablaze with anger and his features stern, a true sign a volcano was raging within him. If a shot had been accidentally fired or an arrow had whizzed, nothing could have kept McKay from starting the ball.

I pushed my horse beside him and spoke to him to keep cool and that later we would make these Blackfeet howl for this conduct of theirs before we were through with them. It was about as ticklish a place as I had been in with a trading outfit. There was not very much danger to ourselves, mounted and armed as we were. We could have each emptied two revolvers among the Blackfeet and probably escaped, for they had nothing in their camp which would equal the speed of our horses, and each of us had extricated ourselves from more difficult positions than this, but if trouble had ensued, we probably would have lost our outfit.

We got out of the village as soon as possible, myself, McKay and one Piegan taking the lead, with Fringe and the other Piegans bringing up the rear. We followed up a draw leading toward the mountains. Please remember that the Blackfeet did not shake hands with any of us. We followed this draw about four miles and when out of sight of the village wheeled to the right, keeping in a low place, travelling at a trot and crossing a low divide with no Blackfeet in sight. We continued north to a *butte* about four miles distant. It was there that Fringe and his warriors intended to return to their village. When we arrived at the *butte*, we drove our outfit on the north side and one of the Piegans crawled on top of the *butte*, while we tightened up the packs.

We had three extra revolvers left which we gave to the Piegans with plenty of ammunition, together with some other presents, which made the young warriors' hearts bound with delight. Fringe pointed out a direct route to the lake, it being a level plain for about five miles. He informed us that he and his men would remain at the *butte* until we disappeared and we shook hands with him and started at a seven-mile gait.

After travelling three hours we got into some rolling hills, and when about half way through these hills, looking off to the right a short distance from us, we discovered three mounted Indians coming at a run, yelling and brandishing their guns. We looked carefully at them and both agreed that they were Blackfeet. The Indians evidently

178

expected to see us run. We could easily tell that from their conduct. When within two hundred yards they swerved to the left, each taking a shot at us. Two of their bullets came unpleasantly close, but that was their last shot, for we were upon them before the smoke had cleared. They were not looking for any such move on our side and there were three good Indians there in very short order, which seemed to operate as a solace to McKay's overwrought feelings. McKay swore he would scalp half of the Blackfeet yet. I told him we might have an opportunity to take a few more topknots before reaching the Kootenai village.

About noon, while crossing a small stream and letting our horses drink and tightening up the packs, we discovered Indian signs but could not tell what tribe left the sign. We thought once of partaking of a lunch, but concluded not to do so until later. It was a good thing we did not, as a large Blackfoot war party was hot on our trail, evidently having come across the three Blackfeet above mentioned and evidently concluding that we would noon on some of these spring gulches. All of this I found out afterwards. Neither did they think we would travel so fast as we did, but we were both expert horsemen, good packers and knew the value of time when hostile Indians were on the trail.

About 3 p.m., when crossing a divide, we discovered the Kootenai village at a distance of about three miles and we were soon there and learned that three good Blackfeet Indians had been spies on this Kootenai village and had previously been discovered by them. They evidently were on their way back to the Blackfeet village when they discovered us. We were met by some forty of the head men outside of the village and escorted to the head chief's lodge, the squaws unpacking and storing our robes and saddles in a lodge adjoining the chief's. We put the goods which we had left in the chief's lodge. The Indians discovered that McKay's hands were bloody and wanted to know the cause and when McKay drew the three scalps from under his belt and passed them over, they examined them closely for about two minutes.

The chief then said something and those present with one accord gave forth a ringing war whoop, which brought up all the warriors in the village on a run. They soon ascertained the cause of the war whoop, and the scalps were passed around so that all could have a chance to examine them. When thoroughly satisfied that the pelts had been taken from Blackfeet, what followed would have made the hair of any delicate person stand on end, for there was a ringing war whoop from every warrior in the village, then the scalps were tied upon the ends of poles and paraded through the village, followed by a procession of old and young singing their war songs, which they kept up until about midnight.

In the course of our previous trading, we had got three sets of bows and arrows which I wanted to retain as my own, intending to present them to the officers back at the fort. As McKay was entitled to half we had got from the Blackfeet, I remarked to him as we entered the lodge to let me have these bows and arrows and for him to take the balance of the stuff, consisting of three horses, three guns and saddles besides blankets. I had seen a large mule tied up near the lodge and told McKay to offer the whole outfit for the mule. He did so. It happened that the mule belonged to the chief. No sooner had McKay made the offer than the mule was led up to the lodge and given into his hands. I believe he might have gotten three mules for the same outfit.

After he had tied up the mule, we again entered the lodge and saw the squaws had been cooking. We sat down to a meal and had a general smoke. The Indians believed us to be very great warriors, coming through the country we had with such a large outfit. The Kootenais are a noble, pleasant looking Indian and very friendly to the white man, a great contrast to the Blackfeet. The chief had taken charge of our stock, making sign they would take good care of them and we felt easy on that score. The reason so much ado was made over those pelts was that three days before our arrival they had a fight with some Blackfeet who were camped on one of the confluences of the Saskatchewan River, and had lost one warrior and had three wounded. They were really glad we had come as the Blackfeet were too many for them.

These Kootenai Indians were slow but beautiful sign talkers and seemed somewhat surprised in discovering that I was very proficient in that art, and asked me what tribe I had been raised by. Upon my replying they seemed to have doubts about my not being raised by some Indians and asked McKay, who understood considerable sign talk. He answered I was a white man, together with a lot of other information.

After answering all of their questions as to where we had come from, they wished to hear how the Yakima and Spokane war had terminated, as those Indians engaged in that war had tried hard to involve the Kootenais as allies. They, however, like the Flatheads, had remained firm friends of the whites. They asked particularly as to the names of the chiefs and head men who were held as prisoners and how they were treated. After answering these questions, they seemed pleased and remarked, "You will get through their country safely." They asked us if we had any powder and lead, as they were getting short. Answering in the affirmative we opened the pack and passed to the chief one ten-pound keg of powder (We had two kegs and two sacks of trade balls).

Speaking about a pleased looking people, here was a picture of gladness displayed on every feature. McKay remarked he had never seen such pleased Indians in his life. The chief asked us how many robes we wanted for the ammunition and I informed him that it was a present. I may remark here that we expected to see all that ammunition expended in keeping these Kootenais and ourselves from being taken in by the Blackfeet, as well also the remainder of the ammunition which we retained; for we were not going to part company with the Kootenais this side of Tobacco Plains, providing we ever got there. The chief, after being informed that the ammunition was a present, made the sign "wait until we cross the mountains to our people."

The squaws had been building a corral for our stock and we asked the chief to have the squaws cut plenty of grass for our stock and we would pay them. No sooner had we made this request than a dozen squaws were off, each with a cord and large knife, and they proved themselves experts in cutting bunch grass. The Crier had gone out and called all the young warriors to the Chiefs lodge, who were out of ammunition, and the powder and balls were then distributed to them, with warnings not to waste any of it, as the Blackfeet were evidently in pursuit. At this time the squaws all returned with fully a thousand pounds of bunch grass hay. We intended to keep our stock in prime condition, especially our saddle horses, as there might be hard work for them to do before we got out of this section of the country.

At this time all the packs were brought in and carefully secured and a general council was held. The young bucks reported they had discovered Blackfeet in the vicinity of the village and I could see the Kootenais felt uneasy; as they only had one hundred and fifty lodges, they could muster about three hundred warriors, young and old. The principal feature of this council was with reference to the route to take across the mountains. McKay and I could discern from their signs that there were three routes, two a little northwest of our camp and one a little south of west.

We could get their location by their constantly pointing in these directions. Neither McKay nor myself could give any advice on the subject, as we had never been in this part of the country before. There was quite an animated discussion among the Indians for about an hour on this matter of route, when it was finally decided to take the southern route.

As we were paying the squaws for cutting the grass, we noticed the Kootenais were wearing heavy caribou *moccasins*, and McKay and I each wished a pair. Upon this information being imparted to the squaws some of them left and soon returned with six pair, which we bought. They fitted us beautifully and McKay felt very proud, making one of his quaint remarks to the effect that the Blackfeet must look out now. We passed a very pleasant evening and did not retire until a late hour, the scalp dance engaging the attention of most of the village. The old chief Black Bear had two noble looking sons of about twenty and twenty-five years of age. The oldest of these sons and myself took the first guard, the others turning in.

Nothing occurred during our watch. Being relieved at the end of our watch by McKay and the younger son we turned in. It was about 4 o'clock when about half asleep I heard gun shots all around the village. I could tell the crack of our double-barrelled shotgun from all the rest. Before the smoke had cleared away myself and young Black Bear were beside McKay and the young buck who was on top of an Indian a little to the left. I could see the flash of his knife and knew that Blackfoot would be bald headed in short order.

McKay had stepped up too and had his foot upon a burly Blackfoot fully six feet tall and was reloading the shot gun. The whole camp was in an uproar. I made signs to the chief to make his Indians stop their noise. Several ponies had broken loose and had stampeded on the prairie. It was most too dangerous to go after them, as we did not know how many Blackfeet might be around. But our stock, as it happened, was all right, thanks to the squaws who had constructed a strong corral. One young Blackfoot had been taken prisoner and brought into the chief's lodge. Speaking about stoicism of Indians, this one at least was the reverse of the common idea.

More abject fear I never saw made manifest than on his part. Upon count after the uproar, it was found that five Blackfeet had been made good Indians, two being credited to McKay. They could not decide what to do with the prisoner, some proposing hanging, some burning, some to knock him in the head with a tomahawk, some to let him go and shoot him as he ran. They asked me my opinion and I replied "cut his hair close, strip him, give him twenty lashes and let him go." They asked McKay and he said "scalp him. If Blackfoot had you, they would kill you." And the Indians present all said "yes" by sign.

On the 27th after breakfast, it was breaking day and many of their young men, mounted upon their best ponies, were scouring the prairie in the endeavour to collect what stock had stampeded during the rumpus of the previous night, and after the ponies were brought in, they took the Blackfoot prisoner outside of the village, stripped him, cut his hair and gave him fully thirty lashes, his yelling being heard all over the village. Afterwards he was told to go, which he did at a fifteen-mile gait until he passed over the ridge and out of sight.

A shot was heard and soon after a young Kootenai, a brother to the one who had been killed in the recent fight with the Blackfeet, made his appearance from the direction the Blackfoot had taken. He passed by near where McKay and myself were standing and I asked him by sign "got Blackfoot?" He smiled, shook his head and went on to his lodge. I found out afterwards that he had got the one that had been captured and released, and that he reported his hair was too short for a scalp.

The lodges being ordered down everybody was busy packing up, the Kootenais being anxious to get away from this camp. McKay and myself had put on our fighting rigs, and it seemed to please the Indians to see us putting everything in fighting order. Everything being ready for a start the order was given for the village to travel in as close order as possible. At this time, I saddled my white mule, McKay mounting his. I asked Black Bear to have his people drive our pack animals with his as we wished to be outside with the warriors. He gave the order and his squaws took charge of our outfit. As about fifty warriors were mounted waiting in the village to start, McKay and myself mounted on our mules and joined them and with them acted as an advance guard.

My horse kept rubbing his nose against my leg as much as to say "ride me". The white mule was the finest saddle animal in the shape of a mule I had ever seen. We were some half a mile in advance of the moving village and had come some fifteen miles, keeping a sharp lookout all the time, when, upon a rise, looking back we discovered on one side and in the rear of the tail end of the village fully two hundred Blackfeet in a draw, out of sight of the other Kootenais. Young Black Bear signalled to those in the rear to close up, and the Blackfeet Indians readily understood the signal. In less time than it takes to write this, the moving village was in a compact circle, we falling back.

183

McKay and I got to our outfits as soon as possible, dismounted and tied the reins to the saddles of the mules, turning them among the village outfit. We then mounted our horses and rejoined the advance and found the warriors stripped to the breech clouts. Whenever you see that, be assured they are prepared to die in the defence of their women and children. They were a noble looking body of brown-skinned warriors. They had no time for painting, for the Blackfeet had been preparing for the attack by stripping themselves in the draw. Many of them did not have a stitch upon them, except a belt and war bonnet and implements of war.

At this time, they showed themselves upon a rise about four hundred yards distant. They gave forth a thrilling yell and then divided in two wings as if going to surround the Kootenai outfit. It was a very interesting sight to see them coming at whirlwind speed, shouting forth yell after yell, and evidently expecting their yelling would stampede some of the Kootenai outfit. In this they were disappointed as the Kotoenais were up to all such manoeuvres and had placed all the squaws and young ones on the outside of the pack animals.

The squaws were nervy, evidently realising that everything they held dear was in danger, at all events they were rustlers on this occasion in keeping the stock from being stampeded. When about one hundred of the Blackfeet, who were charging on our side, got within three hundred yards of us they opened fire with their Hudson Bay flint lock, muzzle-loading guns, but fortunately they were of short range. There was one Blackfoot in advance riding a fine pinto horse and I turned to McKay and said "let us try and stop that fellow." As I have before stated our ponies were thoroughly broken under fire and would scarcely breathe when we took aim. We both fired at the Indian at once and both horse and rider went to the grass and remained there; then the Kootenais sent forth their war yell of defiance.

At this time firing and yelling was going on in the rear at a lively rate. The Blackfeet, when their leader fell, paused a moment and we charged them. I told McKay to look out. I saw the devil was in him and I did not want to lose him. I saw he had prepared his bow and arrows for immediate use and knew then he intended to close on them in close combat. The Kootenais were better mounted than the Blackfeet, who tried to sheer to the left which was a mistake on their part, as it gave us the advantage; they also bunched up which was disastrous to them. I do not think the shots of McKay or myself failed to take effect.

If the Kootenais had at this moment closed in on the Blackfeet they could have put half of them *hors de combat*; as it was, when within forty yards of them they wheeled to the right and commenced a desultory mode of fighting. The Blackfeet at this time being outnumbered beat a retreat. McKay, as I had feared, dashed right up to them, and I expected every moment to see him go down, since fully a dozen Blackfeet were shooting at him and if they had not been unnerved, they would have brought him down. There was only one thing for me to do and do it quickly—go to his assistance, which I did, followed by a few Kootenais. Getting to his side I emptied one of my revolvers and was pleased to see the Blackfeet in full retreat.

I noticed that McKay was wounded and his horse bleeding in a few places from flesh wounds. These were the Blackfeet we had traded with, and they knew McKay and myself by our horses, but as fortune would have it, notwithstanding all the yelling and shooting at us, they failed to do us any material damage. Finally, I got McKay out of danger. He cooled down somewhat but would not be satisfied until he had lifted some hair. We had got some considerable distance from the outfit and Black Bear called off his warriors.

I asked him why he had called off his men. He informed me he was afraid there might be other Blackfeet around and did not wish to endanger his village, which was still kept on the move, that always being the best plan in emergencies like this. The Blackfeet had told the Kootenais they would take revenge as they crossed the mountains, many Kootenais understanding the Blackfeet language.

After all this fighting, yelling and shooting I saw only thirty-five scalps. The Kootenais got all the Blackfeet robes and blankets which had been left in the draw, besides about fifty of their horses, which only replaced what they had lost by being shot or crippled up; the result showing the ineffectiveness of Blackfoot shooting, as the Kootenais lost only four killed and had only twenty wounded. To McKay and myself the fight seemed a failure, it appearing to us that the Kootenais were afraid to kill too many. When the fight commenced the Blackfeet appeared to lose their presence of mind, giving the Kootenais all advantage possible. If they had been determined and followed up their advantage they could have annihilated two-thirds of the Blackfeet, as the Kootenais outnumbered them one hundred warriors without counting McKay who placed at least ten Blackfeet to sleep; there were, however, a great many Blackfeet wounded who escaped.

I got McKay's wounds dressed, having plenty of material for that purpose, and also dressed the wounds of our horses. We then set about to catch our saddle mules and by the time we had gotten them, the Kootenais had their dead and wounded placed upon the travois. Young Black Bear had a close call from an arrow which split his left cheek open; another arrow went through the fleshy part of his breast. Indian-like, he felt proud of his two wounds. I saw him make two good Blackfeet and took pleasure in dressing his wounds and fixing his cheek up with court-plaster. McKay felt stiff and sore. I told him he was foolish to always get mixed up with enemies in a fight. "You will go under some of these times." I could not keep from laughing at him.

He looked at me in a comical manner, remarking "I am no more foolish than you, look at your horse bleeding." I replied to him that it was his fault, I had to get there to help him out, like a mother rushing to her baby to help it out of the fire. He informed me he had lost over half of his arrows and I told him to take the Blackfoot arrows. He said they were no account, "Points too short." I then informed him I had seen long-pointed ones with the Kootenais and would get him some, at which he seemed very much pleased. I thought so much of McKay I would have given the white mule for some arrows that suited him. At this time, we were in advance, moving along as usual before the attack. Riding upon a knoll and looking back upon the moving village I remarked to McKay that if a stranger were to meet us now, he would not be able to discover by any outward appearance that there had been an attack such a short time ago.

There was no danger of being attacked again that day. We were travelling a good five mile an hour gait, the Kootenais wishing to get to the base of the mountains, or as far as possible, since they felt sure the Blackfeet would reinforce and follow, Young Black Bear expressed this opinion while we were advancing and also said there was a good camp, water, grass and wood on ahead, where they could bury their slain. We reached this camp about 3 p.m. The Indian ponies were hungry, having nothing to eat since the day before. Our stock fortunately was all right, thanks to the squaws who had cut grass for them. Unpacking and setting up lodges was the order, every person assisting except about twenty young bucks, who were ordered to keep a good lookout from some knolls.

After the lodges were put up, a council was held by all the head men of the village, and in about half an hour we observed two well mounted young Indians leaving the village. I asked a chief where they were going. He replied, over the mountains to our country to get all the Kootenai young men they could find and send them to join us as soon as possible, upon the theory that plenty of Blackfeet would soon be here before we could cross the mountains. We approved of that measure of sending for reinforcements.

By sundown they had buried the dead and we engaged the squaws to cut grass and busied ourselves in constructing a strong corral. The Indians called me to examine some of their wounded, they having seen me dress McKay's wounds, they very likely thought I was a great medicine man. At all events I could excel them in dressing wounds. The post surgeon had packed me up the needful. After visiting all of the wounded and dressing their wounds, some of which were serious I returned to the chief's lodge. The horses were being driven in, and I saw to it that all our stock was put into the corral which we had constructed. The squaws had cut an abundance of grass, for which favour I had great difficulty in getting them to accept any pay.

By their actions it was manifest they were anxious to do everything in their power for both McKay and myself. I then examined the horses belonging to McKay and myself, and dressed their flesh wounds applying some liniment, and gave them some sugar and salt, which they were very fond of. All men who travel the prairies should teach their horses to eat sugar, as it makes them become attached to the one having them in charge. After this I was called into the lodge and found McKay lying on a pile of robes smoking and looking somewhat pleased. I asked him what pleased him and he replied the Indians had told him the Blackfeet would attack us again in crossing the mountains. "And you are pleased to think we shall be attacked again?"

"Yes," he replied, "I will have a chance to make them pay for some of these scratches."

I said "I should think you would be better pleased to think we would not be bothered any more by the Blackfeet, especially in your condition. A good place for you tomorrow, if we are attacked, would be among the pack animals. You will be stiff as a poker and if you hold on to your mule you will do well."

He replied "I will make 'Kickapoo' think he has never been in a fight before, if we are attacked tomorrow."

After supper I presented Black Bear the other keg of powder and two more sacks of half ounce balls, that being all we had which we could spare, and he called in his warriors and asked each how much ammunition they had and supplied those who had but little or none, and then took one of McKay's arrows and displaying it informed them I wished to trade for thirty like it. It was not over five minutes before the Indians brought in over forty laying them down by McKay whose features brightened up. They would not take any pay for them.

The chief prevailed on me not to stand guard that night, saying they had plenty of young men who would take good care of our stock and that they did not think the Blackfeet would be around, but for all that they were going to keep a lookout. They said further that, if possible, we must get on top of the mountains the following day, as our present camp was a dangerous one, though a good one in many respects. There was, however, a great difference of opinion among the chiefs, some thought it would be best to remain in this camp until they were reinforced.

They thought the couriers they had sent would be able to find from one hundred to one hundred and fifty warriors who would be able to get here in one or two days. This council in courtesy to McKay and myself was held in the sign language, so that we could understand the subject of the conversation; other chiefs thought it would be best to break camp early and get through the timber and canyon as soon as possible, before the Blackfeet became too numerous. We were then asked our opinion on the subject. McKay informed them I would speak for him, as he was no talker, but show him Blackfeet and he would speak.

The Indians all smiled and several of them got up and took him by the hand with a look of high regard that is not often expressed on the countenance of an Indian. As the matter was then referred to me, I first asked the chief how far it was from this camp to the Blackfeet villages which were situated on the Saskatchewan, and how many warriors they would be able to muster, and how soon they could get their warriors to this camp. Black Bear seemed well acquainted with the number of Blackfeet warriors and their method of transmitting signals calling for reinforcements in time of danger, and he replied that the Blackfeet Nation at that very moment had received notice of the fight of that day and also about where our village was in camp that night.

He said that the Blackfeet were their bitter enemies and that all the young men would mount good horses, leading their runners and take a short cut across the country to the place where we would encamp; that all the Blackfeet knew of this pass across the mountains and would not all come in one body, but would come in detached bodies according to where their villages might be. He thought they would be able by the night of the following day to have five or six hundred warriors on hand. Upon hearing these replies to my questions addressed to Black Bear I advised moving the village by sun-up and to get through the canyon and timber before we were outnumbered. If the position on the summit was as stated to us, we would be able to hold any number of Blackfeet at bay until our reinforcements could arrive.

Finally, the Indians agreed to move early in the morning. After having a medicine smoke and taking a look through the village with Black Bear to see that his young men were doing their duty and were keeping guard, we returned to our lodge and went to sleep. Nothing occurred during the night except two or three false alarms, but sufficient to bring forth all the warriors to ascertain what they meant.

The events of the 28th of October are not easily to be forgotten as the sequel will prove. By daylight the squaws had breakfast over. All the wounds of the injured had been dressed and the lodges torn down. One squaw assisted me in packing our animals as I could not allow McKay to assist because he was too stiff and sore. I saddled up his horse and mule and having got some yellow and red ochre and some white clay, painted both of our horses, I was determined that day if we were attacked that our horses should not receive more than their quota of arrows and lead, as it was evident the Blackfeet had a particular spite against McKay and myself and would do their utmost to down us both, if they got the opportunity.

In order to save our pack outfits, I had McKay fix up like an Indian which pleased the Kootenai warriors. A young buck assisted me in transforming myself into a Kootenai warrior. McKay swore I was the best-looking warrior in the village and many of the leading warriors were taken back at my appearance, making sign I was a Kootenai warrior and that the Blackfeet would not know me. It was just what I intended.

Any person who has had experience with Indians can see the wisdom of our transformation, both in respect to our horses and ourselves. At all events the Kootenais felt highly pleased and many squaws came and shook hands with us and smiled and then at once resumed their look of sadness. They were afraid of the Blackfeet, making sign "Blackfeet like grass", (many warriors was what that meant). I told them to cheer up and have strong hearts. They replied that they were not afraid of dying, but were concerned with reference to their little children and were afraid of their being taken prisoners, saying, "If Blackfeet come, we fear they will take them prisoners, as they did once in former years."

I informed Black Bear we wanted our stock animals in advance as it would avoid getting them tangled up among the lodge poles, they not being used to them, and to let two or three boys drive them. All being ready for starting I got McKay to ride the mule in order to save his horse, for I was aware if we were attacked, McKay would make good use of his horse and it was necessary he should be as fresh as possible. I mounted the white mule and about sixty of us took the advance, with myself and Young Black Bear in the lead. The trail being wide enough for two abreast, but rocky and somewhat steep in places.

Old Black Bear with a chosen band of warriors brought up the rear, the balance of the warriors being scattered along the trail amongst the pack animals in order to protect that part of the outfit if attacked. I tried hard to have the chief select some thirty or forty young warriors, nimble of foot, to scout on each side of the trail on foot, in order to discover any Blackfeet that might be concealed in the timber. But I could not prevail upon him to do so, he replying that the Blackfeet were afraid of timber and the Kootenais were their superiors in mountain warfare.

If the Utes or Bannacks had been in the place of the Blackfeet the Kootenais would have suffered a disastrous defeat, as they are superior mountain fighters. We continued up the canyon and through the timber to open country where McKay and I each mounted our war horses, turning the mules among the pack animals. We moved on in advance and saw no sign of Blackfeet as yet. I remarked to McKay that the Blackfeet were no generals to let such an opportunity as this pass without attacking us in the gorge through which our village was moving, travelling slowly, by reason of the wounded being placed upon the travois. Young Black Bear said he did not understand what the Blackfeet meant, as he felt sure they would attack us before we got over the mountains.

At that time about half of our outfit had got clear of the timber and we were in advance of our pack animals about three hundred yards on a small rise looking back at the advancing packs. We then discovered to the west of us some four hundred yards about fifty mounted Indians coming at a canter. In a short time about forty others afoot made their appearance. They all halted. I could tell by their actions they were somewhat taken by surprise at discovering us, it being manifest they had been sent to head us off before we got out of the timber. At this moment war yells came from the canyon and timber, shots following in rapid succession. If Mark Twain with his descriptive pen had been present, he could have written a volume at the pandemonium that broke loose—squaws screaming, *pappooses* howling, dogs barking, pack horses lunging madly about.

Indian warriors sending forth yell after yell intermingled with scattering shots. The Blackfeet, both mounted and afoot, came at us with a yell which would have made a sensitive person's hair stand on end. I asked McKay how he felt and advised him to keep in the rear. He replied, "yes you see Kickapoo in the rear will you." I saw he had his arrows and bow strung, a dangerous weapon in his hands as many a Blackfoot could attest. We met their charge, they acting foolishly and delivering their shots at too great distance, and before they could re-load, we were among them. Their footmen being close were throwing their arrows lively, wounding several Kootenai horses and also some of the Kootenai warriors.

We passed through the footmen and wheeled and then discovered several of the Blackfeet who were mounted had got to our pack animals. One tall Indian had mounted my white mule and was making off with him. That Indian must have been acquainted with the qualities of the mule as a saddle animal, or he would never have attempted to escape with him, although he had a fifty-dollar California saddle on him and a twenty-five-dollar bridle. But be that as it may, he must have known that whoever owned the outfit would make a desperate effort to recapture him.

When I saw the Indian making off with the outfit, he was some two hundred yards distant, heading for the timber on the opposite side, or north of the trail. If I wanted to recapture the mule there was no time to spare, as it was evident the timber be was making for contained other Blackfeet. I threw a cartridge into my gun, which I had just previously emptied and gave the word to Hickory, who seemed to understand that something was up. He fairly flew, and the Kootenais who saw him make the race all declared afterwards be "ran on top of the grass." The Indian saw me after him and applied the whip and heel vigorously.

No common horse could have overtaken him. I was soon fifty yards from the Indian, when he wheeled in the saddle, took aim with an old flint lock and fired. Hickory swerved to the right at exactly the right time and the ball went singing harmlessly by. Before the smoke from the Indian's gun had cleared or he could get an arrow to the bow I was alongside of him, and in less than three seconds be was calmly sleeping, and the mule on his way back to the outfit.

The Blackfeet had been reinforced and made another attempt to stampede our stock and pack animals. The Kootenai boys having them in charge were fighting like little imps. It was truly an amusing sight for anyone who has never witnessed a hostile Indian performance. It cannot be reproduced by any Wild West performance in its reality. I reloaded my two revolvers for I saw there was work to do yet. I was very glad when I saw McKay making Kickapoo fly around our pack animals, keeping them bunched and trying to keep the Blackfeet from getting away with any of them. I saw one of our pack horses fall and roll over downhill and another one with a broken leg.

It was now I saw McKay do an act which is seldom seen, *viz*: drive an arrow through an Indian's body. I joined him at this time saying, "Well done McKay", but was saddened to see that both he and Kickapoo were bleeding. There was no time, however, for comment, everything was in an uproar. As fortune would have it there were about forty Kootenais coming over the mountain, and at sight of what was going on they sent forth their war whoop with a will and were answered by the Kootenais still engaged with the Blackfeet. It evidently appeared to the Blackfeet that the reinforcements were many times greater than they really were, from the manner in which they were scattered out with the best horses in advance.

Accordingly, the Blackfeet were quick to take action and called all their warriors off and beat a retreat and got into the timber, taking a number of their wounded with them, and I know they got several of their dead into the timber also. There should have been ten times more Blackfeet killed than there were. The cause of so many being wounded on both sides was the mix-up among the pack animals. One of the young boys who was driving our pack animals was killed and two were wounded. Those little boys fought more bravely than many of the grown Indians.

Old Black Bear had got the rear of the outfit clear of the timber at last, and the Blackfeet had disappeared in the timber except those who were on the trail to the "Happy Hunting Ground", and from these, several of the Kootenais were making themselves busy taking scalps, instead of dashing to the rear and assisting the old chief. Leaving McKay with the packs, I went to the rear and tried hard to get the old chief to take some of his warriors, dismount and follow the Blackfeet into the timber, but he would not take my advice. As a matter of fact, one hundred and fifty warriors could have made the fight very disastrous for the Blackfeet at that time, as they were nearly out of ammunition, and I so informed Black Bear. I did, however, prevail upon him to leave about one hundred men at the edge of the timber until we could get the packs and wounded beyond range of any guns or arrows.

I then got back to McKay who was trying to get the pack off a dead pack horse; however, he was too weak to accomplish this, as he had lost much blood. I stopped the flow of blood and prevailed on him to sit down. Two squaws came up and soon had the pack off. In the meantime, I shot the pack animal with the broken leg and lassoing two quartermaster mules soon had the packs on them and in about a half an hour we had all things ready for a forward move. There were nine dead tied on pack horses and the wounded were placed upon their own horses.

An Indian will ride his horse until he falls dead, they are so tenacious of life. We had an example of this in the Indian that McKay shot the arrow through. He escaped with the blood streaming from him. It has always been a mystery to me how so much lead can be expended, either in civilized or Indian warfare with so little execution. Some have figured that it takes two hundred pounds of lead to place one man *hors de combat*. That rule, however, would not apply to this previous engagement, because I do not believe there was two hundred pounds of lead in the Kootenai village; but at all events, there should have been more execution for the amount of shooting.

I am well aware why so many were wounded in proportion to the slain. An Indian in a fight never stands still in an open place, but is constantly on the move, dodging from side to side, thus often avoiding a fatal shot. They are also experts in getting their wounded and slain off the field of battle and are also very tenacious of life. I have known Indians who were supposed to be dead, but when approached by their enemies would rise and attempt to shoot.

We got our outfit to the place designated for camp and in course of an hour the lodges were set up. My horse had received two bad flesh wounds by arrows. McKay's horse fared worse, but was not in a dangerous condition. Having dressed their wounds and stopped the flow of blood, we turned them loose. Three of the quartermaster mules had arrow wounds, one somewhat serious, but we saved him.

I next turned my attention to McKay who was reclining on a pile of robes placed there by the squaws, one of whom had placed water by his side. When I entered the lodge, he held out his hand with that peculiar smile of his when he was pleased. I asked him what he was pleased about, was it because he had been cut to pieces with arrows, or what? "No," he replied, "I am pleased to see you come out of this scrape all right. Your medicine is stronger than mine. I saw that arrow strike in your gun stock. That was a close call and made me savage."

I soon had his wounds dressed and placed him in easy position and set the squaws to cooking and making some tea. I was kept busy for two hours going around dressing wounds. Their medicine men got the order to stand back. They appeared to think McKay and myself were invincible and that I was a great medicine man in dressing wounds. It took the remainder of the day to repair all the damage done and bury the dead. The Blackfeet had got away with a few of the Kootenais' loose ponies, but no pack horses. What horses were captured from the Blackfeet made the Kootenais about even.

Take it all in all, the Kootenais had a right to congratulate themselves at the outcome of the fight, for if the Blackfeet had got to timber at the head of the canyon before the advance had reached the open country the result would have been much more disastrous to the Kootenais, although it is possible the Blackfeet might have sustained a heavier loss than they did. Neither had the Blackfeet been reinforced to the extent the Kootenais gave them credit for. I do not think there were over three hundred and fifty Blackfeet, though the Kootenais magnified them to twice that number. This is invariably the case with Indians.

Small bands of Kootenai warriors kept arriving as reinforcements, and went galloping over the battlefield mutilating the dead Blackfeet and picking up arrows and other things that had been dropped in the *mêlée*. The village presented a conflicting scene. Some were crying and making all kinds of diabolical noises, while others were going through the village sending forth yell after yell, and the scalp dance was in progress, while the principal head men were holding solemn council in Black Bear's lodge.

As the chiefs assembled one after the other, they stepped up to McKay and myself shaking us by the hand and calling us chiefs in sign. I informed them that we were not chiefs, but if I had had fifty men equal to McKay in the late muss, they might have called us chiefs, for I was sure many more of the dusky Blackfeet maidens would have mourned the absence of their lovers. The opening of council was commenced by thus complimenting us. I stopped that by informing them it was they who were protecting us and that we simply fought the Blackfeet to protect our packs and to keep our scalps, saying that there was no question that we should have lost both if it had not been for the Kootenais.

This complimentary allusion to them appeared to please them and they asked if we thought the Blackfeet would make an attack upon our present camp. I was somewhat astonished at that question, since they were aware we were strangers in this section of the country and also strangers to the Blackfeet, and I answered that they were the ones who should be the judges as to the movements or possible intentions of this enemy. We could see there were conflicting opinions among them as to the Blackfeet attacking this camp; there was one opinion in which they concurred and that was to move the village early in the morning, as they felt sure the Blackfeet would make another attack, and the sooner they got to Tobacco Plains the better it would be, as they would then be able to concentrate and collect all of the outlying Kootenai camps.

They informed us that the Blackfeet outnumbered them in warriors fully three to one, providing they were all collected together, which seldom if ever occurred, as they were usually scattered over hundreds of miles. We were not molested in this camp, the night passing off without anything worthy of note.

The morning of the 29th was cloudy and looked very much like snow. The sooner we could get clear of the mountains the better it would be for the wounded. I so informed the chiefs and they gave the orders to down the lodges and to pack up as soon as possible. I had dressed McKay's wounds by the time the Indians were ready to move. He was feeling somewhat sore. With the assistance of two squaws, I got our outfits packed up. The Indians brought two good pack ponies to replace the ones we had lost. They said "Pack these ponies, they are yours." I at last got McKay mounted on his mule, and felt very much pleased to know that I still had the white mule. I had become attached to him and he to me, for he began to want his sugar every time I approached him.

The Kootenais being reinforced by about one hundred warriors, the chiefs ordered them in advance to scout both sides of the trail. Young Black Bear with about thirty warriors preceded the advance packs a short distance, our packs being in the lead and boys driving them. Old Black Bear with one hundred picked warriors was bringing up the rear, the remainder of the warriors assisting the squaws with the wounded.

We reached the summit of the mountains when it commenced to

snow. Very fortunately I had provided McKay with a heavy blanket and he sat on his mule as stoically as an old Greek in the midst of pain and danger. We arrived at the base of the mountains when it ceased snowing and at last got to a creek where there was a small prairie; unpacked and set up lodges as soon as possible, with everything secure, stock turned loose attended by a strong guard. About twenty-five young warriors were ordered to keep a good lookout in the rear, as Blackfeet pay no attention to storms, stormy weather being their favourite time to attack or make a raid upon those they are at war with.

The chiefs dispatched two of the young men with robes to the Hudson Bay trading post, which was situated on the north side of Tobacco Plains, to trade for powder and lead, as they were almost out of those commodities, we having given them the last we had to spare. I was kept busy until a late hour going among the different lodges and attending to the wounded. Among the wounded were six squaws, who would not let their medicine men touch them. It would have been amusing to any outside intelligent man to observe what deep interest those squaws and bucks manifested in my manipulation of salves, lint and court plaster applied to their wounds, with a show of confidence in their infallibility equal to that of an old practitioner.

At all events they thought I was superior to any of their medicine men. I afterwards found out that when some of the squaws told Mc-Kay what a great doctor I was, that he informed them I was following a wrong calling in spending my time scouting, and that doctoring was my forte. McKay, of course was very grateful for my assistance to him, for among other services I got him to partake of an abundance of sweet sago tea, which induced him to sleep and to perspire freely during the night; and I informed the chiefs they had better notify all their people to cease making any noise, as it annoyed the wounded and they must be allowed to sleep if possible.

In a short time, the village was quiet, the stock having been driven in and secured and a strong guard placed about the village. Young Black Bear took our shot gun saying, "You sleep, I will watch your stock." I felt I could trust him and after a smoke with the chief turned in and slept until daylight, nothing occurring during the night to disturb the village.

The 30th of October was heralded by a frosty morning. To my great delight I found McKay much better. I dressed his wounds and visited several of the wounded Indians, endeavouring to encourage them by the information that they would be all right in a few days.

After breakfast the sun broke out, which was cheering to the sick and wounded, and by nine o'clock we had everything ready for a forward move. As heretofore, our packs were placed in the advance. We had a few miles of timber to go through and the scouts were sent on ahead and on both flanks, Black Bear bringing up the rear with a numerous band of warriors. In good time we arrived on the south side of Tobacco Plains, where a beautiful location was selected by a small lake and a good spring of water.

In a short time, the lodges were up and as outside bands of Kootenais, who were summoned, commenced to arrive, things looked more cheerful. My greatest desire now was to reach Walla Walla without any further danger of losing our outfits. The two Kootenais who had been sent to the trading post returned with a good supply of ammunition, which was cheering to those who were out of powder and ball. The afternoon passed by with the young bucks and squaws singing and dancing their scalp dance, which was kept up until a late hour. The chiefs and headmen held solemn council as to what the Blackfeet were likely to do. They did not all agree by any means as to the probable action they would take.

I will here state for the benefit of those who are not acquainted with Indians: It is characteristic of Indians when they are the aggressors and suffer defeat to deem it their right and duty to revenge their defeat, and make up what loss they have sustained, and that not to do so is cowardly. The idea of their having provoked the fight and being in the wrong is farthest from their thoughts, and they think that the ones who inflicted the loss are the ones to blame, though they themselves were the aggressors. So, it is with all tribes with which I have mingled. I have conversed with very intelligent gentlemen on this subject, and they admit they cannot conceive how an Indian can hold the attacked party guilty of the offence.

They finally decided they would move their village to the Catholic Mission, which was situated on the southwest side of Tobacco Plains, on the banks of the Kootenai River. I was engaged until late that evening in attending to the wounded and getting our horses in good condition for active service, and the night passed off without any disturbance.

I was up early on the 31st attending to the wounded and found McKay improving rapidly. All being ready for the move our outfit, as usual, was in the advance, and traversing an open country we arrived at the Mission early and selected a favourable place for the village. The lodges were set up in a circle, leaving an abundance of room inside the circle for all the stock, this being a favourite mode of locating the lodges in order to protect the ponies from enemies; for the chiefs were positive the Blackfeet would pay them a visit at this place with additional reinforcements, within four or five days.

The Kootenais sent out runners to bring in all outside hunting bands, so as to be prepared to meet them in the event of their coming. We still remained guests of Black Bear, he would not listen to us putting up our own tent. As a matter of fact, we had used up the last of our sugar, and our provisions generally were consumed. We had, however, an abundance of *pemican*, buffalo tongues and dried meat, so there was no danger of us suffering for the necessaries of life. I was still busy doctoring and getting our things in shape.

Some of our friends have suggested that we should have pulled out here and left the Kootenais, but I think that would have been a cowardly thing to do. After being treated so hospitably by them, we were certainly under obligations to them. It is a matter of great doubt whether we could have got clear of the Blackfeet with our pack outfit without their assistance, and I have no idea that either McKay or myself would have ever returned to the fort at Walla Walla and reported empty handed.

There was also another incentive for our remaining, we had not forgotten the contemptible manner in which we had been treated by the Blackfeet and we both had an inward hatred against them. Even today I have not got over it. By reason of the above considerations, we concluded to remain and take our chances with our benefactors.

The Kootenais set the squaws to work digging rifle pits around the village, they understanding the advantage of having rifle pits as well as the whites. In this they showed great skill, for they were careful in having them dug, if possible, where they could get a cross fire upon the approaching enemy. While the squaws dug, the young people sang and danced, the older ones smoking and looking on. That night a strong guard was placed around the village and nothing unusual occurred during the night.

November 1st, fifty young warriors, well mounted, were dispatched to scour the surrounding country and ordered not to return until sundown, unless Blackfeet were discovered. I informed the chief I would pay a visit to the trading post, as I wished to buy some groceries, and he replied that Young Black Bear would go with me, and giving some orders to an Indian, three good ponies were soon brought in for our use, they not allowing us to use our own stock. The distance to the post was about six miles, it being situated about one-fourth mile north of the boundary line afterwards established, which was disappointing to the Hudson Bay Company, as they thought the whole of Tobacco Plains was north of the line.

I and Linklighter, the trader, had a dispute about where the line would be, he claiming the whole country as Hudson Bay territory, and I claiming the whole of Tobacco Plains for Uncle Sam. Neither of us at that time knew what we were talking about, for the line as run divided the Plain about equally. The trader after all was a good sort of a Scot, but had been educated to think Mr. John Bull had a lease upon all of North America. Upon entering the store, I threw down a double Eagle and he asked me how much that was. Answering, I informed him. He remarked that he would keep the coin himself, saying they were not allowed to trade for money, but for furs only.

As everything was high in those days, I did not expect to get very much for my money, and was pleased to see that "Scotty" put up everything called for in the list, which I handed him, at Walla Walla prices. He made me a present of a quart of Hudson Bay rum as thick as cream. Scotty called his assistant, informing him that he was going to pay the village a visit and requested him to put up sufficient provisions for a great feast. By the time the provisions were packed he had his horse ready and by 2 p. m. we arrived at the village. The trader unloading his pack informed the chiefs he had brought provisions for a feast. This was a good thing for us, for it enabled us to keep more of our provisions until we should finally start on our trip home.

The squaws set to cooking and in a couple of hours the feast being ready there was a general gathering to the chief's lodge. Hides were spread outside for persons of smaller estate, while the chiefs, McKay, Scotty and myself were being entertained on the inside. After the feast, the chiefs held council with Scotty, while I went around among the wounded and attended to our horses. Kickapoo had some bad cuts. The wounded horses appeared to have almost human intelligence, for while dressing their wounds they would stand perfectly still without being tied.

Scotty looked over the wounded in the village and finally came up to where I was doctoring the horses remarking, "You had a glorious fight, I wish I could have been there." I informed him that the chiefs were looking for another attack and that he would have abundant opportunity; that I wanted to see what the descendant of Bruce would do in Indian warfare. He smiled good naturedly, saying, "I will try to be here when the Blackfeet come."

The scouts returned at sundown and reported having seen signals (smoke) on the summit of the mountains, a true indication that the Blackfeet were collecting their warriors for another trial of arms and that to occur inside of three days. I was in hopes they would delay the attack that long at least, on account of our horses and McKay, who was somewhat sore and stiff. For I knew if the attack had been made that day McKay would have mounted Kickapoo and gone into the fight, which likely would have proven fatal to both him and his horse.

The evening passed off in conversing about the Blackfeet and the number of warriors they might bring, the entire Tobacco Plains being their ancient battlefield, and nothing disturbed the village during the night.

On the morning of the second, the scouts were sent out before the stock was turned loose and in course of half an hour a few scouts reported no sign of Blackfeet. I noticed, however, that the Kootenais kept about two hundred of their best horses picketed and ready for use at a moment's warning. We felt easy on account of our own horses, because of the manner in which they were herded, nor did I think that the Blackfeet would attack the village that day; for before they would make an attack, they would try to ascertain what number of lodges the Kootenais had collected and gain information with reference to the forces which they intended to assail.

I talked about this to the chiefs and advised that their young men must keep a good lookout that night, as the moon rose about midnight and the Blackfeet were credited with being experts in approaching a village and ascertaining its location for defence in case of an attack, and the number of warriors, etc. I got the squaws to cut grass for our two horses. My horse was all right and McKay's rapidly improving. Coming upon him unobserved I caught him counting his arrows. I afterwards asked the chief to buy me forty long pointed arrows, and in a short time he brought in fifty good ones, for which he refused to take any pay. After supper I went around among the different lodges dressing wounds, while the chiefs were busy placing the pickets. I saw that they had located one picket by our horses and we let him have our shotgun. Contrary to expectation we were not disturbed during the night.

On the third, a repetition largely of the previous day. Signals discovered, but no sign of Blackfeet. The trader came over from the post and paid us a visit and upon being informed by the chiefs that they thought the Blackfeet would be there the next day, he replied that he would try and be here in the morning. That night all of the stock was brought in and pickets were placed and rifle-pits occupied. I got the squaws to make us a small corral inside of the circle and to get plenty of grass for our two horses.

I also gave McKay those fifty arrows, and he examined them carefully and with great satisfaction before placing them in his quiver. Some of the Kootenais observed him closely and after he put the arrows away, they took him by the hand with a smile. After dressing McKay's wounds, I turned in, but slept lightly, being ready to reinforce pickets at a moment's notice. At about one o'clock there were several shots fired and in a moment all the warriors dashed out of the lodges and joined the pickets, but as everything remained quiet, I got McKay back into the lodge as soon as possible, informing him not to go outside again, as in his weak condition it might result fatally. No further annoyance during the night.

On the morning of the 4th the Kootenais picked up two wolf skins, which had been dropped by the Blackfeet, a tantalising sign that they had been close by and also that an attack by them was close at hand, to a certainty not to be delayed over forty-eight hours. It appeared to me the Kootenais were showing the effect of the constant strain upon their mental faculties in expecting an attack which did not take place as soon as expected. To me it seemed that this delay ought to be favourable to the Kootenais, as several of their bravest warriors were wounded and were rapidly recovering and if an attack were delayed for another day most of them would be in a condition to take a hand in the conflict.

I told the Kootenais the Blackfeet were fools or they would have attacked this camp two days since. About two hundred mounted Kootenais scouted some distance before the stock was turned loose, I keeping the horses up for McKay and myself, getting the squaws to cut grass for them. After a while Scotty, the trader, came leading his warhorse, as he called him, a small pony, but as I afterwards found a good runner, he could run like an antelope. Scotty was disappointed during the day that the Blackfeet did not make their appearance, though the scouts reported numerous signs.

The Kootenai chief believed the Blackfeet were making medicine when and how to attack this village, etc. I asked the chiefs when was the favourite time of attack on the part of the Blackfeet, and they replied at break of day, but they would attack if opportunity was favourable in the daytime. I then expressed the opinion to the chiefs that before the sun set on the morrow the Blackfeet would attack them and for them to be prepared and to see that every Kootenai who had a gun had plenty of ammunition also bows and arrows in fighting trim. McKay had been informing the Indians that day that they should listen to me as I was a great general and a wonderful medicine man, and the Indians certainly seemed to treat me and all my counsel as if they believed everything he said.

I prevailed upon Scotty to remain overnight, as he would probably have an opportunity of gratifying some of his hair lifting propensities on the following day. The night passed off without our being molested. On the morning of the 5th scouts were out early and reported plenty of Blackfeet signs. The stock was turned loose, but with a strong guard. We kept up our two horses, and our two saddle mules, having the squaws cut plenty of grass. I put on the fighting rigging upon my horse and McKay's, and McKay came out of the lodge armed at all points and painted up with some eagle feathers fastened in his hair. The Indians yelled with approval at his appearance.

I felt inwardly pleased to see him step proudly up to Kickapoo and pat him on the neck and ask him how he felt. I afterwards told Scotty if he intended to take a hand in the fight that he had better borrow an Indian rig, and went into the lodge myself and got out my regular rig and was soon transformed from a buckskin mountaineer to what McKay called a splendid Indian. The trader expressed great surprise at the change in appearance and I advised him at once to make a complete change if he wanted an even show with the Blackfeet. I got the Kootenais to paint several of their horses, we painting ours in like manner.

Several young warriors mounted on the swiftest ponies had been sent out to scout along the border of timber and examine some draws or narrow depressions. They had been gone about an hour when three young bucks were seen approaching on full run, making sign "Blackfeet." The chief ordered all stock brought in and made secure, which was done in short order. Indians are quicker at that than the average white man. Inside of five minutes fully three hundred mounted warriors were ready to go to the front. The chief was having a hard time to keep a sufficient number back to protect the village.

Young Black Bear with about a hundred warriors, McKay, Scotty and myself took the advance and opened the ball and to learn their strength. We had not proceeded a half a mile when about one hundred

Blackfeet came out of a neck of timber, shouting their war whoop and sending some lead at us. But as they were distant about four hundred yards, the range was too far for damage. We charged them and they beat a rapid retreat to a small grove some six hundred yards to the rear. We got within two hundred yards of them when they entered this grove. The Kootenais halted, wheeled and beat a retreat some two hundred yards. The reason of this counter-move being that the grove was full of other Blackfeet and a deep, narrow draw to the left was also crowded with them. When we retreated, they sent forth yell after yell of derision, at which the young Kootenais sent back a yell of defiance.

We circled around the Blackfeet at a safe distance to study the condition of affairs. I asked Scotty what he thought of matters and what would be the proper thing to do to get the Blackfeet out of their stronghold. "Do as my ancestors used to do. Charge them!" said he.

"Yes," I replied, "and meet about three hundred leaden messengers, which would empty many a saddle. This is no broad sword and battle axe fight Scotty, I am thinking there is a way to make matters more even. If we cannot dislodge them in any other way than by charging, many of our friends will be paying a visit to their future home, and you and I might be in their company."

McKay was eyeing the Blackfeet with a stern look. Nothing would have been more to his taste than to charge them. I asked McKay what he thought of the state of affairs, and he replied, "Scotty right, get among them."

I then said to him: "Are you acquainted with a handsome half-breed lady and two beautiful little children in Walla Walla, if so you had better be thinking of something else besides charging those Blackfeet in that position of advantage."

After this short interview among ourselves we joined the main body of the Kootenais who were holding a council of war, while several of the young bucks were skirmishing and exchanging shots with the Blackfeet at long range. The Kootenais were not so shrewd as I had given them credit for in counteracting their enemies, this being their home and they having collected all their forces. On the other hand, the Blackfeet had come considerable distance, besides crossing a rugged trail over the Rocky Mountains. In case they suffered a defeat and were pursued energetically by the Kootenais the rout would be disastrous to them.

All this I interpreted to the chiefs in council, they hanging down their heads, as if in deep thought. Black Bear asked Scotty to speak. He replied he had come to fight, not to talk, that the Blackfeet were there, why not fight them. They next asked McKay what his counsel was. He replied that half of the Kootenais should dismount, that the footmen should charge the grove and the mounted warriors charge the draw, and thus get through with the fight. He said this in sign, almost in a savage manner. They asked my advice, I being the last, as each chief and head warrior had previously given in his opinion.

I told them that as there was a light breeze which was favorable and as the grass was dry, to burn or smoke out the Blackfeet from their stronghold; that they should bring up fifty or sixty squaws with wet blankets to put out the fire when the Blackfeet were routed. At the suggestion of this method many of the leading men brightened up, some of the Indians approving my measure and others opposing it, but finally it was adopted. In a short time, the squaws arrived looking very comical I thought coming to fight the Blackfeet with wet blankets. A cluster of Blackfeet showed themselves and quick as a flash Mc's rifle spoke out and an Indian was seen to fall.

The Kootenais sent forth a gratifying yell and the Blackfeet returned several shots and in the meanwhile got out of sight. About fifty bucks crawled within twenty-five yards of the Blackfeet, forming a half circle on the windward side of them, we maintaining our shots upon them while the Kootenais got the fires started. In a few moments, the grass being very dry, the fire swept toward the Blackfeet. Now was the time for the Kootenais to take action and it seemed they were letting the opportunity pass, as the Blackfeet who were afoot would beat a retreat as soon as the fire was started, the grove and smoke screening them from us. I tried every way possible to have the Kootenais charge on two sides as the Blackfeet retreated.

They would not move, however, until the fire had got to the grove, McKay calling them "cowards" in English, which might just as well have been in Dutch. As soon as the fire was fairly started the Blackfeet sent forth a yell, which seemed to me like a yell of despair. I had heard many an Indian yell, but none to equal that. The Blackfeet had planned everything with a shrewdness, both in selection of ground and in their decoys, that I had not given them credit for, and if they had been more deliberate and accurate in their aim when we wheeled from the chase of the decoys, many of us would have gone down.

As it was, there were only a few ponies injured. When the fire reached the grove, we decided upon charging upon each side of the draw and grove, but when clear of smoke we discovered the Blackfeet in full retreat, making for the timber some half mile distant. The Blackfeet footmen numbered about a hundred, and were making better time than I ever saw before. Now was the time for the Kootenais to prove the superior speed of their ponies over the ponies of the Blackfeet, and overtake them before they got to the timber, the opposing forces mounted being about equal. It was amusing to see Scotty trying to keep in front on his little pony, and if he had been more of an expert rider his little charger would have been up with the Kootenais.

We were gaining rapidly on the Blackfeet, they knocking the wind out of their ponies and applying their whips vigorously. I kept close to McKay, it being all I could do to keep him from letting Kickapoo out and getting mixed up with the Blackfeet. As it was, we were fifty yards ahead of the Kootenais. Our two horses could have overtaken the Blackfeet in half the distance we had come. It appeared to me the Blackfeet were panic stricken. They were wheeling in their saddles, firing at random and then swerving from right to left. We crossed in and passed through them some two hundred yards from the timber, the Blackfeet scattering in every direction. We wheeled at the edge of the timber. My revolvers being empty I next emptied my derringers; the only time I ever used them. McKay got another wound in the cheek by a glancing arrow, which bled freely. I accordingly got him away some distance from the timber, informing him he had done enough in this scrap, and to let the Kootenais finish the fight.

I will here state on behalf of the white man, that when properly handled, he is the superior of any of these red men in fighting. I am acquainted with fifty trappers and know if they had been in this skirmish, that fully half of the Blackfeet would never have returned to their country. The heroic Spartan-like bravery accredited to the red man by the novelist exists only in fancy. Some may ask what about McKay, and I would reply that he was half Scotch, and had been with Mountain men from his infancy. Here was an illustration characteristic of Indians in general. In our presence were a few Blackfeet, who had met a warrior's fate, being mutilated by several able-bodied Kootenai warriors who had no hand in putting them to sleep. I made sign to the Kootenais "Stop that and get after the Blackfeet", and their only answer was "hold on."

About this time Scotty joined us leading his pony, both he and his horse limping, Scotty had an arrow stuck through the fleshy part of his thigh. I cut the feather end of the arrow off and taking hold of the point end, got McKay by sign to draw Scotty's attention, and I then jerked the arrow out of his thigh and bound the wound, stopping the flow of blood. He really felt proud of his wound and informed us he shot three times at close quarters at the Blackfeet, but they did not fall, McKay asked him if he put a ball in his gun.

The Kootenais had lost three men and the squaws were carrying them to the village; many wounded were also returning. Yells and shouting could be heard in the timber, but there was not much danger of any great damage being done now on either side. The fire brigade of squaws had been reinforced and when we arrived at the grove the fire was nearly extinguished. Three Blackfeet were found burned in the grove, and the Kootenais cut them up. Arriving at the village I redressed McKay's wounds and also the wound on his horse, the latter fortunately escaping any serious damage.

I also dressed Scotty's wound. He pressed us to remain with him a week or two, but we declined, it being time for us to return to Walla Walla and report. I informed McKay we must have no more foolishness now, but must get back if possible, with our outfits, and as we had some half hostile Indians to pass through, we must save what ammunition we had left for emergencies.

The Kootenais all returned by sundown, showing us a few scalps, they had taken in the timber and assuring us that these scalps belonged to great warriors. I was satisfied, however, that these scalps were taken from some wounded Blackfeet who could not keep up with the main body on the retreat. But of course, I gave the Kootenais credit for driving them out of the country.

If the Blackfeet had had any idea of the Kootenais setting the grass afire they would not have selected the grove and draw for the battle ground. Indians are careful in not setting fire to grass in the close vicinity of their villages, and the Blackfeet had no thought of fire being set out and afterwards extinguished by the squaws and their wet blankets. It is not a difficult undertaking to checkmate or circumvent Indian strategy in war or plan of battle, provided a person has had experience in Indian warfare.

I was kept busy until a late hour dressing wounds, the Indians keeping up a continuous uproar most of the night, some wailing, some singing and dancing and others beating the Indian drum. The stock being secured a few guards were placed around the village. We at last retired, McKay falling asleep, which he stood greatly in need of, as he was still weak from loss of blood and had exerted himself too much that day. The night passed without disturbance.

On the morning of the 6th, at break of day, the scouts who were sent out discovered no signs of Blackfeet and accordingly the stock was turned out with guards attending, as there might be a few Blackfeet with more nerve than the others who might try to get some of the Kootenai ponies. After breakfast was over, I attended the wounded and then notified the Kootenai chiefs that we should leave them in the morning early, as we had to get to Walla Walla as soon as possible. As Scotty departed for his trading post, he made me promise to pay him a visit at some future time. The squaws had rigged up a travois to take him home, his thigh being very stiff and sore.

After Scotty had gone, we opened our packs, having some little trading truck left. I notified the chiefs we would like to trade for marten and fisher skins, this being a great fur country, and these furs being held in high esteem and very costly. The chiefs "harangued" the camp, notifying the Indians what we wanted. And in a short time, the Indians who had been collecting furs came in bringing many prime skins and we traded for one hundred and ten furs. We could have got twice that number if we had had goods. I informed McKay I would certainly have a hand in this fur trade in the near future to the detriment of the Hudson Bay Company. Before closing our packs, we put a few things, which were left, aside as presents for the chiefs, which pleased them highly.

After the midday meal the chiefs retired to another lodge and I went to work remodelling and trimming our packs. We had two hundred and twenty-five prime robes, besides the furs, and were well aware these would be worth money if we once could get them to Walla Walla. By the time I had completed my work, Black Bear called me outside and presented me with a medium sized mule, well saddled and with twelve good robes on his back. The chief said they would have given more good robes but had no more good ones dressed. I informed him we had nothing to give in return and he assured us that we had given plenty.

I then called McKay, asking him to bring the shotgun and all the ammunition to it and asked him to present it to the chief, which he did, the chief being highly pleased. I then engaged the squaws to cut sufficient grass for all our stock, as we intended to start early the following morning. The evening passed very pleasantly in talking and smoking with the Indians. On the 7th we had breakfast by daylight and by eight o'clock were packed, the Indians assembling to bid us good bye. McKay and myself had put on our rough buckskin suits, the Indians thinking the transformation wonderful, having seen us now in three different dresses. The chief sent two young bucks to put us on the nearest route to Lake Pend d'Oreille. Before starting they marked out a map, indicating the route we should take to reach the lower end of this lake, and when once there we would be at home, so far as knowing the country was concerned.

As a general thing the trail from Tobacco Plains to the lower end of the lake was a hard one, through timber most of the way. But as our animals were in prime condition, we were able to make good time. It took us six days to reach the lower end of the lake. An acquaintance of McKay's was camped there, George Montour. He was there for the purpose of trading, having a few goods. We were detained here two days by stormy weather. George posted us as to the whereabouts of the Spokane and Palouse Indians. We intended to avoid their villages, if possible, by passing them in the night.

On the morning of the 16th the sky cleared, the sun making things more pleasant by drying things out. I gave George twenty dollars to place everything we had safely across the river, which he did by 10 o'clock a. m. After the horses got dry, we packed up and made a short drive and camped. On the 17th we camped within three miles of Spokane Plains in the timber, about 3 o'clock in the afternoon. There was a small prairie near us with good grass and water, which was greatly ill our favour, as we intended to make a sixty- or seventy-mile drive from this place before making another camp, in order to get clear of the Spokane and Palouse Indians. We both of us understood that if we were molested in any way that we would have to resist them and run the risk of bringing on a general fight with these tribes.

Everything, however, favoured us, the moon rising about 9 o'clock in the evening and the weather being clear and frosty. A little while before the moon rose, we put the rigging on our horses, so as to be ready for any emergency and by eight o'clock p. m. the packs being all adjusted, we started. As McKay was better acquainted with the route we intended to take, having travelled it many times, I told him to take the lead. In a short time, we got clear of the timber and made a detour of some two miles to avoid an Indian village. We could plainly hear the Indian drums, and getting by them unnoticed got across the Spokane River without any difficulty.

After going about two miles further we tightened all the packs. Up to this time we had been travelling easy, in order to make as little noise as possible, but from now on until daylight we travelled a good six or seven miles an hour, passing Otter Lake at daylight. After fording the Palouse River, we proceeded some two miles and saw five Indians coming mounted, at a distance of about half a mile to the left of us. We mounted our war horses in short order and at once discerned that they were Palouse Indians. They saw by our actions that we were prepared for either peace or war. We let them approach within one hundred and fifty yards and halted them. They took offence at this and called us "fools" in sign, which stirred up McKay somewhat; in fact so much so that he would have opened fire on them if I had not restrained him.

I informed him that it would not do, unless they made clear demonstrations of being hostile. They recognised both of us and wished to examine our outfit. We replied in sign "No, go on about your business". They then attempted to divide so as to approach us from two sides, but we brought our guns to bear upon them and motioned them to keep together and go away. McKay could speak considerable of their language and I told him to tell them to leave quick, or I would arrest them and take them back to Walla Walla. They consulted together for a moment, then wheeled and left.

We then tightened the packs again and resumed our journey. McKay informed me that he knew of a small Camas prairie, where at this season of the year we might find Nez Perces, but that it would be two or three miles out of our way to go there. As this tribe was friendly, I told him to make a bee line for the prairie. We then remounted our mules, saving our horses for any emergencies, and struck out at a lively gait and at 2 p. m., while crossing a low divide we came in sight of the prairie and twenty-five lodges. It was a village of Lawyer's a Nez Perce chief. Both of us were well acquainted with him, and the squaws soon had our outfits unpacked and stored in a lodge; the stock was then turned out, none of them appearing much the worse for over eighteen hours travel.

The Nez Perces were glad to see us safely back. They had all heard of our going to the Blackfeet country and doubted much our ability of bringing back any of our outfit. The chief informed us there had been no news of us since we left the St. Joseph Mission. He also informed us it was good we arrived at this village that day, for on the following day they were going to the mouth of Clearwater. This was the route we intended to take and we would travel together. It was most comical to see the Nez Perces when McKay informed them about the five Palouse Indians whom I was going to arrest if they did not leave immediately.

This threat perhaps was somewhat cheeky, but not so much so as it might appear, since they were aware we were employed by the army as scouts. When you are in contact with Indians, placed in a similar position to ours, assume high importance and bluff big, and the chances are you will get away with it nine times out of ten.

McKay could speak Nez Perce like a native and they kept him busy answering questions. He had a few scalps (Blackfeet) and they created a pleasant furore among the Indians surrounding us, who were the enemies of the Blackfeet. McKay informed the Indians that I had taken those scalps and given them to him and had also given a number to the Kootenais. On the other hand, I informed the chief in answer to his inquiry that McKay had taken all the scalps, and he then smiled and took us both by the hand. That night we retired early, the Indians taking care of our stock and there being no danger.

On the morning of the 19th, we were off by 9 o'clock, feeling much at home now, as there was no danger to be apprehended, except in crossing our outfit in canoes over Snake River. I asked the chief before starting if he had any good canoes, and he informed us that the best place to cross would be below the Clearwater and that he would go with us and see that we got across. On the 20th at 2 p. m., we reached the crossing place and by 4 o'clock had everything over safely, thanks to the chief, who told the Indians not to lose a thing, or he would make them pay for it. I paid the Indians ten dollars, the chief saying it was too much.

We arrived at Walla Walla at 7 o'clock p.m., of the 22nd., and unpacked at my quarters. In a few moments our arrival was rumoured over the quarters. The quartermaster made his appearance and ordered our stock put into his corral. I then paid my respects to the commanding officer, who appeared glad to see us back. After answering a few questions in reply to his inquiries he requested me to report at ten o'clock on the following morning. I then returned to my quarters and found that McKay had supper ready, and had the table adorned with all kinds of fancy cakes, which had been brought in by the orderly, from the ladies of the post.

As McKay was anxious to pay a visit to his family that lived five miles from the post, I put up a lot of cake in a convenient package, together with some buffalo tongues in a sack, and forced him to take them to his home. I asked him to be back early in the morning and bring his family.

Col. Vaughan, the agent of the Piegans, had furnished me with an abstract statement of the disposition and condition of the different bands of Indians in his jurisdiction and I used this as a part of my report and was able to complete it by eleven o'clock that night. I had to lock the door and notify callers that I was too busy to be interviewed and would see them in the morning. That night as my nerves were relaxed, I slept soundly.

On the morning of the 23rd I was up early, dressed in my Sunday buckskin suit and breakfasted with the quartermaster. As several ladies were present, I was kept busy answering questions until nearly time to report. McKay had brought in his family and I had assigned them to my quarters until after I had returned from my interview with the officers. Promptly at ten o'clock I reported at headquarters, the room being full of officers and their families. I felt highly complimented by the greeting extended to me by these officers and their ladies. I made a full report of our experiences and delivered over the statement received from the Indian Agent. After answering all questions, I departed to look after my affairs.

The first thing I did was to settle matters with McKay. He had reported for duty and had got a thirty day's furlough, which he truly merited. Taking him with me to the stable, I had him take all the Indian ponies and saddles we had brought and also his two mules and then opening our packs told him to take what he wanted. The bashful man did not want to take those twelve robes, but I made him take them and I had to force him to let his family take each a garnished robe and six marten skins. I then put twenty-five tongues in a sack for his wife.

After this, Col. Wright and his matronly wife, whom every person at the post worshiped, accompanied by a number of officers' wives made me a visit. I had put aside twenty-five prime marten and ten fisher skins and also four fancy robes for the quartermaster. I then got a large tarpaulin from the quartermaster and had all the robes, furs, tongues, etc. spread out so the ladies could see the whole collection and invited Col. Wright and his lady to make a selection of what they desired, but as they declined, saying that the danger had been too great in getting them for me to give them away, I selected four of the most beautiful robes and two dozen fine furs and presented them to Mrs. Wright with my compliments and asked the orderly to take them to Col. Wright's quarters.

I then selected one robe each for Lieutenant Sheridan and Captain

Dent and as the ladies were backward in taking anything I divided the fine furs among them, informing them I had traded for them expressly for their use. I then presented to the quartermaster the skins and robes which I had laid aside for him and also sent to his lady a number of Indian curios. I now had left one hundred and fifty robes and the white mule. The robes afterwards brought me from twenty-five to forty dollars each and I was offered for the mule two hundred and fifty dollars, but refused to part with him, as he was worth five hundred dollars in any market for a saddle animal.

That evening, I had a half dozen invitations to dine, but accepted the one from the quartermaster and when I arrived at his quarters, I found there a bevy of ladies commenting upon the beautiful furs. For four days I was feasted by the officers and their families, the ladies especially being very desirous of learning all the news of our experiences on the late trip. McKay had done considerable talking and had informed them that I had saved the Kootenais from annihilation and had been very destructive to the Blackfeet, etc., and also informed them of those three medicine arrows which Little Dog had given me.

The officer of the day informed me that the commanding officer wished to see me, and when I arrived at headquarters Col. Wright asked me if I had any objection to letting him see those arrows. I went at once to my quarters and got the arrows with all the curios which I had left and spread the outfit on a centre table before them. The colonel examined the arrows very closely and remarked that he would like to retain them if I had no objections. I think he was getting up a museum or curio collection and I took great pleasure in letting him have them. It was now that he complimented me on my report, saying that it was valuable to the War Department as being authentic

That evening those seven mules which the quartermaster had furnished for the trip were led up to my quarters with a bill of sale and presented to me as a present.

As the Indian war in this country was over, I discontinued my connection with the army, strongly against the desires of the officers, and I was pleased when Col. Wright informed me that I could remain in the service indefinitely if I desired. I thanked them all for their kindness and appreciation and informed them of my intention of establishing myself in the Flathead country.

The Indian hostages which had been held during our trip were that evening, called into council and were informed by Col. Wright through an interpreter that they would be held responsible for any hostile acts of their people in the future, and that they would be at liberty on the following morning to depart to their villages. During this council McKay acted as interpreter, and the hostages asked him how their people acted toward us when we passed through their country. He replied that they were sullen and not over-friendly and informed them of the hostile interview with those five Palouse Indians.

If all government officers would follow the example of Col. Wright when in council with Indians, such interviews would have a moral effect upon them that few would scarcely credit. His method was to use few words and to mean what he said. For example: If the commanding officer when in council with the chiefs would tell them to notify all their people that in case any white men were molested or lost their stock through any of their warriors, he would hang the last one of them and then dismissed them, ever afterwards the whites could pass through their country with comparative safety.

I remained at the post a few days after this, arranging my affairs, and when about ready to leave, I was summoned to the quartermaster's. Col. Wright asked me if I could deliver some dispatches at Fort Dalles inside of twenty-four hours, and stated it was imperative that they be there at that time. I consented to go and he said that I could select any animal belonging to the government that I wished. It was one hundred and seventy-five measured miles and I was well acquainted with every foot of the route. I went to the stable and brought out my white mule. He was in prime condition. I saddled up a horse belonging to the quartermaster and at 8:30 a. m. started out on this trip with the dispatches and delivered them at Fort Dalles at 6:15 a. m. the next morning.

On this trip I rode the quartermaster's horse sixty miles, then leaving him made the rest of the trip on the mule. I could have reached the Post three hours earlier if positively necessary. I took three days to return and upon my return handed Col. Wright a letter stating the time the dispatches had been received. The colonel and his officers could hardly credit it and all of them came out to examine the mule, which looked none the worse for the trip. For this trip I received five hundred dollars, and one week after I sold the mule for a like amount and have cursed myself ever since for parting with him.

McKay assisted me in making my final arrangements for the trip to the Flathead country and in packing up all my things. I took supplies sufficient to last me two years. I sold all the mules but kept Hickory, and after stopping for a few days with McKay I made my final *adieu* to the officers and their ladies and made my way back again over the lonely trail to the land of the Flatheads and took up a permanent abode within the boundaries of what is now called "Montana."

Conclusion

It may be of interest to mention that my companion McKay was an older brother of Donald McKay, who with the Warm Spring Indians operated as scouts for our soldiers in the Modoc War in 1872. He wished to accompany me with his family to the Flathead country, but it was not right for me to allow it as he had a good position in the post at Walla Walla and also a good ranch. He visited me twice at the Bitter Root, coming with a number of Nez Perce Indians. Little Dog and his son Fringe also paid me several visits and we remained fast friends until their death, which occurred in 1867. Little Dog was one of the most remarkable Indians on the Plains, and as he often narrated to me his experiences, especially of his younger days, I want to write out a history of him at some future time.

More than forty years have passed since the expedition narrated in these previous pages, and I have been requested and encouraged to thus put into permanent shape the memorandum, notes, and memories of this chapter of my life. I have endeavoured to portray in a correct manner the true character of those Indians, good and bad, and at the same time to give an idea of the trials and dangers of the trader and scout. And I now close this chapter of my experiences, hoping that what I have written may be of some interest and profit to my friends who read it and some advantage to the generations that follow, in gaining a correct knowledge of these bygone days whose incidents can thus be found only in the annals of the past.

www.ingramcontent.com/pod-product-compliance
Lightning Source LLC
Chambersburg PA
CBHW032055080426
42733CB00006B/279